HOW TO WIN A CULTURE WAR

Lisa M. Stulberg

HOW TO WIN A CULTURE WAR

LGBTQ+ Social Change Through Pop Culture

THE UNIVERSITY OF CHICAGO PRESS
CHICAGO AND LONDON

The University of Chicago Press, Chicago 60637
The University of Chicago Press, Ltd., London

Published 2026
Printed in the United States of America

35 34 33 32 31 30 29 28 27 26   1 2 3 4 5

ISBN-13: 978-0-226-82207-5 (cloth)
ISBN-13: 978-0-226-85168-6 (ebook)
DOI: https://doi.org/10.7208/chicago/9780226851686.001.0001

Library of Congress Cataloging-in-Publication Data

Names: Stulberg, Lisa M., author.
Title: How to win a culture war : LGBTQ+ social change through pop culture / Lisa M. Stulberg.
Description: Chicago : The University of Chicago Press, 2026. | Includes bibliographical references and index.
Identifiers: LCCN 2026008373 | ISBN 9780226822075 (cloth) | ISBN 9780226851686 (ebook)
Subjects: LCSH: Sexual minorities—United States. | Social change—United States. | Popular culture—United States.
Classification: LCC HQ73.3.U5 S78 2026
LC record available at https://lccn.loc.gov/2026008373

♾ This paper meets the requirements of ANSI/NISO Z39.48-1992 (Permanence of Paper).

Authorized Representative for EU General Product Safety Regulation (GPSR) queries:
Easy Access System Europe—Mustamäe tee 50, 10621 Tallinn, Estonia,
gpsr.requests@easproject.com
Any other queries: https://press.uchicago.edu/press/contact.html

To IRV and BOB, and BRYAN:
Three true mensches without whom
this book would not have been
possible—or nearly as fun to write

CONTENTS

PREFACE

The first notes of the songs that were the soundtrack to your youth can erase decades. You feel them in your stomach, and you know all the words. Forever. Your first on-screen crush is the same way. You were drawn to them the first time and did not understand why. Now you will always hold a soft spot for what they taught you about yourself. Navigating life, you have looked to people you see on TV, encounter in movies, and hear through your headphones. They are both role models and salvation. They bring comfort and community. You can lose yourself in their stories and beauty. They open up a space in the world.

People have created these moments and this art and put themselves purposefully and lovingly into them. Some explicitly have hoped to break barriers and make a political statement. Some emphatically have not. Yet their existence in popular culture and popular imagination has been revolutionary.

For this book, I talked with 170 smart, talented LGBTQ+ people and their allies in Hollywood and elite sports.[1] *How to Win a Culture War*[2] is about them and the way that they think about and do their work—and the barriers they face along the way. The caricature we have of athletes and Hollywood types is that they are uninformed, self-centered, and not entitled to have a public voice. But this is wrong. People in Hollywood, onstage, and in sports *are* actively engaged and are authentically working to change American culture. Despite these very difficult times, they are succeeding.

INTRODUCTION

Do you want to know what waging a culture war looks like now? If you are presidential candidate Donald J. Trump, it means spending over $45 million—more than any other ad buy of your campaign—to relentlessly run transphobic commercials.[1] You bombard viewers, especially during televised sports,[2] with the message that your opponent is for "they/them" while you, Donald J. Trump, are for "you."[3] And you know who *you* are, football-watching Pennsylvanian or baseball-watching Ohioan. If you are newly reelected Trump, waging a culture war looks like forcing federal employees to remove their pronouns from their email signatures.[4] It looks like declaring that the American flag is the *only* flag that matters and prohibiting Pride or Black Lives Matter flags at federal facilities in the United States and around the world.[5] These are not small or inconsequential things. No, no not at all.

There are many ways to try to understand our current politics. Why turn to culture wars? Sociologist James Davison Hunter has been credited with bringing the culture wars framing to prominence with his 1991 book, *Culture Wars*. Hunter wrote that what divides post-Reagan-era Americans is primarily differences in *worldview* and morality: "The contemporary culture war is ultimately a struggle over national identity—*over the meaning of America*, who we have been in the past, who we are now, and perhaps most important, who we, as a nation, will aspire to become in the new millennium."[6] In 1998 activist and writer Michael Bronski connected culture wars to gay liberation and identity: "The culture wars, in all of their manifestations, are the public forum where issues of what it means to be an 'American' and a citizen are being debated and decided."[7]

In short, culture wars are not trivial or tangential or *merely* about beliefs and values. They are about who can claim American identity and have American institutions work for them and protect them. They are about who belongs.[8]

The idea of a culture war can be off-putting because it implies winners and losers. The idea of the LGBTQ+ community *winning* a culture war seems to declare premature victory when there is clearly *lots* of unfinished business in the battle for LGBTQ+ justice, especially now. But when we really look at LGBTQ+ social justice movements and the conservative backlash against them, the idea of culture wars has indeed been a big part of the broader fight for gender and sexual equality in the United States.

The 1980s and early 1990s were the height of the AIDS crisis and the Reagan revolution. At this time, social and religious conservatives enthusiastically demonized gay people and activists. Right-wingers like Patrick Buchanan and Senator Jesse Helms directly invoked culture war imagery to frame their despicable homophobia. In the summer of 1992, conservative commentator and presidential-hopeful Buchanan opened the Republican National Convention with this notorious framing: "There is a religious war going on in this country for the soul of America. It is a culture war as critical to the kind of nation we shall be as the Cold War itself."[9] Culture wars framing, then, is a most useful and appropriate way of understanding LGBTQ+ politics and social movements[10] in the United States since World War II,[11] with the caveat that LGBTQ+ Americans are still in the *process* of winning a culture war. The *win* is an active verb, not a settled state.[12]

The nation has repeatedly failed LGBTQ+ people throughout US history and in recent decades. It has prevented them from serving their country in the military. It has willfully ignored the AIDS crisis and refused to mobilize the resources of the federal government to fight it. It has weaponized police against queer people in their homes and their community institutions. It has neglected to create laws to protect against discrimination. In response, LGBTQ+ Americans have turned to art and popular culture—among other tools—to hold the country accountable for its failures and promises. For their part, LGBTQ+ cultural warriors and their allies are actively working toward opening up the nation to them, to reshaping American institutions to serve them. Through art and popular culture, LGBTQ+ Americans have asserted their national belonging and have carved out a space of self-determination, unapologetic love and sexuality, and community building.[13]

THE CURRENT STATE OF LGBTQ+ CIVIL RIGHTS IN THE UNITED STATES

We are living now through a truly horrifying inflection point in LGBTQ+ politics. This might seem counterintuitive because, for decades, American public attitudes about LGBTQ+ people and civil rights have become substantially more pro-LGBTQ+. The identities in this umbrella term do not all draw the same public support, and intersectional power and marginalization is at work here, as it always is. Yet this is broadly true.

Some numbers help tell this story. When Gallup asked in 2003 if "gay and lesbian relations" were "*morally* acceptable," only 44 percent of Americans said they were. Twenty years later, that number had risen to 64 percent.[14] In 2004, the year that the first state began certifying same-sex marriages, 60 percent of Americans opposed and only 31 percent supported these unions. By 2021 the reverse was true: 68 percent of Americans supported and 30 percent opposed marriage equality. On broader civil rights protections, in 2021, 79 percent of Americans supported laws to protect LGBTQ+ people from discrimination, up from 71 percent in 2015.[15] Public opinion, especially on gay and lesbian civil rights and on marriage equality, has truly shifted quite (relatively) quickly. This shift also cannot be explained by "generational turnover"[16]—older, more conservative people being replaced by younger, more liberal people. Rather, individuals' actual views have changed with time. Sociologists Kevin Kiley and Stephen Vaisey call this an "active updating" of public opinion.[17]

In recent decades, there have been some substantial wins in LGBTQ+ law and policy, too. It took until 2003, in *Lawrence v. Texas*, for the Supreme Court to overturn its own decision and finally decriminalize consensual, adult, private same-sex sex. On marriage equality, Massachusetts became the first state to perform same-sex unions in 2004. Following this ruling, state laws around the country changed rapidly. The Supreme Court, in a 5–4 decision written by Reagan-appointed Justice Anthony Kennedy, affirmed the constitutional right to marriage equality in 2015. The case, *Obergefell v. Hodges*, was brought by a man seeking the right to be listed on his husband's death certificate. The court's decision in the case established marriage equality nationwide.

Even after these steps forward, it was still legal to discriminate in employment against LGBTQ+ people in almost half of all US states. Many in the LGBTQ+ civil rights movement liked to say that you could get married on Sunday and fired on Monday. But in June 2020, President Donald Trump's first appointee to the court, Justice Neil Gorsuch, wrote the landmark 6–3 Supreme Court opinion in *Bostock v. Clayton County, Georgia*. This decision finally held that federal law protected employees from discrimination on the basis of sexual orientation and gender identity.[18]

American institutions also have become broadly more LGBTQ+ inclusive in recent decades. President Bill Clinton instituted a policy of "Don't Ask, Don't Tell" in the US military in early 1994. This discriminatory policy that kept gay, lesbian, and bisexual service members in the closet remained in place for seventeen years, until President Barack Obama overturned it. It was not until 2016 that Obama lifted the ban on transgender service members. Obama also worked to extend civil rights protections to transgender young people in schools in unprecedented ways, especially during his last two years in office.

Despite this historic progress, LGBTQ+ Americans still do not have general protections from discrimination in health care, housing, public accommodation, parenting, and schooling. And recent legal and political action threaten even the partial civil rights protections that are in place in US states.[19] Even though most of these attempts were unsuccessful from 2013 to 2016, "bathroom bills" or other restrictive public access bills—aimed to force trans people to use the facilities that correspond with their sex assigned at birth—were introduced in at least twenty-four states. After 2016 the Trump administration wasted no time in rolling back civil rights gains, especially for transgender Americans. Anti-LGBTQ+ hate crimes and discrimination also escalated after Trump became president the first time.[20]

As the Republican Party set its sights on the White House again in 2024, it doubled down on transphobia in the Republican Party platform. It never specifically mentioned trans and nonbinary people. But it employed all of the right-wing buzzwords and dog whistles that it could possibly fit into one platform item, entitled "Republicans Will End Left-wing Gender Insanity." The item reads (with some unusual capitalization choices that I have not corrected here): "We will keep men out of women's sports, ban Taxpayer funding for sex change surgeries, and stop Taxpayer-funded Schools from promoting gender transition, reverse Biden's radical rewrite of Title IX Education Regulations, and restore protections for women and girls."[21]

Once he took office again, Trump 2.0 made it a day-one priority to continue to target hatred and bigotry at LGBTQ+ people, especially trans and nonbinary people. This is a cynical strategy by Trump and his supporters to grow and maintain a base of right-wing allegiance. It truly often seems as if Republican politicians are competing to be as anti-queer as possible. Despite legal challenges, some state-level pushback, and federal congressional action to protect marriage equality,[22] there is substantial evidence that the right-wing strategy is taking hold in the states.[23] The year 2023 was record-setting in anti-LGBTQ+ legislation. More than five hundred bills were introduced in states, nearly tripling the number of laws proposed just one year before. Of these, eighty-four bills passed in twenty-three states in 2023.[24] And this was topped in 2024. By the end of the year, the number of proposed anti-LGBTQ+ bills was at least 533, and 49 of them were passed into law. In 2025, emboldened by Trump's win, states had considered 616 new bills and had passed 71 into law by mid-September.[25] These bills include attacks on trans athlete participation and health care—even going so far as to criminalize gender-affirming care.[26]

There is also a newly aggressive and mean-spirited anti-LGBTQ+ focus on young people and schooling. The Trump administration pulled funding for LGBTQ+ youth suicide prevention measures in the summer of 2025.[27] In addition, hundreds of proposed bills would mirror Florida's "Don't Say Gay" law of 2022.[28] These would restrict what is taught in public schools and compel "forced outing," requiring teachers to notify parents if their children begin using new names or pronouns.[29] And this comes at a time when teens are already really struggling after the COVID pandemic. In 2021–22, 14 percent of straight teens reported that they had seriously considered suicide, while almost half of LGBTQ+ teens had.[30] Private institutions that rely on federal funding have pre-complied with Trump's anti-trans push or have bowed to explicit pressure from his administration. In the summer of 2025, several hospitals began eliminating gender-affirming care for young people.[31] And the Supreme Court, stacked with Trump's three appointees, made its own contributions. It ruled, in the summer of 2025, *for* parents who sought to opt out of LGBTQ+ content in their Maryland schools. And, in a highly anticipated decision, the court ruled in *Skrmetti* that Tennessee's ban on gender-affirming care for minors was *not* unconstitutional. This allowed the law—and others like it—to stand.[32]

These hateful and dangerous anti-LGBTQ+ strategies accompany an expansive assault on bodily autonomy and self-determination—and are part of a broader national and global rush to the political right on gender and sexuality and a rise of White supremacy and nativism.[33] They also demonstrate a willingness by states, federal lawmakers, and the Supreme Court to reconsider settled law. We have seen this, of course, with abortion rights. In 2022, in *Dobbs v. Jackson Women's Health Organization*, the Supreme Court overturned its 1973 *Roe v. Wade* decision and held that the Constitution did not protect the right to an abortion. This ruling put other fundamental rights on the table. In his concurring opinion in *Dobbs*, Justice Clarence Thomas wrote that other due process rulings should be reconsidered as well, including *Obergefell* and *Lawrence*.[34] A regression in reproductive freedom could bring with it huge steps back in sexual and marriage rights and freedoms.

Anti-democratic gerrymandering, voter suppression, "disinformation-based politics,"[35] and a Supreme Court that President Trump has stacked have produced lawmaking that does not reflect majority public opinion.[36] Yet the hardening of some of the right-wing politics *does* seem to be having some impact on public opinion, such as a reduction of support on trans rights since 2020. For example, Gallup found that the proportion of respondents who said that "changing one's gender"—already a problematic framing—was "morally acceptable" (vs. "morally wrong") fell from 46 to 43 to 40 percent, while the proportion who responded that transgender athletes "should be able to play on sports teams that match their current gender identity" fell from 34 to 26 to 24 percent from May 2021 to May 2023 to May 2025. The proportion of respondents who *opposed* "allowing openly transgender men and women to serve in the military" rose from 26 to 33 to 35 percent from May 2019 to May 2021 to January 2025.[37] It will be important to watch how Trump's assault on trans and nonbinary people continues to impact public opinion in the upcoming years.

Even the current level of public support for LGBTQ+ civil rights does not translate to full *cultural* acceptance. Many non-LGBTQ+ Americans still report personal discomfort with LGBTQ+ people, lives, and histories. In early 2021, 25 percent or more said they would be uncomfortable even seeing a gay or lesbian coworker's wedding photo at work, seeing a same-sex couple holding hands, or learning than a family member identified as LGBTQ. A full 37 percent said they would be uncomfortable to learn that their child had a lesson in LGBTQ history at school.[38] And, in mid-2022, 38 percent of respondents on a Pew Research Center survey indicated that "our society has gone too far in accepting" trans people.[39]

This cultural discomfort has life-and-death consequences. Anti-transgender harassment and violence, especially against women of color, is a hate-fueled injustice that gets little mainstream attention and has been on the rise in recent years. In 2024, at least thirty-two transgender and gender-expansive people—disproportionately Black women—were violently killed.[40] It is no wonder that LGBTQ+ Americans report that their elected officials are not doing enough to protect them.[41]

At the same time, as Trump and right-wing lawmakers have set their sights on transgender and nonbinary Americans, some high-profile voices with long-standing connections to the gay rights movement have joined them. In June 2025, *The New York Times* gave a lot of real estate to Andrew Sullivan, a cisgender gay conservative writer who had been especially active in the marriage equality fight. Sullivan blamed electoral and public opinion losses on fights for trans health care, civil rights, and cultural acceptance, calling these an "overreach" perpetrated by "gender revolutionaries" and "trans extremism."[42] Here, the transphobia of the current moment is being laid at the feet of trans and nonbinary people themselves.

ENTER POP CULTURE

The current moment in LGBTQ+ social change presents a paradox: At the same time that LGBTQ+ civil rights protections are in severe danger, there has been a monumental shift in representation of queer people in popular culture. Of course, again, the extent of this representation varies by gender and gender identity—not to mention other forms of identity and power. Yet these cultural spaces, almost hidden in plain sight, are major sites of politics and drivers of social change.[43] And they have been for generations.[44] Current social justice efforts derive from a long history of agitation and activism. These earlier movements, too, used media, art, and sport in creative and radical ways. Colin Kaepernick's bent knee on the football field has its origins in Tommie Smith's and John Carlos's raised fists on the 1968

Olympics medal podium: these athletes using their platform to challenge the enduring nature of American White supremacy. #BlackLivesMatter Spotify playlists and the wide range of artists responding to racist police brutality call back to Tupac Shakur singing in "Changes" in the mid-1990s, "Instead of war on poverty / they got a war on drugs so the police can bother me," and, before him, to Marvin Gaye, singing in 1971's "What's Going On": "picket lines and picket signs / Don't punish me with brutality."[45] The "Real Beauty" Dove soap campaign or the Billie razor company proclaiming women's self-determination in body hair care recall the 1968 protest of the Miss America pageant with the plan to burn bras in the "freedom trash can": commercialized spaces engaging with feminist critique over standards of beauty for women.[46] And the family TV drama *The Fosters* (2013–18), featuring a multiracial family headed by two loving and overextended moms, can find its roots in the revolutionary *All in the Family*, which depicted a complicated television family explicitly and messily confronting the political issues of the 1970s.[47]

For its part in pop culture, Hollywood's connection to political and social movements dates back a century. Hollywood as we know it was originally built by outsiders: Jewish immigrants and refugees who helmed the creation of the movie studio system in the early part of the twentieth century. This impacted the culture of the business, its relationship to American politics, and its cultural products.[48] Hollywood—the community of people and institutions engaged in the culture industry by making or supporting US movies and TV shows[49]—has become more and more politically involved. More broadly, *culture* has been part of movements for social change, and social movements have had a substantial impact on culture and cultural change.[50]

For social change around gender and sexuality, activists began in the 1950s to demand visibility, community, and equality. The Stonewall uprising in the summer of 1969, when bar-goers and their allies fought back against police repression, spurred and energized a movement. That movement for LGBTQ+ equality demanded the right to come out, live openly, gain acceptance in families and institutions, and have equal protection under the law. Activists marched in the street, challenged laws and policies, and eventually organized online. Culture and cultural strategies tend to be ignored by scholars of social movements. Yet pop culture is one very important front in LGBTQ+ social movements, and cultural tools have been central to movements' successes in changing hearts and minds. They have been since the beginning, when previous generations drew on the culture available to them to build community, defy oppression and erasure, open up resistant institutions, and push for systemic change.[51]

THE INTERVIEWS

All the way back in the fall of 2011, I could not stop thinking about fourteen-year-old Jamey Rodemeyer and singer Lady Gaga. The self-identified bisexual boy from upstate New York was inspired by Gaga's lyrics. He said so in a video he posted to the It Gets Better Project. The video was designed to give the hopeful message to other young people like him—young people who were being relentlessly bullied and who were lonely, unheard, and scared—that they could persevere. Gaga, he said, "makes me so happy, and she lets me know that I was born this way." But the words were not enough. Jamey took his own life on September 18, 2011. His parents buried him in his "Born This Way" T-shirt. Lady Gaga, for her part, responded via tweet, angry and upset and mentioning Jamey by name. She pledged to her millions of Twitter followers that she would fight to make bullying illegal.[52]

That was when I first set out to talk with the artists and culture workers who seemed to be using their talents to contribute to LGBTQ+ social change. A New York University PhD student, Bryan Rosenberg, joined me in talking with people who make and participate in the pop culture that was so meaningful to Jamey and others. This was well before marriage equality was legal nationwide, before President Obama had even offered his public support for same-sex marriage, and long before there was anything close to federal protections for LGBTQ+ job discrimination. Streaming services like Netflix, Hulu, and Amazon

Prime Video were in the first stages of shedding their roles as high-tech Blockbuster video rental hubs. (Google this if you're too young to remember brick-and-mortar video rental stores!) Many fewer of us carried around mobile TVs and movie theaters in our pockets.

Bryan and I went out to Los Angeles in October 2011 for four initial interviews and, on our very first day, found ourselves on a studio lot talking with an Academy Award winner. In the years that followed, our overworked backpacks and sensible academics' shoes saw the insides of swanky hotel rooms and lobbies, amazingly appointed homes, more studio lots, a recording studio and the backstage of a concert, and so many gloriously cute LA and New York City cafés. Over the years, we (or I alone, from 2019 on[53]) conducted interviews with 170 people in three main batches, first in 2012–15, then after Trump's first election in 2017–19, and then a set of update interviews with thirty-six people in 2021–25 (some of whom I spoke with more than once in these years). Despite all the changes in this country since 2011, most of the interviewees would say many of the same things today. That said, I checked all interview quotes with my participants. If anything they said felt outdated or inaccurate, it is noted.

So, who said yes to being interviewed by two academic randos? The answer, happily, is a wide range of "culture makers,"[54] including Super Bowl and Olympic champions; Academy Award, Emmy, and Tony Award nominees and winners; and many who are involved with some of the most iconic and groundbreaking television shows, films, and theater productions with respect to LGBTQ+ content, as well as those who will go into history books as forerunners and activists.[55] I would have loved to talk with every A-lister who identifies as LGBTQ+ (if you can think of a show/character/publicly out LGBTQ+ celebrity, I probably tried to contact them and have in my archives an unreturned or quickly batted-back email from a manager or agent or an unread Twitter or Instagram DM).[56] But, in the course of my research, I learned that there are many creative, technical, and executive people, as well as people who support their careers, who are absolutely essential to how culture gets produced and who could teach me so much about their industries. You will find stars in this book. And you will also find smart, creative, hardworking people who may have never had their face on an *Us Weekly* cover but who do the work that powers Hollywood, professional sports, and LGBTQ+ culture and social change.

"IT'S A BUSINESS": HOLLYWOOD TODAY

Hollywood—the entertainment industry, broadly—is a business that has changed in dizzying ways in recent decades. It even changes month by month if we take into consideration the past few years' response to the COVID-19 pandemic and to Trump 2.0. These changes have profound implications for who gets to belong in the industry and for how Hollywood contributes to social change, especially because what the Hollywood business cares about most is making money.[57]

The exact phrase "it's a business" was uttered dozens of times by people I interviewed about Hollywood. It was partly offered during our interviews as a way to keep my sociological presumptions and my fangirl enthusiasm in check. It was a warning that to expect culture workers to do the job of social movements is to fundamentally misunderstand the nature and limitations of their work. It captured the sentiment, shared by many, that there might be collateral benefits to the creative work done in Hollywood when it comes to LGBTQ+ social change. But concerns for art for its own sake or for social justice will never be fundamental drivers of television and film. To expect otherwise is naive and misplaced. Show business is show *business*.[58]

It would be tough to overstate the changes to the business of mass culture in recent decades. Television looks nothing like it did in 1969, when Stonewall activists at the birth of the modern LGBTQ+ movement could not even break into the local television news.[59] Those few shared TV channels that broadcast limited, scheduled programming have blossomed into prolific, on-demand cable and streaming platforms. Our interconnected, online world means we have 24/7 access to not just content but content creators, producers, and celebrities. Cultural producers and consumers have a level of control and choice that is unparalleled. This new world could not have been imagined by the cultural outsiders who built Hollywood—or studied it. In anthropologist Hortense Powdermaker's famous 1950 examination of Hollywood, she wrote plainly: "Hollywood represents totalitarianism."[60] Similarly, sociologist Todd Gitlin, in his classic 1983 study of prime-time television, derisively called the medium "junk food for the mind."[61] These disdainful views of cultural creation and consumption do not accurately capture the reality that actors, writers, athletes, musicians, and their fans now have an active role in shaping popular culture and the place it holds in their lives.[62]

I am going to fast-forward past a lot of the history of Hollywood: the business that was built via the success of the movie studios in the first half of the twentieth century. For those interested, there are some excellent written histories of the industry.[63] I will just say that by the time we land in the twenty-first century, Hollywood has been shaped by decades of deregulation, mega-conglomeration, and globalization of entertainment companies. By the end of the twentieth century, with ubiquitous newer-on-the-scene cable television came new business models. While network television relied on advertiser revenue, cable outlets were financially supported by both advertisers and by individual user subscriptions.[64] And there was a lot of creative excellence in television. A series of critically acclaimed original programs by HBO, and then other premium cable companies, ushered in a "Third Golden Age" of television that began in the 1990s. This brought in TV writers and showrunners who were attracted to a medium that had seemed bland and constrained before.[65]

Even in the years right before streaming services were fully up and running, people I interviewed in the early 2010s felt that they were in the middle of a renaissance of television. Even by this point, there were just so many outlets and so much content for viewers to choose from. The best of the best in the industry found themselves writing and producing for TV and celebrating the impact of this intimate medium. Many of the people I spoke with, some of the giants of paid premium cable, felt that it was in *this* television space, which is not publicly regulated[66] and does not rely on advertiser dollars, that they initially had the freedom to push boundaries and tell the stories that compelled them. And, in fact, as Ron Cowen and Daniel Lipman, the creators of the American version of *Queer as Folk* (2000–2005) on Showtime, told me, they felt that creative freedom and even risk-taking were part of what was wanted and expected of them. "It was at a certain point in the development of paid cable," Cowen said, "where they were making their name being as daring as they could be because they had to compete with network TV. And if they're expecting potential viewers to pay for their service, they believed they had better give them a good reason to do so."[67]

Of course now, streaming platforms have become dominant. I had already started interviewing people for this book by the time the first original streaming show launched on Netflix. While the company had been streaming existing movies and TV shows, acquired content, since 2007, it introduced its first original programming in February 2012. The following year, Netflix launched the shows that put it on the map for original content: the massive hits *House of Cards*, then *Orange Is the New Black*.[68] Amazon soon introduced original programming of its own: *Alpha House*, also in 2013.[69] A decade later, there are almost fifty streaming services in the United States and more than two hundred worldwide—and in May 2025, for the first time, streamers in the United States drew more viewers than cable and broadcast TV combined. To provide these options, networks and cable channels generally do not have to compete for revenue, because often media conglomerates own a range of platforms. This means that these gigantic companies can profit from viewers choosing to watch either "linear TV" at a set time and on a specific channel or OTT, "over-the-top TV," which is delivered online, often on demand, by streamers—like Disney+, HBO Max, and NBC's Peacock.[70]

Streaming platforms do not just represent a new way to deliver storytelling in Hollywood. They also signal that the culture of the workplace has been changing in new and unfamiliar ways. Several people I interviewed remarked on the tech culture of the big streaming companies like Netflix, Amazon, Apple, and YouTube. Netflix, for instance, got its start and is headquartered in Silicon Valley. As one television producer/executive said to me: "The streamers are tech companies first and foremost" that were created in a different ecosystem. "For a while they were like visiting guests in our industry and now they are the big guns in town."[71] These companies have a different investment model and may simply see TV and film viewers as customers rather than as audiences with an attachment to the stories they put into the world.[72] Their decision-making and workplace culture also seems to work differently than the studios and networks that were created for the sole purpose of making television and film.

These days the multinational "entertainment conglomerates"[73] own just about all aspects of television, streaming, and film—not to mention other forms of media and entertainment, like news programming and theme parks.[74] For instance, in March 2019, Disney moved to rival newer tech/streaming companies by making its largest-ever acquisition: buying, for $71.3 billion, most of 21st Century Fox's companies, which included most of Hulu and the 20th Century Fox movie and TV studio.[75] Even movie studios and cable companies or streamers that have a reputation for cutting-edge content and independence often now have conglomerate parent companies.[76] For film, this means a rise in reboots and a franchise model of filmmaking that results in fewer movies being made each year. The movies that are green-lit tend to be huge, familiar stories (based on intellectual property already owned by the parent company), with familiar characters and storylines, and the possibility of sequels and spin-offs.[77] At the same time, with the rise of streaming platforms—and especially in the years since the COVID-19 virus cleared out movie theaters in early 2020—feature films in theaters have lost a lot of ground. And with conglomerates owning both movie studios and streaming platforms, they have a choice as to how to release movies—in theaters or on streamers, or both simultaneously—that does not impact their bottom line but that does endanger the traditional movie business.[78] The December 2025 (and now-failed) Netflix bid to buy Warner Bros. Discovery is one of the most recent and consequential examples of this trend.[79]

POP CULTURE AND LGBTQ+ SOCIAL CHANGE

The people I spoke with who make their living in popular culture openly reflected on the connection between their art or sport and their politics, the meaning they make of their work, and the politics and the business necessities in their industries. They had a lot to say about the risks, uncertainties, and stresses involved in professional culture-making. As one actor/writer said to me, "There are probably four, or let's be generous and say six, actors in town who aren't worried about where their next job is coming from."[80] Many in Hollywood and professional sports see their work as political and believe that they are using their talents to make social change in the best way they can. Others are assiduously trying to entertain or do their art, or play their sport or their music, separate from any political goals. But they, too, feel they have a place in the world and something to say. These culture makers have a savvy sense of the possibilities and the constraints of their roles.

In the chapters that follow, I tell a story broadly about pop culture and LGBTQ+ social change in the United States. But my interviews focus primarily on television (including streaming shows) and sports. There are some circumstantial reasons for this: I did have limits to who I was able to access, and my interviews were so social network dependent that if I could not break into one area of pop culture, I had a tough time doing many interviews in that area. But there is also a substantive reason for this focus on television and sports: it is in these areas of pop culture where we have seen tremendous transformation in the past ten to fifteen years. Sports and television have been at the forefront of recent LGBTQ+ politics and social change.[81]

Recent mainstream network television hits like *Modern Family* and *Will & Grace* have been credited by many with the speed with which public attitudes have shifted on marriage equality, LGBTQ+

participation in sports, and employment nondiscrimination—even though Hollywood and elite sports are conservative institutions that are primarily driven by consumer and advertiser interests. By those lights, any involvement in LGBTQ+ social change efforts in pop culture is merely commodifying social change and co-opting queer culture and visibility. And this is true: Hollywood and sports insiders acknowledge that their industries *are* businesses that are not primarily driven by an interest in social change. And yet! Culture workers *are* actively and deliberately working to make change. Even if the bottom line is king, and even if the current time is quite dire, many of those in pop culture *are* in the process of winning a culture war, and they are largely doing so by using the same playbook. This playbook outlines the six primary steps for winning the culture war, and each of the following chapters covers one or two of those primary steps in detail. They are

1. Be visible.
2. Use available platforms.
3. Change your workplace.
4. Overachieve.
5. Become normal.
6. Stay queer.

I am beyond grateful to the many brave individuals who shared their opportunities and barriers and have committed their life's work to making and excelling at their art or sport and making change. You'll hear much more from them in the chapters that follow.

1. BE VISIBLE

The current wave of anti-trans laws is made "by people who don't want trans people to exist in public spaces," elite athlete and trans sports activist Chris Mosier said to me. "The goal," he said, "is to eliminate trans people from public life."[1] Mosier is a high-profile athlete who has also built his career around public advocacy and social media visibility. He is also someone who has faced a *lot* of stomach-turning transphobic violence online. In the days after Trump's reelection in the fall of 2024, Mosier regularly posted some of his hate mail on social media, overlaid onto joyful photos of himself. On November 7, for instance, Mosier posted a screenshot of a message with the subject line "it's almost time" and the message "Don't worry, he'll make it quick! Day 1, you're a fucking goner." Mosier responded: "Here's what they're missing: My people get stronger in the face of adversity. Trans people have always been here & we will always be here."[2]

Visibility *is* this kind of a treacherous double-edged sword.[3]

On the one hand, becoming and remaining visible has been a central tactic for LGBTQ+ people for decades. Visibility has mattered to LGBTQ+ social change because it helps to change hearts and minds, and it boosts support for LGBTQ+ civil rights. Generally, the more that straight and cisgender people see LGBTQ+ people in their lives and in public, the more commonplace and sympathetic they become.[4] Visibility can also bring personal triumph. Those who have come out in pop culture tend to have had a much more personally affirming experience than they expected or feared.[5] Actors and athletes that I interviewed reported that they steeled for a backlash when they came out personally or publicly. They were mostly relieved that this did not come to pass. For many, there was grace and support where they dared not hope for it. There was also a kind of pride in achieving this vulnerable, often difficult thing and coming out on the other side of it.

On the other hand, alongside these moments of personal pride and public gain, visibility can be fraught and dangerous. It can be a personal burden: a weight that people bear of being a trailblazer, a role model, or a token. Visibility can also bring substantial risk and vulnerability. "Gays do not realize that the more we become visible, the more we come out of the closet, the more we are hated," wrote AIDS/LGBTQ+ activist Larry Kramer back in 2007.[6] The danger of visibility is particularly great for those who are most marginalized and subjugated as they become more visible. In short, invisibility can sometimes be lifesaving.[7]

Placing too much stock in *commodified* visibility can also be misguided, even harmful. Commercial "visibility traps" mean that sometimes visible queer people are misrepresented, stereotyped, or dehumanized—or simply included for profit or prestige. Or this kind of visibility might only celebrate LGBTQ+ people being *seen* without ensuring that they are *safe* and legally protected.[8]

Even with these complexities, so many culture workers make personal and professional choices that contribute to visibility. They choose to come out or disclose, support others in doing so, or create content that contributes to increased LGBTQ+ representation. In this chapter, we hear from them about how they view LGBTQ+ visibility and understand their role in it. Their experiences are about navigating the closet, coming out publicly, and telling LGBTQ+ stories. Their visibility brings joy and recognition. At the same time, these culture workers offer up their labor and their personal stories. They shoulder a burden—and sometimes pay a price—for their work.

PROGRESS IN FICTIONAL LGBTQ+ VISIBILITY

Fictional representation is key to LGBTQ+ visibility. And it started out bleak. In his classic 1980s exposé and call to arms, *The Celluloid Closet*, activist and writer Vito Russo railed against the old "lazy" tropes of gay people: the pitiful, the misanthropes, the masochists, the murderers, the relentless sexual predators, the sexless, the "powerless sissies," and the "homosexual villains, fools and queens." He wrote plainly that "the history of the portrayal of lesbians and gay men in mainstream cinema is politically indefensible and aesthetically revolting." Think of the suicidal repressed lesbian played by Shirley MacLaine in the 1961 film *The Children's Hour*; the self-hating ennui presented in the 1970 film version of *The Boys in the Band*; and two of many murderous movie gays, a couple played by Christopher Reeve and Michael Caine in 1982's *Deathtrap*. Russo relentlessly took Hollywood players to task. He viewed them as being driven by their own ambition and cowardice, writing: "Hollywood is where a gay director makes anti-homosexual films so that he can continue to work with the big boys. . . . Hollywood is yesterday, forever catching up tomorrow with what's happening today."[9]

Since Russo's time, there has been a revolution in the representation of LGBTQ+ people in American popular culture.[10] After the social movements of the late 1960s and early 1970s, *in*visibility was replaced by *fraught* visibility. Increased representation presented the sinister opportunity to portray queer people as dangerous, marginal, or laughingstocks. Yet, in the 1970s, homosexuality began to have a more human face, especially on television. And as the 1970s gave way to the 1980s, the AIDS epidemic brought new visibility to gay men, both in public and in families and communities.[11] LGBTQ+ and AIDS activists began to hold Hollywood to account for its representation. They became consultants on and watchdogs of queer visibility.[12] They also advocated for queer people to come out in their everyday lives. "We're here! We're Queer! Get used to it!" was a slogan of both radical and mundane visibility.[13]

The 1990s brought an incomplete but undeniable transformation in LGBTQ+ mainstream representation in popular culture. The combined impact of the AIDS crisis, the social movements of the previous generation, and dramatic changes in the television and film industries produced this turning point. In November 1989, ABC aired a landmark episode of the popular TV show *Thirtysomething* with a scene of a male couple in bed together, with just the *hint* of sex. The show faced protests, and some advertisers pulled their spots from the episode.[14] Yet just a few years later, *Entertainment Weekly* proclaimed the decade to be "The Gay '90s" in a cover story that remarked triumphantly: "In 1995, the gay stream flows freely into the mainstream." Gay and lesbian TV and film characters (if not yet bi, trans, and nonbinary characters) were slowly becoming less pathological. They were not quite as tragic—and were more part of the everyday fabric of the worlds they inhabited. They also tended to be disproportionately White, gender-conforming men, and middle class. For these '90s characters, coming-out stories were not always central to their narratives. They could be gay or lesbian, but they also had other identities. And they were just as well-adjusted or messed up as their straight counterparts.

Now, in the third decade of the twenty-first century, LGBTQ+ representation and visibility are still too limited but are truly mainstream. There are so many LGBTQ+ television characters, storylines, artists, comedians, actors, and athletes that a list of them here would be inspiring but also dull to read. There has been a true spike in the number of lesbian, gay, and bisexual characters portrayed on television and in the movies (though films lag far behind TV)—even if this number still underrepresents the population and *still* disproportionately consists of gay, White, cisgender male characters.[15] For young people now, in particular, the LGBTQ+ characters on hit television shows and films would be completely unrecognizable to the closeted, tortured, and/or virginal teens of the 1980s and early '90s.[16] Today's queer characters often have full, out, connected lives and the freedom to fumble publicly through awkward first kisses and loves.[17]

There is still so much work to be done in transgender, genderqueer, gender-expansive, and nonbinary representative and visibility. But there has also been marked progress since *Time* magazine declared, in 2014, a "transgender tipping point" in its cover story featuring actress Laverne Cox.[18] Pop cultural transphobia is still tragically mainstream (see Harry Potter's creator, J. K. Rowling, for just one high-profile example of someone who inexplicably continues to defend her transphobia[19]). Yet it is being called out by the mainstream as well[20] (even on network reality shows, like *Survivor*[21]). Through the intentional and hard work of many in Hollywood whom we meet in this book, there is numerically more, more positive, and more varied and complex LGBTQ+ representation than ever before.

"WE CAN BE VILLAINS NOW"

Increased commercial and personal visibility for LGBTQ+ people means that there are more LGBTQ+ stories and openly LGBTQ+ people in the culture. This provides for another kind of a cultural payoff beyond the possibility of changing public opinion and policy. It allows for LGBTQ+ people to have their full humanity. They can be complicated people who do not have to represent an entire, large, and very diverse community.[22]

The people I interviewed who were responsible for creating and portraying LGBTQ+ characters were incredibly self-reflective about the images they were putting out into the world and their historical context. Some had lived and worked through a period of creative history when LGBTQ+ people and allies felt they had to create wholly positive representation to correct for the aggressively anti-queer culture of mid-century America. In the 1990s, "there was a sense that you had to offer positive imagery to lift people's self-esteem, that there was a negative balance that had to be redressed," said Alan Poul, a gay producer and director known for his work on the hit shows *My So-Called Life*, *Six Feet Under*, and the *Tales of the City* productions. "Everything became tilted toward the halo" for queer characters as a form of remediation for invisibility and negative representation.[23] AIDS, too, produced a kind of turning point in gay representation: a shift from negative stereotypes to a kind of "safe nobility," according to Paris Barclay, an award-winning director who was the first openly gay and African American president of the Directors Guild of America.[24]

Now, because there is so much *more*, especially on TV but also in film, there is less at stake for any one character to combat every single negative characterization. The people I interviewed also felt that they no longer had to make up for the past by portraying only queer angels and heroes. There was finally a new freedom to be complicated and flawed. This is not an issue that is unique to LGBTQ+ people. For example, Jews, African Americans, and Muslims have also wrestled with how to counteract old Hollywood stereotypes and tropes with their full complexity and humanity.[25] And, of course, the angel/villain categories themselves are messy and not at all mutually exclusive.[26] The artists I spoke with knew and welcomed this. Characters and storylines that might be read as "negative" allow for engaging storytelling and are therefore likely good for business.[27] They free up creatives to leave behind a narrow respectability politics.[28] They also may provide a more open space, as one scholar of Black representation noted, for "possibilities for nonnormative feelings, experiences, and allegiances that . . . are simply not possible in the image-policed spaces of positive texts."[29]

"There is no better medium," actor Wilson Cruz said, "to communicate complexity than art." When we spoke, he was serving as the Strategic Giving Officer for GLAAD, an organization that has worked on LGBTQ+ media representation since the 1980s. He has been a successful actor since he was young, playing teenager Rickie Vasquez on *My So-Called Life*, then other iconic queer roles like Angel in the Broadway tour production of *Rent*. He has also served in several political roles. In our conversation, Cruz talked about how progress could be measured by the complexity of LGBTQ+ representation. "We deserve," Cruz said, "the right to be complicated." The way that Cruz summed this up reflects many of the conversations I had. He celebrated the progress that had been made in the Hollywood representation of LGBTQ+ people since the 1990s, when he was coming of age as a young actor: "We can be villains now. It's okay if we're murderers and thieves, and people know that we are complicated people just like everybody else."[30] Director Barclay, too, celebrated the move out of 1990s nobility and best friend status into gay-you-love-to-hate territory: "We can also be dark, and we can be villains, and it can be okay. You hopefully won't get a letter from GLAAD because the villain is gay."

Queer show creators and writers talked with me as well about being committed to taking this creative liberty to convey queer complexity. "I am going to treat a gay character exactly like I'm going to treat a straight character, which means they're going to be just as fucked up. Because I'm interested in characters that are fucked up. I'm not interested in heroes. I'm not interested in people who get everything right. They intimidate me. They make me feel inadequate, because I'm not one of those people myself," said Alan Ball, the creator of HBO's *Six Feet Under* and *True Blood*, and the Academy Award–winning screenplay writer of the film *American Beauty*.[31] Actor Samy Nour Younes Figaredo reminded me that this kind of complexity does not just make for good storytelling, but it also makes connection to audiences all the more possible. "When it comes to people who are genuinely trying to be allies," he said, "the worst thing you can do is make us perfect and good in *every single way*" as a way to counterbalance negative representation. "We watch TV to kind of get that catharsis and empathize with other people's struggles. And if a person doesn't have a struggle, we can't empathize with that person. So, putting someone up on a pedestal, we can't reach them."[32]

Even still, there is a long way to go toward full, diverse, humane LGBTQ+ inclusion. Because of the way that Hollywood runs (as I will say much more about in chapter 3), and because of the cultural endurance of patriarchal White supremacy, it is still the case that White, cisgender, gender-conforming gay men are cast as the norm in LGBTQ+ representation. Many women I spoke with pointed to the sexism and queerphobia with which queer women are presented in television and film—when they are included at all. "Lesbians are tired of being killed off," pop culture writer and editor Trish Bendix said plainly.[33] Similarly, Lea DeLaria, the self-identified butch actor and comedian who played Big Boo in the Netflix hit *Orange Is the New Black*, talked with me about the narratives that still prevail when butch women are portrayed in pop culture: "If you saw any butch representation, in almost anything, butches were always played as stupid, as truck drivers, as hitting their girlfriends, getting drunk, getting into fights, you know, that was it."[34]

Racial exclusion joins misogyny to produce an overrepresentation of White gay men in mainstream pop culture. "If you're using sex to help sell, you're trying to sell something that people think is sexy, and for a lot of people a good-looking White male is sexy, especially for a lot of people with expendable cash. They see that as a sexy figure and if they can use sex to sell, they're going to use a good-looking White guy because that's what's going to move the needle," said politics and sports journalist LZ Granderson, who is Black and gay.[35] But, he said, "in reality, the community is a lot more diverse than that."[36]

And transgender characters on TV and film still are not given the space to be fully and complicatedly human. There has been some progress from the across-the-board "disgusting villains" phase of the 1990s. But it is still the case that "trans lives and trans experience have the tendency to become spectacle really, really quickly and easily," according to writer Meredith Talusan.[37] Or, to counteract this, trans characters and stories still need to be flawless. Actor and writer Jen Richards said to me in 2018 that, at that time, she looked at "this kind of moment in trans representation as being this Sidney Poitier phase of respectability politics where everyone has to be so unimpugnable." She talked about her hope that she could, moving forward, "make a complicated anti-hero, the kind of character that only, you know, straight men have traditionally been able to do."[38] This kind of complexity, the room to be imperfect yet still human and sympathetic, is *progress*. It is also an achievement of LGBTQ+ visibility that is still incomplete.

THE CLOSET AS A BARRIER TO VISIBILITY

There are still real barriers to being out in sports, Hollywood, music, and theater, and those barriers tend to be more substantial for anyone who is not a White, well-off, cisgender man.[39] The persistence of the closet stifles the voices of people who have a public platform. The closet also works to deny visibility to celebrities and others who might otherwise be out in their public lives. As theorist Eve Kosofsky Sedgwick put it all the way back in 1990, "The closet is the defining structure for gay oppression in this century."[40]

Of course, much has changed since Sedgwick published these words. But many people I interviewed—both in 2012 and more than a decade later—spoke about how the modern closet operates in their line of work: the way that the lack of job security in sports or Hollywood and the realities of discriminatory casting decisions make them afraid to come out; the way that representatives like agents and managers keep their clients in the closet; and the way that public people feel pressure to downplay their LGBTQ+ identities.

"The closet" is not an accident. It is a deliberate accomplishment of history. The term itself, historian George Chauncey tells us, was not used before the 1960s. The repressive 1950s helped to build the closet, and the movements of the late 1960s and early '70s took aim at it. Then the AIDS epidemic of the 1980s threw open closet doors for many ailing men who demanded new support from loved ones or who came out to families and friends on deathbeds. Yet the AIDS crisis also shut closet doors tight for many gay men who were trying to live and work while the world was afraid of them.[41] In Hollywood, too, the closet has a long, tortured history, dating back to its beginnings when early twentieth-century studios fired gay stars and/or "contractually married" them to mixed-gender partners.[42] In these years, there *were* thriving and visible gay cultural scenes in cities like New York and Los Angeles. But a repressive legal regime also censored and criminalized queer content on stage and screen.[43]

The percentage of people in the United States who identify as LGBTQ+ is tough to accurately determine and varies widely by identity category and age/generation. In 2024, according to Gallup, a record-high 9.3 percent of US adults self-identified as LGBTQ or "something other than heterosexual"—a proportion that has almost doubled since 2020. Breaking this down a bit, 1.4 percent of respondents identified as lesbian, 2.0 percent as gay, and 5.2 percent as bisexual. In this survey as well, Gallup found that 1.3 percent of respondents identified as transgender, while a Pew Research Center study from 2022 found that 1.6 percent of US adults identify as transgender or nonbinary. Both polls identified substantial generational differences. In the Gallup 2024 poll, while 23.1 percent of Gen Z adults and 14.2 percent of Millennials identified as LGBTQ+, only 5.1 percent of Gen Xers and 3.0 percent of Baby Boomers did. Gen Z is driving the rise in the proportion of LGBTQ+-identified adults.[44]

With almost a quarter of Gen Zers identifying as LGBTQ+, clearly this population is not being fully represented in popular culture. The closet endures. In recent years, the pop cultural closet, especially the Hollywood closet, hasn't operated in the strict, constraining way that it did historically. The modern closet is often described by insiders as a *glass closet*: a closet still, but one that is not hiding its inhabitants effectively.[45] A related form in current pop culture is a closet that has quite a few people in it, in which public figures are "out" in their private lives but have not publicly come out. I have come to think of this as a "walk-in closet," and I admit to being pretty pleased with myself when I (wrongly) thought I had come up with this term. It turns out, not surprisingly, that I had not. Apparently, an activist in the Stonewall era dubbed gay bars "walk-in closets," and others since then have used the term in the way that I considered it.[46]

Several people spoke with me about the walk-in closets of Hollywood and elite sports. "There's a big community of closeted actors, yet it's very tight-knit. It's existed for sixty years, you know, Rock Hudson, Montgomery Clift, Tab Hunter—that little secret group has existed for a long time within gay Hollywood, most of its members are closeted, and everybody's protecting each other and supporting each other: supporting one another to remain closeted,"[47] said James Duke Mason, a young out gay writer, activist, and former West Hollywood city official (he served on the WeHo LGBTQ+ Advisory Board from 2015 to 2020)—also the son of singer Belinda Carlisle. The walk-in closet, then, makes room for a circle of supportive people around an athlete or celebrity who has not come out publicly and who relies on the discretion of their walk-in closet friends.

We could think of the glass and walk-in closets as being related to a form of identity work called *covering*. This term was popularized by law professor Kenji Yoshino, in his 2006 book by this name. Yoshino, citing the original idea by sociologist Erving Goffman in his 1963 book *Stigma*, writes that there have been three ways that people have historically negotiated their marginalized or "spoiled" identities: by *conversion* to a new identity, by *passing* as that socially acceptable identity, or by *covering*. Yoshino explained that covering means "to tone down a disfavored identity to fit into the mainstream." When someone covers, they do not pretend to be someone they are not, but they play down a stigmatized part of themselves.[48] Covering is part of how the closet functions. It completely obscures or at least downplays LGBTQ+ people's queer identity, thus serving as a barrier to visibility. This is an important concept, because it reminds us that visibility is not a simple binary concept (you are either visible or you are not). It is, rather, a complex and context-specific set of negotiations.

THE MECHANISMS OF THE MODERN CLOSET

The closet—in its various forms—is maintained in many ways and for many reasons for the culture workers I interviewed. First, and simply, *fear* operates as a mechanism of the modern closet, and there is quite a lot of fear of what will happen to public people if they publicly come out.[49] This "fear of the unknown"[50] maintains the closet, even today, for people who are trying to break into a business that is so competitive—like Hollywood—and for which they have been training assiduously and dreaming of since childhood—like elite sports. "I still feel like my queerness is an obstacle to reaching my potential on my career route. I hope I'm wrong," said Amin El Gamal, an Egyptian American and Muslim actor, in 2022. He has been on television shows such as *The Newsroom*, *Prison Break*, and *Good Trouble*, and films such as *Breaking Fast*. El Gamal acknowledged a lot of progress in LGBTQ+

inclusion in the industry, but they still expressed trepidation about being out in Hollywood. He still feels that he has to ask himself: "Do I have to hide this aspect of me" during auditions?[51]

Beyond fear, many culture workers noted that people in Hollywood and elite sports uphold and support the closet themselves. Representatives like agents, managers, and public relations people are hired to do "relationship work," image management, and gatekeeping for their clients.[52] These professionals can and do get involved when it comes to the romantic, sexual, and family lives of their clients, so reps can wittingly or unwittingly contribute to keeping people in the closet. For instance, they might counsel their clients not to come out publicly if they think it will close doors to career opportunities.[53] Many people I spoke with believed that queer gatekeepers, too, maintained closets around individuals and stifled queer creative content.[54]

In my more recent interviews, there has been some sense that it has become a *bit* less remarkable or risky to be publicly out as lesbian, gay, or bisexual in Hollywood. However, this is not yet the case for trans and nonbinary culture workers. "It feels like people don't want to see trans people anymore. They don't want to see them on television. They don't want to see them in the press," said TV writer and producer Shadi Petosky in 2021.[55]

The mechanisms of the closet, the barriers to LGBTQ+ visibility, are slightly different in sports. Fear plays an important role in maintaining this sport closet, as does pressure from coaches and others to remain silent about LGBTQ+ identity.[56] There is also a pervasive narrative in sports that if athletes come out as LGBTQ+, they would "distract" from a singular focus on athletic performance.[57] Sport has been incredibly slow to change for LGBTQ+ athlete inclusion and equity. It is also, as I discuss further in chapter 3, now one of the primary targets of the political Right, which has relentlessly targeted trans athlete participation as one of the issues to unify and energize its base in recent years. The experience of the closet is not universal, and forms of privilege that operate more broadly in the United States cannot help but inform the ways in which the closet impacts its inhabitants.

This is certainly true with respect to gender privilege in sports. Many assume that it has been historically easier to be a queer woman in sports than a queer man, because the general narrative is that sports is chock-full of queer women. But this is not what experts, coaches, and athletes have reported. In fact, because of this public narrative, which is both sexist and homophobic, women's sports and women athletes are often highly visible and heavily scrutinized.

Former athlete, coach, and vanguard sports activist and scholar Pat Griffin described in 1998 a "glass-closet bargain" between closeted lesbians and their ostensibly straight teammates and coaches—a kind of "don't ask, don't tell" détente. One of the ways that this dynamic works is by policing gender presentation of women athletes and maintaining a sense that veering from traditional femininity marks an athlete as gay.[58] Griffin said to me that if you watch women's softball, you will notice that a lot of the players have bows in their hair; ribbons superfluously tied to their functional ponytails. She said that this is code: "no bow, lesbo." The bow is "not just a fashion. It's a statement of heterosexuality."[59] (I should add, parenthetically, that "no bow, lesbo" is a theory that received a substantial counterexample in the winter of 2021, when seventeen-year-old dancer and social media phenom JoJo Siwa—who now identifies as queer rather than as a lesbian[60]—announced online that she had a girlfriend, all while wearing a rainbow version of her signature *massive* hair bow).[61]

Another mechanism of the closet that I heard a lot about in my interviews with respect to women's sports is *negative recruiting*. This pertains especially to women coaches, but it has been a broader cultural tool of control, silence, and invisibility on women's sports teams. Negative recruiting is historically widespread but is not actually allowed by the NCAA in college sports. It describes a practice in which a team tries to recruit away prospective players from another team by painting a negative picture of that competing team.[62] As it applies to sexuality, one college coach might try to convince a high school recruit to join their team by telling her and her family that the coach of another prospective team is a lesbian and that this team is filled with lesbian players. This coach would not only be playing here on a "guilt by association" narrative but also on a kind of "recruitment" trope that the lesbian coach could "convert" her players into lesbians. For coaches, whose precarious jobs depend on winning games, their ability to successfully recruit top players is central to their professional success and security. Negative recruiting, then, has been a pervasive part of the mechanism of the closet in women's sports, in that it has kept women coaches—and even their players—in the closet.

Sherri Murrell, the now-former head coach of the Portland State University women's basketball team, was the only publicly out Division I women's college basketball head coach at the time I interviewed her in September 2013. She came out publicly by the mundane but news-making act of agreeing, when asked, to include a family photo of herself, her wife, and their two kids in her team's media guide. Over the years, Murrell received quite a bit of press attention for this trailblazing role.[63] She talked with me about the role of negative recruiting in her experience. She said it was "the number-one thing that I was worried about when I was closeted." She tied this to job security, saying that coaches in more than three hundred colleges are competing for the best basketball players, so any disadvantage in the recruiting process has high stakes. In her experience over the years with parents of prospective students, she had both "coded" and direct conversations with parents about sexuality. "That's one of the fears, that 'Hey, there! You've got a lesbian coach. She's out. Oh, she must have an entire lesbian team. She must recruit lesbian athletes.' And that couldn't be further from the truth." It has been this kind of fear of being publicly out, though—stoked through the practice of negative recruiting—that has helped to maintain the closet for some LGBTQ+ coaches and their players. It has deterred queer prospects from getting into coaching for fear of reprisal or fear of not being able to do their jobs effectively. It keeps queer coaches in the closet, denying their visibility in sports and in the broader culture.[64]

Thankfully, this practice seems to have receded in recent years. Nevin Caple—a former college basketball player and current inclusion consultant and educator and NIL (name, image, and likeness) strategist—said of negative recruiting: "In the early 2000s, coaches were often subjected to negative recruiting and had a difficult time landing top recruits if rival coaches questioned the 'traditional family values' of a particular coach or program. Very subtle, but very intentional, deliberate, and dangerous behavior. This has changed significantly as society has become increasingly more accepting of LGBTQ student-athletes, and families of high school recruits are more likely to question the intentions of a college coach who uses this tactic to recruit."[65]

In early 2023, Outsports noted that the number of publicly out coaches in women's college basketball "has exploded" since Murrell's coaching days. They noted that athletes are more publicly out than ever, especially women. They counted 186 publicly out LGBTQ+ athletes in the 2021 Summer Olympics (170 of whom were women) and noted that at least 20 percent of women playing in the Women's National Basketball Association (WNBA) at the time were publicly out.[66] Outsports also found, in a 2021 study, that athletes in the United States and Canada who come out while they are high school or college students report "widespread acceptance from teammates." In their survey of 820 student-athletes reporting on 1,000 experiences, more than 95 percent reported that their teammates' responses when they came out were somewhere between "neutral" and "perfect," and that the majority of respondents had a better experience coming out to teammates than they had expected to have. Few of the athletes in this survey, however, reported coming out as transgender (just twenty-nine of the one thousand coming-out experiences).[67]

It is still rare for elite athletes to be out as gay, lesbian, or bisexual. But, as is the case in Hollywood, it is a bit less remarkable. It is still transgender and nonbinary culture workers, athletes, and artists for whom the closet is the most durable and most assiduously constructed by policies and institutions. The closet can operate differently for them than for those who hold a minoritized sexual identity. Transgender activist, director, and writer Janet Mock explained this distinction in her autobiography: "People often transpose the coming-out experience on me, asking how it felt to be in the closet, to have been stealth. These questions have always puzzled me. . . . I never hid my gender. . . . People assume that I was in the closet because I didn't disclose that I was assigned male at birth."[68]

THE COST OF THE CLOSET

This denial of public visibility is one significant cultural cost of the closet. The *individual* cost of the closet is also quite profound, and this is what can make coming out desirable or even necessary.[69] Here, again, I focus on sports, where there is still a very active closet. There are a number of high-profile examples of men who came out as gay after they left their sport and reflected back on how much they gave up to the closet.[70] From published memoirs of gay athletes or others in sports (like umpires), we know that one cost of the closet is a lack of an open romantic or sexual life and/or relying on inauthentic relationships in an attempt to pass as straight.[71] Another devastating cost of the closet for athletes is living with the constant fear of having their first love—their sport—taken away from them if they come out or are involuntarily "outed."[72] This anxiety comes with a severe cost to mental health and happiness. Esera Tuaolo, an NFL nose guard for nine years, wrote in his 2006 memoir: "It's rough down in the trenches, where linemen weighing more than three-hundred pounds hurl themselves at one another in brutal hand-to-hand combat, but it is nothing compared to the pain I kept buried inside so I could play out my dream." Over his years in the closet in the NFL, he became suicidal.[73]

The closet also cost former Major League Baseball player Billy Bean quite a lot. Bean, a White gay man who passed away at age sixty in the summer of 2024, was an outfielder in the MLB for at least part of six seasons during the years from 1987 to 1995. He wrote in his 2003 autobiography that he was not out as gay to anyone on his team in his playing days. He believed that he would have to quit professional baseball, a game he loved so much, if he wanted to live openly as a gay man.[74] He simply felt that being out as gay was incompatible with playing professional baseball, and he made a trade-off to play the game. "I never loved anything more than baseball," he said to me in 2012.[75] He was married to his college girlfriend at the beginning of his career, and she learned early on that whatever was happening on the field for Bean was going to determine his mood and his focus. Baseball was going to come first. "Sports," he said to me, "is not easy, even for the greatest players in the world," and "I think for all athletes, their main goal is to eliminate distractions so they can focus exclusively on what they're trying to do." Bean, with a singular focus on baseball, envisioned a potential cost of being out as gay. He described not wanting to stand out for anything other than his performance on the baseball diamond.

As a result, Bean did not give his friends, teammates, and family a chance to support him in coming out. He had witnessed the homophobia of many of his coaches, from elementary school to pro baseball, and he had no role models in other out athletes to pave the way, no other gay friends, and no gay community. So, he *presumed* that he should not come out to his loved ones. This became a burden that he carried with him into baseball. A tragic cost of the closet for Bean was that he was not able to openly mourn the death of his male partner. While he was playing with the San Diego Padres, Bean lost Sam to AIDS-related complications. On the very day of Sam's death, after a grueling night attending to Sam's illness, Bean had to show up to play an exhibition baseball game. He felt that he had to play rather than take time to grieve, because he felt that he could not show how much he was mourning this loss of the man he had presented publicly as just a friend. He wrote that he did not attend Sam's funeral, either, worried that it would look suspicious if he even missed one game.

Ultimately, after Sam's death, Bean gave up a game he truly loved because he could not reconcile being out as gay and being a professional baseball player. He wrote: "I quit playing baseball in 1996, after playing a whole season pretending that my partner's death from

AIDS-related causes didn't happen. That's what happens when you live in the closet. You start to believe your own lies."[76] Bean's life and career, though, did not remain in the closet. Bean came out publicly in 1999, published his autobiography in 2003, and then became a high-profile, highly involved advocate for sports inclusion.[77] He returned to the MLB in the summer of 2014, when he was appointed the league's first Ambassador for Inclusion, taking with him the lesson that he did not ultimately have to give up a game he loved for a full and open life as a publicly out gay man.[78]

THE COMING-OUT IMPERATIVE[79]

Visibility was a key strategy and goal of the LGBTQ+ social movement that flourished after the 1969 Stonewall uprising. Activists of the 1950s and early 1960s (known as the "homophile movement") met in secret, used pseudonyms in their public writings, and feared that exposure could cost them jobs and loved ones.[80] But their counterparts in the next generation explicitly urged queer people to *come out* and to *be* out and visible in their lives. This was both for personal fulfillment and was a political tactic. Drawing on the social movements that preceded them, especially the Black Power movement that urged unapologetic Black pride, visibility politics were central to the early campaigns of the gay liberation movement. As activist Carl Wittman plainly urged in his "Gay Manifesto" in 1970: "If we are liberated we are open with our sexuality. Closet queenery must end. Come out."[81]

Decades later, LGBTQ+ people and activists still see coming out as a necessary part of changing culture and politics. People in Hollywood, music, theater, and elite sports also recognize the benefits and responsibilities of coming out. They understand that their personal visibility opens up their workplaces and the culture. Many LGBTQ+ culture workers I spoke with felt that there were many reasons to come out publicly, even if—and sometimes because—the stakes were so high. For some, publicly coming out alleviated the pressure of the closet and created a personal and professional space of comfort, openness, and ease. Jamie Babbit, a White lesbian Gen Xer and hugely successful director and writer, has to establish rapport and authority quickly on new TV and film sets. She is often in charge of hundreds of people at a time. "That's why," she said, "I'd rather be out, moment one, like gay, gay, gay. Just own it, because, otherwise, it just gets weird, you know?" She noted, too, that coming out like this was not a onetime accomplishment. It had to be negotiated over and over again in the span of a career and a life.[82]

Many also believe they can do public good by coming out publicly. They take this role seriously, even if it might be personally burdensome. Some spoke with me of the way that visibility begets visibility. Having publicly out role models in their fields could pave the way for their own work. Former basketball player Nevin Caple said of her own career choices:

> Part of the reason I chose not to go into coaching was because I didn't know any lesbian coaches who were out publicly at the time. I knew I wouldn't survive a profession where my success would be closely tied to hiding salient parts of my identity. Who knows how different my career path would have been had the experiences of lesbian coaches been celebrated and personalized for me earlier in life?

Former lacrosse goalie Andrew Goldstein also understands what coming out might do for others. He holds the distinction of being the first American male professional athlete to publicly come out as gay (in 2005) on a team sport while he was actively playing. He said to me that he had had a positive experience coming out to teammates and friends. But when ESPN wanted to do a coming-out story on him in 2005, he was apprehensive. He wanted to be known for his lacrosse skills, not for his sexuality, and he was not comfortable with the attention. But he believed that coming out made new things possible in sports. "For me growing up," he said, "one of the biggest things was there were no role models. So literally it wasn't possible to be a gay athlete and even play in college." When he was being recruited to play in college, at Dartmouth, he thought: "So that means I'm either going to never be gay again and play sports or I'm going to be gay and never play sports."[83]

There has been so much attention to individual gay men in the big team sports coming out, like Jason Collins in basketball and Michael Sam in football, because these individual publicly out athletes are almost always *firsts* in their sport. People in and around elite sports recognize that coming out does not in and of itself accomplish broad cultural change, but it is an important step in this direction. "People don't think that the guy who's at the plate, the bottom of the ninth with two outs, and they're praying to God for him to make contact, is gay," said Brian Ellner, who is a communications and political strategist in New York City and an LGBTQ+ and marriage equality advocate.[84] For fans or teammates, knowing that your sports hero is gay can change stereotypical views of how gay men look and act. It can also change attitudes and behavior once fans know that they have such a strong connection and sense of loyalty to a gay man.

Patrick Burke is a straight ally whose father was a high-profile elite hockey executive. Burke co-founded the organization You Can Play to open up sports to LGBTQ+ athletes after his younger brother, Brendan, who was gay and a hockey player, died in a car accident when he was twenty-one. Burke said to me that when athletes come out, it changes the way that their teammates and friends think about their own homophobia. "We call it a real 'holy shit' moment when you put a human face on it": for instance, when athletes can see that their homophobic language makes their gay teammates feel unsafe in their locker rooms.[85]

Some I spoke with drew a connection directly from pervasive homophobic language and bullying to LGBTQ+ suicides. They believe that tragedies could be prevented if LGBTQ+ people could give their teammates and loved ones a chance to see firsthand the impact of their own homophobia. As recently as 2021, in an Outsports survey of high school and college athletes, nearly 70 percent reported that they heard anti-LGBTQ+ language "from at least one teammate on a weekly basis" before they came out to their team, and that this then diminished once they had come out.[86]

THE COMING-OUT APPARATUS

When public LGBTQ+ people consider publicly coming out, they usually have a lot of help. The apparatus behind them includes the mainstream media. It also includes within-community media outlets like Outsports, which breaks and tells stories of LGBTQ+ athletes. Public people also often rely on the social capital—or networks—of others who have come out before them. This is something I will talk more about in chapter 4. In this case, people who are considering coming out publicly can look to others within their community—like gay football players relying on other gay professional athletes who have already come out—to provide guidance and support on the experience of coming out in the international spotlight.[87] The within-community support also includes the LGBTQ+ movement itself, which mobilizes celebrity visibility through, for instance, National Coming Out Day and International Transgender Day of Visibility each year.

The coming-out apparatus also includes professionals, like PR reps, who help public people manage the public coming-out process. If I had to cast one person in the leading role here, it would be Howard Bragman. White, gay, and in his sixties when he passed away in early 2023, Bragman was considered to be *the* coming-out broker for celebrities. His clients included professional basketball player John Amaechi, the first NBA player to come out publicly; the WNBA's Sheryl Swoopes; and football's Esera Tuaolo and Michael Sam. When I interviewed Bragman, he handed me a copy of his book as soon as I walked into his office. In *Where's My Fifteen Minutes?*, Bragman wrote about the importance of controlling the public narrative and getting out ahead of any secret you might be keeping. He shared that he, personally, made the choice to come out early in his professional life, and he believed in this process and its outcome: "I can't think of a person who came out and was less happy or was displeased with the results, because truth is so powerful. . . . In Hollywood, most publicists spend their time keeping their clients *in* the closet. I'm the guy you come to when you want to come out." In my conversation with him, without my prompting, Bragman connected his work to social change. "I've always believed that you have a couple of ways to move: you have the political movement and the culture wars. And I think we're winning the culture wars."[88]

Amaechi, one of Bragman's highest-profile clients, said to me in 2014 that for athletes coming out publicly, "Howard Bragman is the one." Amaechi explained how this kind of PR work is useful to LGBTQ+ public people. He described Bragman as a kind of a "membrane" and a "funnel" between him, the media, and the broader public during what Amaechi described as a "frightening experience" of coming out through the 2007 publication of his best-selling memoir. Even though it is more common for people to come out as LGBTQ+ now, it still becomes news, especially for those who are trailblazers. Amaechi was absolutely one of those trailblazers, and he faced a barrage of media attention at the time. Not only did Bragman and his PR company schedule Amaechi's interviews and the logistics of those engagements; they also stepped in to handle mismanagements by the press—like when Amaechi was asked offensive questions in interviews. "Howard," Amaechi said, "filters out some of the bullshit."[89]

Amaechi—who came out publicly after he retired from basketball and is now a Professor of Leadership at the University of Exeter (UK), a psychologist, and an executive coach—lived in a glass closet while he was playing in the NBA. He was born in the United States to a White, English mother and a Nigerian father, was raised in England, and then came back to the States to play high school and then college basketball. He told me that there were a few times when NBA teammates asked him, either directly or obliquely, and that he never lied about his sexuality to them, never invented stories of women in his life. But he *was* purposefully evasive. According to Amaechi, this was a tactic that served both him and his teammates well at the time. He has recounted, both in writing and to me,[90] that a teammate of his on the Utah Jazz, Greg Ostertag, once asked him, as they were walking onto the court before a game: "You gay, dude?" Amaechi's response, delivered lightly, was "You have nothing to worry about." Another teammate in Orlando was sent by teammates during a plane ride to inquire, according to Amaechi: "You never talk about girls, do you, Meech?" Amaechi's response was a quintessentially British and elusive "Indeed," and the conversation ended there. He said that if he had been asked more directly, and when he could have a fuller conversation about it, he would not have lied about being gay. But he felt that the glass closet of his playing days served to preserve stability on his teams and was maintained by his teammates. Amaechi said to me: "People are complicit. The existence of the closet is not simply for the benefit of the person in it. It is for the benefit of people outside of it also. They are the ones who truly benefit by not ever having to deal with the issue."

Amaechi did not upset the delicate equilibrium of his glass closet while he was in the NBA. But he did recognize the toll it took on him. "It's exhausting," he said to me, "to withhold data from people. It's tiring, because it means you're constantly thinking about what you're going to say next, and you can't pre-censor the next sentence while delivering the previous one in any kind of really authentic way." When he decided to publicly come out, the reaction was largely positive, with some of the biggest names in basketball offering public support.[91] At the same time, the revelation brought immediate danger: "Literally, in the first tranche of emails," Amaechi said, "were three death threats." Being out in a homophobic culture has its price, too.

COMING-OUT BURDENS: CONTENDING WITH THE MEDIA

The media—broadly defined—is often a central part of the coming-out apparatus for those who choose to come out and those who are publicly "outed." The mainstream media, and some high-profile gay writers and activists, participated in a controversial practice in the 1990s of forced "outing" of celebrities and public figures. At the height of the AIDS epidemic and conservative anti-queer politics, this practice was, in part, about exposing the hypocrisy of supposedly closeted public figures and their silence and/or public policy assaults on queer people.[92] But in the twenty-first century, as celebrities work to exercise their *own* control and choice to come out publicly, their process often includes carefully orchestrated cover stories and press interviews. In 2013, when basketball's Jason Collins became the first gay man in the top four professional US team sports to publicly come out while actively playing, he chose to do so via a cover story in *Sports Illustrated* under the headline "The Gay Athlete." The lede read: "I'm a 34-year-old NBA center. I'm black. And I'm gay. I didn't set out to be the first openly gay athlete playing in a major American team sport. But since I am, I'm happy to start the conversation."[93]

The media is not just a *conduit* for public people—it is an active player in the public coming-out process. It vies for the high-profile stories of barrier breaking and history making that will sell magazines or attract clicks. It is not, though, a *neutral* player in the public coming-out process. Reporters have a point of view, a focus, a story that they want to tell. Many people I spoke with understood and had experienced, for instance, that sexism and racism shape public attention and narrative. These dynamics inform the media's intense focus on cis male athletes coming out, ignoring or downplaying trailblazing women athletes. Journalist LZ Granderson spoke with me in 2013 about the gender and race dynamic of coming out in the media. He pointed out that if you are a White, gender-conforming, cis gay guy, you are celebrated for coming out as gay in a way that others are not. He mentioned the public's response to basketball star Brittney Griner[94]:

> It goes back to the phenomenon of being in love with the gay White male. Part of that eliminates ethnic minorities, racial minorities, but then it obviously also eliminates women being held up in the proper light as the heroes that they're supposed to be and that they actually are. I mean Brittney Griner comes out, and she's like one of the

> greatest basketball players of all time, and yet we're still waiting for the "gay athlete" to come out?

He not only blamed external media for this dynamic, but also LGBTQ+ people themselves. He was once on a panel where there was a comment that a top athlete had not yet come out as gay while they were still playing. Granderson countered by mentioning a number of elite women athletes: "I mean, how many top athletes have come out while still playing do you need before you start saying the fact that you're just a sexist pig and you're waiting for a dude to come out?"

The mainstream media can also display insensitive ignorance when it participates in the coming-out process. People do not always get to choose the way their story is told or to choose *how* they become visible. This has been especially true when it comes to the media treatment of transgender and gender-expansive people.[95] Kye Allums became the first publicly out transgender Division I college basketball player in the fall of 2010 while playing at George Washington University. Allums said to me:

> The media coverage back then was overwhelming, not just because of the volume, but because of how uninformed and performative it often felt. I learned quickly that media reporting also exists on a spectrum, and many weren't equipped to understand trans experience beyond cultural projections. A few got it right, and by right, I mean they listened, asked better questions, and didn't try to make my story "just fit" their headline.[96]

Chris Mosier first came out publicly in 2010. One of the first things he said to me was that he had had negative experiences with other interviews. He recounted a terrible experience with a reporter for a high-profile publication that pathologized Mosier and transgender people and experiences. "He was really digging for the story he wanted to write. He kept asking me, 'Were you bullied in high school? Were you picked on as a kid?' And I was like 'No, I wasn't. I had a fine experience.' What he was really pulling for was the damaged child" story.[97]

COMING-OUT OPPORTUNITIES

Of course, the media has changed in recent years, which has naturally impacted the way it participates in the coming-out process. Social media doesn't quite make the Howard Bragmans and the *Sports Illustrateds* of the world obsolete, but it certainly changes their public roles. And as publicly coming out becomes more common, some feel it does not have to be as carefully orchestrated and can happen more informally. Social media provides a means for this. It even provides more agency, control, and immediacy in the coming-out process.

For athletes in high-profile men's sports who have come out as gay or bisexual in the years since Jason Collins and Michael Sam made headlines, some still use traditional media opportunities. NFL defensive end Ryan Russell came out as bi in an ESPN story in the summer of 2019, and professional hockey player Luke Prokop publicly came out as gay in an article in *The Athletic* in the summer of 2021.[98] Others, however, have turned to social media to come out publicly. Defensive lineman Carl Nassib, the first player in the NFL to come out publicly as gay while he was *actively* playing on a team, relied on an Instagram video post in June 2021, saying, "What's up, people . . . I just wanted to take a quick moment to say that I'm gay. . . . I'm a pretty private person so I hope you guys know that I'm not doing this for attention. I just think that representation and visibility are so important."[99]

Beyond sports, some of the most high-profile public coming-out events in recent years have happened via social media, like singer Lil Nas X coming out via Twitter at the end of Pride month in June 2019, JoJo Siwa coming out on TikTok in 2021, or hip-hop artist Lil Uzi Vert making news in the summer of 2022 by changing their pronouns on Instagram to they/them.[100]

For some artists, their *creative* roles serve as a catalyst to come out in both their private and public lives. Their workplaces and the specifics of their jobs become an opportunity for increased LGBTQ+ visibility. I spoke with several actors who came out publicly as gay around the time they played a gay character on television. Wilson Cruz was nineteen years old when he auditioned for the role of teenager

Rickie Vasquez on *My So-Called Life*. Even then, he recognized the significance of this young, trailblazing character. Cruz told me that he was not out, even to his parents, when he filmed the pilot for the show, but he planned to come out if the show got picked up and went to series. He felt that staying in the closet would be to undermine the show itself:

> I just felt like it was an important role, and if I went around in the closet while playing it, and then it came out that I was gay? Then I felt like everything that we did on the show would be negated. That it would have been all for naught because this character, which was really about self-acceptance and dignity in the end, if I wasn't doing that, then what message was I sending out, and what good would the series be?

When Cruz was preparing to shoot the episode of the show that addressed Rickie's coming out, he remembers going into the office of Alan Poul, a gay man who came in to produce the last ten episodes of the show. Cruz remembers that he was resolute about coming out publicly, and he remembers fondly the way that Poul, who had come to be a mentor, supported him through the process:

> When I walked into Alan Poul, I didn't go in and say, "Do you think I should?" And I had the same conversation with my agent at the time, and people who represented me. I didn't go in and say, "I'm wondering if." I had already made up my mind, and I was asking them for help in *how*.

Cruz knew he was doing something risky but also believed it was something—given his portrayal of Rickie—that was the right thing to do.

Commercial visibility is one way that married couple Larry Sullivan and David Monahan have been out publicly through their careers as actors.[101] White gay men now in their mid-fifties, Monahan and Sullivan have been professional actors since they were in their twenties. Monahan was part of a pathbreaking storyline on *Dawson's Creek* in 2001, when he shared a 5.5-second kiss with Jack at the senior prom.[102] Sullivan and Monahan have been successful working actors for decades, cast in both gay and straight roles. Monahan is also a successful television writer. They are unique in the way they have approached being out, bringing their real-life partnership and family into public view. Not only did they play a couple on HBO's *Big Little Lies*, but they have made a bit of a name for themselves in the commercial space, as big mainstream brands embraced a modicum of LGBTQ+ visibility.[103] The couple has appeared with their real-life son in high-profile television commercials for Campbell's soup, Sabra hummus, and Target. The 2015 Campbell's soup commercial for the brand's Star Wars line first shows Sullivan and his son, as Sullivan does his best Darth Vader impression while spoon-feeding soup: "Cooper, I am your father." The camera pans back as Monahan says, in *his* Vader voice, "No, no, no, *I* am your father." This spot made international news, warranted commentary from Stephen Colbert, and attracted backlash from the right-wing One Million Moms. It also earned Monahan and Sullivan the title of "sexiest pitchmen" in the November 2015 "Sexiest Man Alive" issue of *People* magazine.[104]

In our conversations, Monahan and Sullivan were self-reflective about coming out publicly and how to manage it in their careers. They talked about the decisions they made to *be* out. They didn't come out publicly in a grand way, but they were open and honest in their lives and careers. They didn't lie earlier in their careers if they were asked about their sexuality. They then chose to be visible as a couple and a family when they had the opportunity. "I don't know if I ever needed to come out," Monahan said. "I mean, we are out gay actors living our lives." In the context of societal homophobia and its consequences for young people's mental health, Sullivan said, "It's just the least that we can do: live as openly and honestly as possible." They also have had the experience of getting feedback on their work that has allowed them to recognize the importance of their visibility. Monahan remembered that when he was on *Dawson's Creek*, he got a piece of fan mail from a young person that said they had watched the prom episode and immediately turned off the TV and came out to their parents. "You're thinking you're just living your life in a bubble," Monahan reflected, "that you do a TV show, and you don't realize that your work does have those kinds of ramifications."[105]

VISIBILITY IS CRITICAL, BUT AT A COST

The award-winning teen Netflix hit *Heartstopper* debuted in 2022 and was an instant heart-warmer. It featured the kind of representation that could not have even been remotely imagined in the 1990s. One of the lead characters is a rugby player, Nick Nelson. He had only ever seemed to like girls until he falls for his new friend, Charlie Spring, in their British boys' school. The show follows their developing relationship, which includes Nick exploring his identity and eventually coming out as bisexual. They are two cisgender White boys falling in love and kissing, a *lot*, on-screen. They have a group of multiracial friends that includes a mixed-race lesbian couple; cis boy Tao Xu and his best friend and love interest, Elle, who is trans and played by the young trans, Black British actress Yasmin Finney; and Isaac, a White cisgender boy who is never on-screen without a book in his hands and is actively exploring asexual identity in season two. The show explores themes of coming out, bullying, defying stereotypes, and navigating ignorant family members. But it also joyfully centers around a group of young people who show tenderness and care and form a supportive and loving community for each other.

The show and its cast received a lot of media and social media attention when it first aired. The actor who plays Charlie, Joe Locke, was already publicly out. His costar, Kit Connor, was not. After a September 2022 video of Connor holding hands with a woman surfaced on social media, he was subject to increased speculation about his sexuality. He also faced vitriolic public charges that he was portraying an important pop cultural character with whom he did not share a sexual identity.

This upset him publicly quite a lot. By the end of the following month, he felt he was forced to come out before he was ready to do so. He tweeted: "back for a minute. i'm bi. congrats on forcing an 18 year old to out himself. i think some of you missed the point of the show. bye." The more thoughtful media coverage after Connor's tweet focused on the fact that it might be important to raise legitimate concerns about casting and professional opportunities for queer actors (more on this in chapter 3), but it was not okay to pressure a young actor to reveal anything about himself to the public.[106] Connor, himself, almost a year later, reflected that what was most upsetting to him was the fact that his visibility did not allow him the privacy that he needed as a young person who was just gaining fame.[107]

On the one hand, *Heartstopper* provides beautiful queer storylines and characters that have been so important to young people and others.[108] On the other hand, its popularity and visibility brought a coming-out imperative that was experienced as personally vulnerable and difficult by at least some of its young stars. This is just one recent example of the double-edged and complex nature of visibility—especially now, and especially for those who are most targeted. "Each to their own" when it comes to visibility, said trans artist and filmmaker Zackary Drucker in the summer of 2025. "But for those of us who have the freedom to be visible without tremendous risk and consequence, it's more important than ever."[109] At the same time: "We are in a sociopolitical moment wherein the most visible parts of trans life are being weaponized," trans filmmaker and writer Chase Joynt said to me in the summer of 2025, "and it is thus *very* important to render certain things unseen or unfindable, and to recognize that being unseen and unfindable was—and still remains—a way that trans people survived."[110] Another trans writer offered, in 2022, "As a trans femme person of color, I know all too well the simultaneous importance of visibility and the imminent danger of it." Perhaps, instead, "radical invisibility" could be not only a "form of trans care," but also "an act of resistance."[111]

These commentaries—and the experiences of culture workers we have heard from here—provide an important warning: visibility both speaks back to a power that wants you to disappear *and* puts you in harm's way of that power. We should not equate mainstream pop cultural visibility with institutional or interpersonal equity, justice, or safety. We need to keep the complexities and even dangers of visibility front of mind as we celebrate the explosion of queer characters on television and the shattering of celebrity glass closets. LGBTQ+ visibility has made tremendous strides in the past thirty years. It is complicated, insufficient, imperfect, and hard work. It is also not always safe or desirable. At the same time, it is triumphant and transformative. It can bring familiarity, acceptance, new communities, and new intimacy across difference. It can be both a joy and a burden for those who do it. Culture cannot be won without it.

2. USE YOUR PLATFORM

Once you have people's attention, you need to use it. Or as former professional basketball player John Amaechi put it: "If people are going to look at you like you're a god, then you should probably work a miracle every once in a while."[1] Using your public platform is another key step in winning the culture war. This chapter highlights the way that LGBTQ+ people and their allies in Hollywood and elite sports use their fame and visibility as a "cultural strategy"[2] for social change. It takes seriously the choice or *agency* of celebrities to think critically about their public role, to wade into movement debates about their participation (as in the case of allies), and to act in ways that they feel are aligned with their professional and political values.[3]

Celebrities and culture workers both in front of and behind the camera *do* play a central role in people's lives. This gives them a platform from which to speak out on issues that matter to them.[4] In recent decades, social media has created more fame, amplified celebrity voice, extended reach, and provided near-infinite opportunities for celebrities to speak directly to their fans. Yet this public celebrity has a long history dating back at least a century in Hollywood.[5] When public people, drawing on this history, use their platform for LGBTQ+ social change, they confront stereotypes, raise broader awareness, direct new resources, change policy, and make human connections in ways that move people.

PLATFORM OF THE SELF

I asked almost everyone I interviewed some version of the question: "Do you consider yourself political?" Many enthusiastically said that they did, while others were uncomfortable with the label—and the question. Some talked their way into an understanding of political contribution that they *did* feel comfortable with. They identified a kind of platform of the self: that their very way of being in the world, generally as a publicly out LGBTQ+ person, contributed something to LGBTQ+ social change.[6]

It is hard to overstate the cultural and athletic impact of diver Greg Louganis. Of course, his excellence in his sport is legendary. He is also in a tiny group of elite athletes who has drawn attention to HIV/AIDS, as well as to the participation of gay men in sports. Louganis became an Olympic medal winner at age sixteen, in the 1976 Montreal games, and won gold in his next two Olympics, in 1984 and 1988. One of the most iconic moments in sports history was when Louganis smashed his head on the board during a preliminary dive in the 1988 Seoul Olympics then came back in the finals to win the gold medal. He had been diagnosed as HIV-positive six months before the Seoul games. But he had revealed this to only a few people until 1995, when he came out publicly as HIV-positive in his memoir, *Breaking the Surface*.[7]

In the years since, Louganis has engaged in both US-based and international HIV/AIDS and LGBTQ+-related advocacy. He said to me, however, that he does not consider himself to be very political: "I mean, all I know is my own experience and the stories that people share with me."[8] He said of his own work: "I think that's the best way that I can be effective is just being who I am." Part of this kind of platform of the self—just showing up and being who you are—relates to something that I heard from a few people: that Louganis played *against type*, and this may have had a more substantial impact on how his fans viewed gay men. He said of his 1988 Olympic experience—climbing back up on the diving board after his head injury and winning gold—"I joke that in that moment in time I became the toughest sissy in the world."

Others, too, understood, that just being yourself as a publicly out LGBTQ+ person can matter. Actor Denis O'Hare talked with me in 2011 about how he did not feel that people necessarily knew he was gay as he went through his daily life, but that having a husband—and talking about that husband as a *husband* (rather than a presumably gender-neutral "partner")—and having a child together made him visible as gay in ways that had an impact on people. "For me," he said almost four years before marriage equality was legal nationwide, "that's a form of activism" that confronts people's assumptions about what it means to love and parent as a gay man: "Every time I say 'husband' someone's mind goes 'That's not right.' That little voice inside of them gets dimmer and dimmer, the more it's said. You just wear people down in a weird way. You just kind of show up, show up, show up."[9]

I heard a poignant example of the impact of this platform of self from Shadi Petosky, a TV writer and producer who has been active in fighting for transgender inclusion and equity in Hollywood. I first spoke with her in the summer of 2014, when Netflix's *Orange Is the New Black* and Amazon's *Transparent* were beginning to break barriers with trans representation. Petosky spoke with me about Laverne Cox, the trans actress who played trans character Sophia Burset on *Orange Is the New Black* and who is, herself, explicitly change-oriented in her artistic work. Petosky talked about the way that Cox's very presence on the screen mattered to Petosky, who also identifies as trans:

> Laverne Cox just personally standing up tall in a photo. We're around the same height, and she just fucking wears it and just stands up. And then talks about, like, "Oh, I didn't think I was feminine enough and little enough, and it wasn't going to be me," and it is her, and it's amazing. So, I stand taller in photos. Like when somebody's going to take a photo of me, I used to hunch down to stereotype women level, LA women level. And she wasn't a person I know. She wasn't a friend giving me that. She's just a person on TV talking, on the Internet talking. It really matters. I think about that stuff all the time just to live.[10]

Here, and in these examples, we see the way that public people have and use a platform that can make a difference in how LGBTQ+ people see and understand themselves and how straight and/or cisgender people can come to understand LGBTQ+ lives and experiences. They may or may not identify as *activists*—or even as explicitly political people. But they have an impact on the world just by being authentically who they are in public, even when social change is not necessarily their primary goal.

PERSONAL PLATFORM

The activist background and genuine political commitments run deep for some of the people I interviewed. In fact, part of their vocational identity is to marry their artistic or athletic work to their politics. "If a burning building is on fire and I've been given a bullhorn, I'm not useful to anyone unless I start shouting for a fire engine to arrive and for the occupants to get out," actor and writer Alec Mapa said to me.[11] Public culture workers like Mapa use their personal platform—the visibility that they have gained through their culture work—and they put it to work for social change.

Many people I spoke with were quite thoughtful about the way their activism has developed over time and how it connects with their professional work and identities. This has changed over the years, as the politics of the country and the world have shifted. Culture workers I spoke with have been activated in recent years over Trump's first election; the Black Lives Matter push after George Floyd's murder in 2020; the Hollywood writers' and actors' strikes of 2023; the fight for justice in Palestine; and now the second Trump presidency and its very local LA-based Immigration and Customs Enforcement (ICE) raids in 2025.[12] One actor, Amin El Gamal, has been a local organizer and activist for years—and has always organized with and through his artistic identities and communities. They started what they described as an "LGBT support group for Muslim people" in Los Angeles and also have been actively involved in a coalition in Hollywood to "lobby on behalf of Middle Eastern and North African actors" around the way that they are racially categorized for purposes of hiring and diversity accounting in Hollywood. In our earlier conversations, El Gamal downplayed his role, noting to me that while he considers himself political and outspoken and "involved in advocacy on many different levels," he hesitated to call himself an activist. By the summer of 2025, when we talked again, this had changed. They have been involved in advocacy work through their union, SAG-AFTRA, as vice chair, then chair of the Middle Eastern/North Africa (MENA) Committee since it began in 2022. El Gamal also has been centrally involved, in many ways, in organizing through artists' groups and unions for justice and a ceasefire in Palestine, co-founding a group that is now called Entertainment Labor for Palestine.[13] El Gamal could now say, "I feel like I'm actually a true organizer."[14]

Culture workers can also use their personal platform by institutionalizing their politics. Wilson Cruz—who, as described in the last chapter, came out through his experience as a teenage actor playing the pathbreaking character of Rickie Vasquez—calls himself an "actorvist" (actor + activist). He is authentically and deeply committed to bringing together his artistic and his political work. Cruz worked with the Obama campaign, was a field organizer for the (formerly named) National Gay and Lesbian Task Force, and has written editorials on and gives speeches about LGBTQ+-related issues. When I interviewed him, he was working at GLAAD. Actor Rory O'Malley also uses the term actorvist to describe himself and his dual commitment to and pride in art and politics. Tony-nominated for his role of Elder McKinley in *The Book of Mormon*, O'Malley is a self-described "political junkie" who campaigned for Obama in 2008 in his hometown of Cleveland. In 2009, after the passage of California's Proposition 8, which banned same-sex marriage in the state, O'Malley was in a bit of an acting lull during the financial crisis and had some free time, during which he co-founded Broadway Impact, a highly successful nonprofit that fought for marriage equality through theater and the theater community.[15]

I interviewed both O'Malley and one of the friends with whom he co-founded his organization, Jenny Kanelos (the third co-founder was the late actor Gavin Creel). From the beginning, the organization's founders understood that their extensive contacts in the Broadway community could be put to use to energize an involved and enthusiastic fan base. Drawing on organizing skills and lessons that he had learned from the Obama campaign, O'Malley and his co-founders initially organized Broadway celebrities to attract fans to write letters on behalf of New York marriage equality, lobbying lawmakers in Albany. They also organized phone bank sessions where they advertised that Creel, one of the stars of a Broadway production of *Hair* at that time, would be there phone banking alongside fans. O'Malley said that this way of mobilizing celebrity was effective because they were asking fans to do something they might not be comfortable with. Having the Broadway celebrity draw helped to make new activists comfortable.

In sports, Chris Mosier has successfully mobilized and institutionalized his personal platform for education, policy change, and mainstream pop cultural visibility. In 2015, as a member of Team USA as a duathlete (a run-bike-run event), he was the first out transgender athlete on a men's US national team. Mosier is a longtime LGBTQ+ sports activist. Among many other leadership roles, he is the founder of TransAthlete.com, a superb source of information about national and international trans athlete policies and practices. When he qualified for Team USA, he did not know whether he was going to be allowed to compete in the World Championship in 2016, because the team relied on International Olympic Committee (IOC) restrictive guidelines for transgender athlete participation. Mosier publicly and actively challenged these guidelines, and in January 2016, the IOC dropped its surgery requirements for trans participation. Mosier not only used his platform as a trailblazing athlete to change international sport policies, but he also took the opportunity of his success to raise the visibility of trans athletes. He earned sponsorships with the fitness brand TRX; the juice brand Odwalla; and, in the summer of 2016, he became the first trans athlete to be featured in *ESPN The Magazine*'s "Body Issue"[16] and to have a (high-profile) Nike commercial, entitled "Unlimited Courage."[17]

Though Mosier's sport is not the world's most popular or well-known, his elite status at the top of his sport allowed him a platform that he has fully embraced. Mosier's identity as an *athlete* has been paramount, but he also has understood that being an out *transgender* athlete has allowed him to be a committed, effective, and highly visible force for change in trans participation and equity in sports. When he first began competing in men's races, he shared his story and sat for several press interviews. Mosier was always intentional about this: "I was trying to gauge my comfort in being a voice for the athletic community because I felt really alone as a trans athlete."[18] He said that he sought out opportunities to tell his story, with an express purpose of creating change in sports:

> As I became more comfortable with myself and felt like there'd be less scrutiny about maybe my performance of masculinity as an athlete, I've been more comfortable in assuming that public role. And I think it was something that I knew that I was going to do when I came out. I want to use my voice and my history as an educator to push forward toward eliminating transphobia in athletics.

It is difficult to overestimate Mosier's impact on the conversation and policymaking, especially the more inclusive IOC policy on trans inclusion,[19] which was widely adopted in sports at many levels until the regressive years of the early 2020s and the Trump-fueled assault of the mid-2020s.

Overall, people I spoke with were thoughtful about the limits and possibilities of their platform and the exigencies of their business, each with their own calculus about using this platform. They had a range of strategies, especially in their social media presence in the early years of Twitter, Instagram, and other platforms. Some reined in their politics, feeling that their followers were fans of their *artistic* work and were not there for their politics. Others felt strongly that they were going to use their social media opportunity to call attention to the issues that mattered to them, and they reasoned that they were unlikely to lose viewers or fans because they were politically outspoken. Others simply became *activists* in their personal lives, whether this meant using their professionally earned platforms or not.

Some I spoke with felt the traits that allowed them to be artistically successful, and the structure of the work itself, informed how they participated in social change efforts.[20] Wilson Cruz said that he actively drew on the skills he had as an actor for his political work, like engaging with strangers about the importance of LGBTQ+ civil rights: "It's one of the most vulnerable things in the world to walk up to somebody's home, knock on their door, and ask for their time, to talk about an issue that affects me and people I love. And I think being an actor helps me to do that. I know how to speak to people, and I think I can read people really well."[21] There are other aspects of the acting profession that can lend themselves to activism and advocacy as well. The episodic nature of acting in theater, TV, and film means that there is little job security, leading to risk aversion (as I will say more about in the next chapter). But this aspect of the work can also free up time for political engagement. While there are barriers and challenges to actors using their platform in this way, some working conditions make it *easier* for actors to be activists.

ARTISTIC PLATFORM

When Vice President Joe Biden came out in favor of marriage equality in 2012, he surmised that the television hit *Will & Grace* had done more to change public opinion about marriage than almost anything else.[22] Politically engaged culture workers do not see their work as *only* political. They value being able to use their artistic position for the purpose of LGBTQ+ social change. But they absolutely care deeply about their artistic work for its own sake, too. Using an artistic platform includes telling stories and creating change-making iconic content.

Storytelling itself has been a form of artistic platform for LGBTQ+ social change, in part because it has served an educational function when there is an information void. This was particularly true with HIV/AIDS-related stories in the early years of the epidemic. I want to take a longer look at this example, since it has been so central to the history of LGBTQ+ people, social action, and popular culture. Since the beginning of the AIDS crisis in the early 1980s, popular culture and art have been critical vehicles for HIV/AIDS politics and social change. They have also been a tool for community building and education.[23] Of course, there have been celebrities—like Greg Louganis—who became HIV-positive and taught the whole world about the virus. Movie star Rock Hudson's disclosure of his fatal diagnosis in 1985 drew international media fascination in the same way.[24] And the positive diagnosis of emphatically straight basketball legend Earvin "Magic" Johnson in 1991 put a new focus on the broad reach of HIV/AIDS.[25] Johnson embraced his role as educator, even doing a 1992 special on the children's television network Nickelodeon for the express purpose of reaching young people about HIV/AIDS.[26]

Theater, too, was quick to respond to the AIDS crisis, confronting audience members with the ravages of early AIDS diagnoses and galvanizing them to care. Some of the watershed stories here are the award-winning *The Normal Heart* by Larry Kramer (1985), *Angels in America* by Tony Kushner (1991), *Falsettos* by William Finn and James Lapine (1992), *Rent* by Jonathan Larson (1996), and *The Inheritance* by Matthew López (2018).[27] When I spoke with lifelong activist and author, the late Larry Kramer, he said that he produced art, theater, and literature out of the "necessity" of the early AIDS crisis and his urgent sense that he needed to do something in the moment.[28] He, like others we meet in this chapter, mobilized the resources, talent, and platform that he had at his disposal. He said that he wrote *The Normal Heart* as a play for the sake of speed:

> I wrote it as a play because that was pragmatically the fastest thing I could do. I knew how long it took me to write my novel. And I knew

> that no one would make it as a movie, both of which I would have preferred to write: a novel or a screenplay. Plays are very difficult. For me, anyway. But I could write the play faster and get it out there faster.

There were also some award-winning films that brought the AIDS crisis to mainstream audiences during the early days of the pandemic, *Philadelphia* (1993), starring Tom Hanks and Denzel Washington, and HBO's *And the Band Played On* (1993), adapted from the nonfiction best-selling critical investigation of AIDS science and politics by journalist Randy Shilts.[29]

There are two standout TV moments in the early days of AIDS. These programs used their artistic platform for storytelling in a way that informed mass audiences about an unknown, highly stigmatized virus that disproportionately impacted queer communities. The first was a made-for-television movie that aired on NBC in November 1985, more than four years into the global pandemic and just a little more than a month after Rock Hudson had died. *An Early Frost* was the first of its kind to meet the AIDS epidemic head-on. NBC approached Ron Cowen and Daniel Lipman, both personal and professional partners, to write the screenplay. They delivered a story about a young, White Chicago lawyer who was gay and in a long-term relationship but was not out to his family. When he was diagnosed with AIDS and then became sick, the story followed his coming out to his family and the way that they contended with his sexuality and his illness. The show (which, of course, was produced at a time when it was not available for on-demand viewing—you had to watch or record it when it aired) reached a wide audience of 34 million people, outperforming Monday Night Football on the night that it was broadcast. It even drew more viewers than a controversial, abortion-focused episode of the hit show *Cagney & Lacey* that was airing in the same time slot on CBS. *An Early Frost* was also critically acclaimed, receiving several awards, including fourteen Emmy nominations and four wins.[30]

NBC execs had wanted to air a show about AIDS. But they nevertheless significantly curtailed the representation of gay male sexuality and affection in *An Early Frost*.[31] The show garnered some criticism for either being not really centrally about AIDS as the protagonist experienced it[32] or for being overly focused on the trope of gay men as a diseased "problem."[33] But the focus on the virus itself served as a source of "dissemination of knowledge through fiction"[34] that was much needed in these early years of AIDS. Cowen and Lipman reminded me that in 1985 there was so little information, so much stigma and brutal imagery in the news media, and a terrifying amount of death around AIDS. Their storytelling, by contrast, served as education. They visited hospitals to meet with patients who were living with AIDS, and they had medical advisers for the show. They kept up-to-date on the most recent scientific knowledge, knowing that they were taking on a responsibility beyond what most television writers would expect from their work.

Lipman recounted to me how this worked in their creative process while filming the movie: "Terry O'Quinn played one of the doctors. Research was revealing the latest discoveries of the virus almost every day. So, we placed Terry under a contract that would allow us to quickly script and shoot any new updates to film up until twenty-four hours of the broadcast." He remembers that friends and colleagues knew that they were working on a film that allowed them access to up-to-date medical information, and that they were approached at parties by terrified guests with medical questions. "We would be invited to dinner parties and the guests would pull us aside and say, 'Could you look at this spot on my arm—is it KS [Kaposi sarcoma]?' Or 'Could you feel my glands—are they swollen?' And we'd say, 'We're just the writers, we're not doctors.' But that's how terrified people were at the time that they had AIDS."[35]

The second TV moment in HIV/AIDS education was a breakthrough in reality television programming, the third season of MTV's *The Real World*, which aired in 1994.[36] Set in San Francisco, it featured its usual house full of young adults trying to make their way in the world as they navigated the strong personalities of their roommates and the constant camera presence. Cast member Pedro Zamora was a charismatic, Cuban American gay man in his early twenties. He was an AIDS educator and was HIV-positive when he was cast on the show, which he knew would give him a substantial platform to educate young people.[37] Throughout the run of the show, and until his death also in 1994, he spoke openly and regularly about living with HIV, and he was a television first in many ways.[38]

Zamora's "entire goal was to make himself visible," said his *Real World* housemate and close friend, Judd Winick.[39] Zamora's presence on the popular *Real World* season gave many young people their first understanding of HIV/AIDS. "I don't think young people even know what T cells were until Pedro told them," Winick said. Many people I interviewed mentioned—unprompted—the importance of Zamora to their own experience as they were growing up as young gay people. Zamora's impact was helped by the way that MTV allowed Zamora the space to tell his story in a compelling way, said Dave Karger, who was a senior writer with *Entertainment Weekly* when I interviewed him. "I know it's been said before: for many people Pedro was the first person they knew with HIV—at a time when there was such stigma around it. For so many people, he was just a total eye-opener and started the conversation, internally but then also externally in a lot of families and groups of friends."[40]

Writers Cowen and Lipman went on to be able to portray HIV/AIDS in new ways as their careers progressed. They developed, wrote, and produced the American version of *Queer as Folk* for Showtime, where they were able to tell full stories about gay men's sexuality and relationships but also stories about HIV/AIDS, especially in the character of Ben Bruckner (played by Robert Gant). Even by the year 2000, when their *Queer as Folk* began, almost twenty years after the beginning of the AIDS epidemic, it was unusual for television shows to tell HIV/AIDS stories. Even now, there are still very few stories about HIV/AIDS on television or in film, and those on-screen tend to be about the earlier period of the epidemic, rather than about what it means to live with HIV in the twenty-first century.[41] But in these early stories, we see the ways in which an artistic platform can be used to educate. In this case, storytelling filled a void by publicly tackling a topic that was so taboo and about which so little was initially known.

Stories are told by story*tellers*, of course, and they, too, sometimes embrace their artistic platform for social change. If you have watched any comedy television in the past decade, you have probably seen something directed by Nisha Ganatra. She not only directs some of the best television shows in recent years, but she is also an award-winning writer and producer, known for her work on LGBTQ+-focused projects like *Transparent*. Ganatra was a budding activist when she graduated from college in the early 1990s. She also loved film and chose to go to graduate school for film at New York University's Tisch School of the Arts. "The whole reason I wanted to go to film school was to tell these stories that I just wasn't seeing represented on-screen," she told me.[42] But she was not sure that this was going to measure up to the social justice work that her friends were pursuing in their first jobs.

Ganatra had a bit of an epiphany that allowed her to think about her work in new ways. In January 1996, the hit TV show *Friends* aired an episode called "The One with the Lesbian Wedding," in which Ross's ex-wife, Carol, marries her longtime partner, Susan. Ganatra remembers this as a turning point: "When *Friends* had a lesbian wedding episode, and it felt like the next day a lot of our country was talking about lesbians, I thought, 'Wow, you know what? That *Friends* episode really caused a national conversation on lesbians and gay weddings. It had impact.' It seems so obvious now, but then I was just starting to understand the connection between film and TV and how it shapes our culture. And to see that shaping as a form of activism." This realization allowed her to think about her career choice in new ways and to view her creative work as a contribution to social change. She went on to direct, star in, and co-write the 1999 award-winning film *Chutney Popcorn*: the story of a young, lesbian Indian American woman, played by Ganatra.

Ganatra has had a lot of professional success in the decades since, and one of the ways that she uses her artistic platform now is to choose to do work that she believes can tell untold stories. Her current success and clout give her a sense of freedom and choice, and she uses this freedom to be very deliberate about, as she said, "what story am I trying to tell in society and what am I trying to push forward in culture and why?" Ganatra has adopted a particular view of pop culture as potentially powerful for social change—and then she contributes to that through the stories she chooses to tell in her career.

Angela Robinson—also a director, writer, and producer who came out of NYU Tisch during the same era as Ganatra—has a similar professional story, even down to the importance of the *Friends* lesbians in coming to see her own artistic work as a contribution to politics. Robinson has been connected to some of the most successful shows in recent years, like *How to Get Away with Murder*, *True Blood*, and the original *L Word*, and her film credits range from the fairly independent to Disney (*Herbie Fully Loaded*, starring Lindsay Lohan in 2005). Robinson, too, recounted her *Friends* moment and its impact on her career choices. When she was in college at Brown University, she wanted to be a theater director and moved to New York to pursue this after graduation. She recalled marching in a Pride parade in New York City around the time that *Friends* introduced the lesbian moms and thinking to herself: "More than 30 million people watched the *Friends* with the lesbian moms, and now 30 million people probably think it's cool for lesbians to be moms, and what's actually more political? To walk up Fifth Avenue to maybe five thousand eyeballs on you or 30 million people who have an experience that, whether they know it or not, is probably really changing their perspective?" In her career since, she said to me, she has been interested in marrying her "pop sensibility" and desire to work on big-budget projects with her explicit interest in creating work that is political. She accomplishes this through the kind of storytelling she does, both visually and on the page.[43]

Peter Paige is of the same generation as Ganatra and Robinson, a Gen Xer who came of age during a critical period of LGBTQ+ change. He played Emmett Honeycutt on Showtime's *Queer as Folk*. He then went on to co-create two recent television shows that told queer stories, Freeform's *The Fosters* and *Good Trouble*. Paige identifies strongly as a political person from birth, a "devout Democrat" and "unapologetic progressive."[44] "I really, really believe in the power of pop culture to change minds. I really do. I've seen it work," he said. In his career, he has been able tell new kinds of stories that he believes can change viewers' understanding and relationships to queer sexuality and LGBTQ+ people. He believes that *Queer as Folk* provided a "vocabulary for gay sexuality" that did not exist for non-queer people before. And he has used his platform as a co-creator and writer on his Freeform shows to highlight trans experience; to show attraction and affection between middle school boys; and to respond directly to the early Trump years by telling stories not just about gender and sexuality but also about racial injustice and the persecution of immigrant Americans.[45]

Along with storytelling, acting also gives people a way to embrace their artistic platform. I spoke with several LGBTQ+ actors who played queer roles. I also spoke with straight cisgender actors who played iconic queer roles. In both cases, audience responses and connection to their characters often *changed* something in the actor. It politicized them or strengthened an existing political identity and inspired them to recognize that they had a new platform at their disposal. They came to understand that the character they gave life to had power, that audiences were connecting with them in intimate ways, and that they could work to mobilize that power and connection for social change.

Some actors didn't need much prompting to activate their already-held political identity and commitment. Paige, for instance, as Emmett on *Queer as Folk*, drew on a lifelong dedication to liberal politics but took the platform he was given through the hit show. "I mean, I was raised by a hard-core feminist from the '70s," he said. "My mother worked at, like, Uterus Rising bookstore. So, for me, it provided a platform to express myself politically and, in doing so, I got better at it and more engaged with it."

Other actors developed a new sense of public responsibility through the roles they played. Mark Indelicato was just thirteen years old in 2006 when he began his four-year run on the ABC hit show *Ugly Betty*. He played the role of Justin Suarez, Betty's young, eventually out gay nephew. Justin was groundbreaking in a number of ways: he was a gay Latine character in a mostly White TV world; an out gay boy who got to share an on-screen kiss with his high school boyfriend; and a family member whose sexuality was not just accepted but fully celebrated by his mother, aunt, and grandfather.[46] Indelicato identifies as gay himself, but this was not a part of his identity that he had begun to express or explore when he began playing Justin. He also, as a young teen, had not yet paid much attention to societal homophobia and its impact on people, because his own childhood was not marked by homophobia. Yet the character of Justin inspired audiences, and Indelicato began hearing from young queer fans who wanted to share their experiences. This gave Indelicato a new understanding of the role he could play as an actor and a new sense of responsibility, even at such a young age.

"I was unaware of the weight of the character," Indelicato reflected to me. "I remember being thirteen years old and going to the GLAAD Awards with the cast, because we were nominated for an award, and a journalist asked me at thirteen if I was gay personally. And it was never something that I had thought about. And that was, I think, the first time that I thought that this is actually really important. When it went from the scrutiny of the character to personal is when I kind of realized the importance of it."[47] Indelicato said that when fans wrote to him, they expressed both a strong connection to Justin and their own pain. He was also impacted by just being on set with older cast members who were, themselves, quite politically engaged. His castmates and mentors on the show included America Ferrera, who played Betty. She is an active Democrat and voting rights advocate, and in 2018 she became one of the founding members of the TIME'S UP Legal Defense Fund to respond to workplace sexual misconduct. Through his own artistic community, Indelicato gained a political awareness and a sense of his own responsibility.

Straight actors playing high-profile gay roles also have cultivated a new sense of political engagement through their roles. Two of the most high-profile network television gay men's roles of the past generation have been played by straight actors: Will Truman on *Will & Grace* and Cameron Tucker on *Modern Family*. Eric McCormack, who played Will, noted to me that he came to understand the responsibility he had in playing such a groundbreaking and visible role, and that he embraced the artistic platform that came with the role:

> Will was a great, funny leading man part in a smart and touching NBC comedy. And he happened to be gay—wasn't much of *that* on TV in '98. This scared me a little, not because I was afraid of failure—I'd played several gay roles prior, and I knew the script was fantastic and respectful—but because I knew that, in success, I might very well become *more* than an actor in a role. I might become a spokesman and a symbol for the LGBTQ community. As it turns out, I *did* . . . and it's been one of the great privileges of my life.[48]

Eric Stonestreet—who played Cam on *Modern Family* beginning in 2009, just a few years after the original run of *Will & Grace* ended—is famously not much like his character in real life. And he has enthusiastically and regularly used this in the service of LGBTQ+ social change. He has fully embraced his artistic platform, and as a football- and NASCAR-loving White Midwesterner, he has access to spaces that are not necessarily known for being queer-friendly. He spoke with me about the ways that he has been able to use his fans' love of and connection to Cam to impact their views on LGBTQ+ people and civil rights.

"I happen to be one of those actors that thinks actors should just shut the hell up," Stonestreet said to me in 2012.[49] But "there's no doubt that because of the role on the show and the character that I get to play that I have to have something to say about this specific thing. I would be *wrong* to not have something to say." His own perspective has changed as a result of his career choice, and then his role on *Modern Family*:

> You know, I'm a Kansas guy, born and raised in Kansas. I didn't know any gay people until I went to college and started doing theater. I say that just because of the sort of people I grew up around—and I had a

> way in which I was raised and thought of people. Obviously, through my industry and my work, my eyes opened and life opened and I realized that people aren't defined by their sexuality.

Stonestreet gained a sense of empathy and connection as an ally by virtue of playing and having such high visibility as a gay character: "I realized at the beginning of the show that I was going to have, potentially, a real front-row seat" to the experience of being gay—"just being able to experience someone else's life."

Stonestreet said that he thought his own experience would prove helpful: "I thought I had a really great opportunity to have a perspective of where I came from, to be able to change people's ideas and hearts and minds, based on where I'm from and the people I grew up with, the people that I know and still know that have backwards opinions." He had the access that he has because of who he is: "my football-playing, sports-loving, regular dude from the Midwest guy." He was preparing for a fight—for backlash and for a hostile or violent public reaction to his costar Jesse Tyler Ferguson, who played his husband on the show and who is publicly out as gay. It was a huge surprise to him that this homophobic backlash did not happen to the extent he feared. When he encounters fans of Mitch and Cam at a NASCAR race or a game, he can be "a bit of a go-to for people that have trouble understanding what it means to be gay." He said that he has experienced this: guys at NASCAR races asking where Cam buys his colorful shirts, or people at football games asking if they can snap a picture for their father who is a huge fan. He believes, because he has been told over and over again by fans, that this makes a difference: "Jesse and I have both been in conversations, publicly and privately, where people have said things like 'You cured my dad of his homophobia. You single-handedly made my dad understand about gay people.'"

COMMERCIAL PLATFORM

In recent years, if your algorithms are aligned in June, your inbox and social media accounts probably have been flooded with rainbow-adorned sneakers, T-shirts, even special coffee drinks created especially for Pride month. Or, at your local Pride event, you have probably encountered floats, merch, and marching contingents sponsored by banks, vodka, or any number of corporate brands.[50] And, of course, it is not only in June when companies have demonstrated visible LGBTQ+ inclusion and support. Many household name brands have raised the visibility of LGBTQ+ people, relationships, and families. They also have actively courted LGBTQ+ consumers and their sizable "pink dollar."[51] In one of my favorite examples, in 2019 the razor company Gillette debuted a commercial featuring the father of a young transgender man teaching him how to shave, with the tag line: "Whenever, wherever, however it happens—your first shave is special."[52]

Like individuals, brands and companies have sometimes thrown their capital and influence into social justice causes, including LGBTQ+ social change. Elite sports provides a fascinating example. It's difficult to imagine a pop cultural space with more access to the mainstream and, therefore, more of a potential platform. For just one of many measures of the reach of professional US sports, especially *men's* sports, the Super Bowl dominates television ratings each year. According to Nielsen ratings, of the top-twenty TV programs in history, eighteen of these were Super Bowls, as of 2018.[53] Sports can both powerfully maintain the status quo *and* powerfully interrupt it. Athletes, the sports they play, and the brands they promote are central actors in American and global culture. Collegiate and professional sports are national pastimes that shape community and provide common allegiances (and rivalries). For young people, participation in organized sports from even an early age often shapes identity, especially as it relates to gender and sexuality. For youth, as well, athletes as public figures and celebrities influence style trends and provide models for good and bad behavior.[54]

It should come as no surprise, then, that sports organizations and *brands* are well-positioned to use their platform for LGBTQ+ social justice. They have done so—imperfectly but actively. Nike, for instance, is known internationally for its labor violations. Yet it, too, has used its brand platform for LGBTQ+ inclusion through, among other things, its Be True line of sneakers and workout wear; its endorsement deal with number-one draft pick, basketball star Brittney Griner; and its institutional and financial support of the high-profile LGBT Sports Coalition and Sports Summit for a number of years beginning in 2012.[55] The WNBA, which has been a leader in sports advocacy for racial justice, provides another example that what is best for business is often best for equity and inclusion. Recognizing its sizable and loyal lesbian fan base, the basketball league became the first professional sports organization to develop an LGBTQ+-focused marketing campaign, in 2014, featuring WNBA Pride merch, special events, and marketing and nonprofit partnerships.[56]

As with so many things, this is changing with Trump 2.0, as right-wing market responses and fear of political retribution impel corporate rollbacks to broad diversity commitments.[57] Commercial actors, like sports leagues and corporate brands, are making both a business calculation and a political one when they use their commercial platform. They make a political calculation and act—as I say much more about in the following chapter—when they believe that doing good is good for their bottom line, when being visible proponents of LGBTQ+ inclusion, equity, and pride can pay off.

This means sometimes, too, that businesses suffer consequences in the market—or *believe* they will—when they do use their platform in this way. In the lead-up to Pride Month in 2023, Target was just one of a number of companies "to rethink its approach" to its Pride marketing and merch, citing concerns for employee safety after some anti-LGBTQ+ hostility in their stores and on social media.[58] Another recent high-profile example is that of Anheuser-Busch's Bud Light and its spring 2023 campaign with transgender social media influencer Dylan Mulvaney.[59] When an Instagram post featured Mulvaney drinking a Bud Light and showing off a custom can with her face on it, anti-trans vitriol was swift and harsh. Sales of the beer dropped by 24.6 percent, losing even more ground in some regional markets, amidst calls for a brand boycott. Mulvaney said that the company did not publicly respond to defend its campaign or privately contact her in the aftermath.[60]

When businesses and brands use their platform for LGBTQ+ visibility and politics, they don't just anger the homophobes and transphobes. They upset the political Left, as well. Public skepticism of commodified queer inclusion comes from two primary places. The first is a general doubt that private, profit-driven corporations can be authentic social change actors. As progressive sports politics writer Dave Zirin rightfully asked of Nike's involvement in social causes: "Will the revolution be branded?" In response, he wrote: "This is Nike. Asking them to be a voice for social justice is like asking a dog to meow." Multinational billionaire companies like Nike, Zirin argued, "don't underwrite rebellions. They co-opt and quash them."[61] There is specific concern with respect to LGBTQ+ social change: that corporations like Nike are making a show of support for queer people and causes when it serves their business interests and/or as a form of "pinkwashing" to cover up for labor and other human rights abuses.[62]

LGBTQ+ advocates are also understandably wary that their communities are just market props when they are in political favor—and are easily expendable when the politics go the other way and corporate support would be costly for big business. During the second week of the second Trump administration, in January 2025, one popular queer social media commentator, Matt Bernstein, called this out. Under the heading "corporations when it's cool for us to exist in public," Bernstein posted a number of rainbow-adorned ads and photos from Target, McDonald's, Amazon, Ford, and other giants. Bernstein then contrasted this with headlines of corporate rollback under the heading "corporations when the government wants us dead"—for example, "Jeff Bezos deletes 'LGBTQ+ rights' and 'equity for Black people' from Amazon corporate policies."[63]

A second aspect of skepticism of corporate involvement in LGBTQ+ social change relates to a long-standing debate over the best path to social change for queer people: Is assimilation—blending in to mainstream American culture—the best route to social justice? Or is maintaining distinct—sometimes separate—identities and institutions more desirable and authentic? Those who reject integration and appeals to sameness tend to be skeptical of corporate sponsorship and brand allyship. They see these as mainstream and *mainstreaming*, capitalistic, desexualized, and insufficient to respond to structural and material inequalities.[64] Yet, what is the alternative? As media scholar Katherine Sender wrote: "No pristine GLBT culture existed before, or outside of, consumer culture."[65]

ALLY PLATFORM

Along with the question of who can advocate for social change is the question that most social movements confront: What is the proper role of allies—non-LGBTQ+-identified supporters—as voices and leaders for social change?[66] My strong belief—admittedly self-serving, since this is how I identify—is that allies or accomplices do have a role to play in social justice movements, but that our allyship requires a lot of humility and a lifelong, daily commitment to self-awareness and self-examination of our proper role.[67] Allies have been a sizable part of LGBTQ+ social movements since the mobilization of the Religious Right drew them into the movement in the late 1970s.[68] The work of high-profile allies has been a source of division within LGBTQ+ communities and movements. It has raised questions about who gets to use their platform—and how—for social change, and how a culture war can and should be won.

You wouldn't necessarily think that sports would be such a central place for LGBTQ+ cultural politics in the twenty-first century. But they have been. The promises and pitfalls of allyship in sports are instructive for the broader conversation about how platforms get used for social change. In recent years, cisgender straight male athletes have mobilized their masculine capital and privilege for LGBTQ+ social change. By this I mean that these allies have a commodity that is valuable in American culture—cisgender straight maleness—and they can *spend* this commodity for LGBTQ+ social change. They often leverage sports aphorisms about teamwork, having your teammates' backs, working together, and winning as a team. They have also worked to change what it means to be a man: an ally of queer people rather than a homophobe or transphobe.[69]

In US sports, public and celebrated LGBTQ+ allyship has primarily been a men's game. This is, in part, a by-product of male privilege and misogyny. Cisgender women athletes simply do not typically receive the same public recognition and adoration as their cisgender male peers. This is true for both allies and LGBTQ+-identified women athletes. Some of the most talented and celebrated women athletes in recent memory identify as lesbian or queer, including basketball and soccer superstars Brittney Griner and Megan Rapinoe. Yet these incredible athletes have received much less public consideration for several reasons: the lower profile and cachet of women's sports, general sexism in our public culture that devalues the voices and experiences of women, and a widespread stereotype that women's sports are already brimming with lesbians. So, too, there actually *have* been fewer cis/straight women high-profile athlete allies. Experts have read this, in part, as a "fear of association": that because women athletes are already assumed to be gay, their advocacy might further confirm this, even if they do identify as straight. As Pat Griffin put it, "the lesbian label" has "continuing effectiveness in silencing women about homophobia in sport."[70]

By contrast, a number of cisgender straight men in high-status team sports have become vocal and visible LGBTQ+ allies, especially since the marriage equality fights of the early 2010s. The marriage movement served as a well-organized gateway for allies to begin to use their platform for LGBTQ+ social change. They then could move into other spaces, like changing the culture of sports so that it is more open to LGBTQ+ athletes. Football players, including Khalen Saunders,[71] Michael Irvin, Michael Strahan, Domonique Foxworth,[72] Sean James,[73] Scott Fujita, Brendon Ayanbadejo, and Chris Kluwe; and basketball players Charles Barkley, Steve Nash, Kenneth Faried, and Dwyane Wade are among those who have been interested in using their status to change public perception of LGBTQ+ people, to change law, and to change culture.[74] I would also include sports and politics writer Dave Zirin among the sports guys who embody many forms of thoughtful and authentic allyship with respect to gender, sexuality, and race and who actively uses his platform for social change.[75] And, like British rugby player Ben Cohen, many cisgender straight male athletes have demonstrated their allyship in a way that also recruits their classic good looks and athletic bodies to bring attention and support to LGBTQ+ fights, drawing on what Griffin has called a "hunk factor."[76]

Brian Ellner—a New York City lawyer and political and communications strategist—is a huge proponent and practitioner of using the celebrity platform, particularly when it comes to marshaling masculine capital.[77] Ellner has been central to many of the celebrity campaigns for LGBTQ+ marriage and broader civil rights in recent years. In his view, celebrity endorsement is a "cost-effective way" to get the word out about a campaign and energize support. Just as the big LGBTQ+ civil rights groups organize celebrity *visibility*, they also rely on celebrity endorsement, support, and talent to call attention to and bring resources to their work.

Ellner, who identifies as gay, also has had a clear strategy when it comes to mobilizing celebrity for LGBTQ+ civil rights. He believes that relying on "unusual suspects"—those who wouldn't be expected to be vocal advocates for LGBTQ+ equality—is especially effective.[78] He also has a theory about sports and male athletes: that they are revered, godlike heroes who bring people together in a kind of American religion. They have "a disproportionate space in society" that they have historically used for political involvement in civil rights.[79] In his campaigns for marriage equality, Ellner specifically turned to straight cisgender men in the "helmet" sports, like football and hockey—those sports that are considered the roughest and, therefore, the most traditionally masculine. Ellner acknowledged, in 2013, that athletes choosing to use their platform for politics is risky, but that it could also be a win-win for social change and for individual careers. "This is like the smartest thing you can do to get exposure to make a name and be beloved and to create a second career." This kind of public allyship could land you on late-night talk shows or cable news. "These guys are sophisticated," he said. They believe in the work, and they get positive exposure from it. And, on the other side of the equation, the impact of these allies can be "seismic" for LGBTQ+ social change.

Perhaps surprisingly, given the conservative reputation (which is warranted[80]) of the National Football League, several of the most high-profile LGBTQ+ allies have been pro football players. They have deliberately activated their masculine and athletic capital to bring a pro-LGBTQ+ message to a wider audience.[81] And they have a *massive* audience. Football is the most popular sport in the United States and the most revenue generating.[82] Allyship in pro football actually dates all the way back to the iconic Hall of Famer coach Vince Lombardi. He had a gay brother and, even in the late 1960s, he was actively protective of gay players on his team, like Dave Kopay and the Washington football team's number-one draft pick in 1967, Ray McDonald. He reportedly said to a member of his coaching staff, about McDonald, "If I hear one of you people make reference to his manhood you'll be out of here before your ass hits the ground."[83]

Linebacker, Super Bowl champ, and University of California, Berkeley, political science graduate Scott Fujita was a true trailblazer in his public support of LGBTQ+ civil rights. He is a White adoptee of a Japanese American dad who was born in an internment camp. And this personal story informs his worldview, including his support for family diversity. Even before the surge of marriage equality efforts in the early 2010s, Fujita publicly came out for LGBTQ+ social equality and supported the National Equality March of 2009. He then contributed a video to the Americans for Marriage Equality campaign in 2011 and wrote a *New York Times* editorial in 2013 in which he acknowledged the historical role of athletes in social movements: "Some think football players like me should just keep our mouths shut and focus on the game," he wrote. "But we're people first, and football players a distant second. Football is a big part of what we do, but a very small part of who we are."[84]

Fujita spent eleven years in the NFL, longer than many pros. But, even so, he knew he had a limited time with a platform—a chance to bring the issues he cared about into locker rooms and the pages and airwaves of sports news—and he explicitly took advantage of this opportunity. "I think there was a time and a place where athletes were encouraged and almost expected to stand for something," he said to me. "I look back at guys like Jackie Robinson, Muhammad Ali, Roberto Clemente, Pee Wee Reese. People almost expected and encouraged them to do that at that time. Nowadays, for a while at least, you didn't see that so much." But he looked to this history for inspiration for his own role.[85]

Brendon Ayanbadejo is a UCLA football grad and history major and a thirteen-year pro football veteran. He was another linebacker and Super Bowl champ to become a tireless and outspoken LGBTQ+ ally. This support is central to the way he defines himself and his work. In his support of marriage equality, he has drawn parallels to his own upbringing, as the child of an interracial couple, an Irish American mother and a Nigerian father.[86] In the spring of 2009, Ayanbadejo wrote an editorial for the *Huffington Post* entitled "Same Sex Marriages: What's the Big Deal?"[87] This use of platform was not something that straight pro athlete men in high-profile sports—or really any pro athletes—did at the time, and Ayanbadejo drew a huge amount of attention for it. In the years that followed, Ayanbadejo went on to write a number of additional pro-LGBTQ+ pieces and was a frequent guest on news segments in support of marriage equality and LGBTQ+ inclusion in sports.[88]

Chris Kluwe is yet another cisgender straight football player who took deliberate advantage of his platform to advocate for LGBTQ+ social change while he was a punter with the Minnesota Vikings—and who is still a headline-making progressive activist in Southern California.[89] This UCLA grad and eight-year NFL veteran made a name for himself as an LGBTQ+ ally when, in September 2012, he wrote an open letter to a Maryland state official who had criticized Ayanbadejo's marriage equality advocacy.[90] Kluwe's letter was published on Deadspin, and it went absolutely viral. In a book he published the following year, Kluwe said he felt that letter got so much attention because it "had a bunch of naughty words in it."[91] The phrase that was reprinted the most was "lustful cockmonster." As in "I can assure you that gay people getting married will have zero effect on your life. They won't come into your house and steal your children. They won't magically turn you into a lustful cockmonster."[92]

Kluwe was also a visible ally in a number of other ways: appearing on the cover of *Out* magazine in November 2012, doing a range of news media spots, vocally quitting his blogging work with the *St. Paul Pioneer Press* because of their stance on the Minnesota marriage initiative, and writing a number of pro-equality editorials and blog posts.[93] He and Ayanbadejo also led the effort to organize athletes to file an *amicus* brief with the Supreme Court in 2013, in one of the landmark marriage rights cases, *Hollingsworth v. Perry*.[94] Kluwe said to me that he recognized that he and others, like Fujita and Ayanbadejo, were bucking the stereotype of football players as "dumb jocks." But, he said, in his experience, the pro players he knew were "a normal mix of humanity who just happen to run very fast and play football." And while he considers himself "more of a 'stay on my couch at home and play video games' kind of guy," he recognizes that he had a responsibility as a pro football player with a wide reach. "Athletes," he said, have "a platform to reach people that just wouldn't otherwise think about the message."[95]

Kluwe was ultimately removed from the Vikings' roster in May 2013, when he was thirty-one years old. He believes that this was the cost of using his platform, as noted by the headline of his Deadspin piece in January 2014, "I Was an NFL Player Until I Was Fired by Two Cowards and a Bigot."[96] Kluwe also filed a lawsuit over his termination, which he settled in the summer of 2014 with, apparently, no personal financial award but a commitment by the Vikings to make sizable donations to LGBTQ+-related organizations.[97] Despite Ellner's point noted earlier, that using a public platform can be professionally *beneficial* to public allies, it can also come at a professional cost—or at least can be a professional risk.

The active marriage fight of the early 2010s gave an organizational space for allies to speak out. So did the LGBTQ+ sports movement that gained traction during this time. During these years, there was an active public conversation about what it meant to be an ally and the responsibilities and boundaries of this role. In the sports movement, some have felt that cisgender straight male athletes have been particularly effective vehicles through which to deliver a message of LGBTQ+ equity and inclusion, because they could best persuade people like themselves. This has not come without controversy, though. Some have felt that high-profile straight allies—particularly cis straight men (who are often, though not always, White)—have received a disproportionate amount of attention and praise for their work. Some also have felt that these allies' voices have been too loud and their leadership too visible or self-serving.

Pat Griffin has been working to change the culture of sports for LGBTQ+ athletes since before many of the Millennial advocates mentioned in this section picked up their first ball. She has extensively expressed both her gratitude and her discomfort with LGBTQ+ allies. She has written of the need to recognize the privilege that allies have and the ways in which they, too, benefit from the homophobia that they confront:

> Allies need to understand and be mindful of the privilege they have as they speak out. There is a disturbing benevolence that reinforces inequality when well-intentioned allies do not understand that they too are part of the oppression equation, whether they like it or not. They benefit by being heterosexual in a heterosexist world. Allies need to understand how their privilege is part of what enables them to speak out and be heard. Challenging homophobia is a great way to use privilege, but it is privilege nonetheless.[98]

This echoes what Griffin said plainly in her first interview with me: "I get a little nervous when I feel like the allies are kind of driving the agenda. It's partly because of that concern that I don't want them speaking for me. You know, I don't need that."

Some of these allies, too, have drawn particular criticism from other cis straight White male sports advocates. Patrick Burke, a co-founder of You Can Play, an organization that got its start mobilizing allies, has been one such critical ally. "Straight people," he wrote in 2013, "have co-opted and abused this movement," and it is time they recognize their proper place. "We have reached a point in the LGBT sports movement where a true ally has only one ethical move left to make: Get the hell out of the way."[99]

The organization Athlete Ally is an instructive example in the recent conversation about the complicated role of LGBTQ+ allies. Athlete Ally was founded at the beginning of 2011 by Hudson Taylor, a White cisgender straight former college wrestler now in his late thirties. Taylor initially gained public attention for wearing the logo of the LGBTQ+ civil rights group the Human Rights Campaign on his headgear during his college wrestling matches.[100] His organization has institutionalized allyship and has, from the beginning, been interested in changing sports culture and policy at the K–12, college, and pro levels through athlete education and training, policy work, and advocacy.[101]

By the mid-2010s, some early critics of Taylor and Athlete Ally felt that they centered *themselves* in the fight for LGBTQ+ social justice, and that they failed to recognize the extent to which their advocacy might push aside LGBTQ+ voices and activists.[102] Over the decade that followed, Athlete Ally did work to course correct. By late 2021, sports activists reported to me that Athlete Ally was focusing its work at the institutional level to broadly change sports culture and also to advocate for trans and nonbinary athlete inclusion at all levels of sport. Taylor worked to earn back trust by sticking around, listening to his critics within the movement, and being a "vigorous ally"[103] who moved himself out of the spotlight while promoting LGBTQ+ leadership within the organization. And movement insiders recognized that Taylor had access and influence that he likely would *not* have had if he were not a straight White cisgender man, and that this was a substantial political asset. He was, for example, able to speak with conservative legislators in states where Athlete Ally was working to fight anti-trans laws.

Taylor himself, when I spoke with him in early 2022, said that he felt that the early work of building a viable organization necessarily involved a lot of forward-facing engagement on his part, and that he came to understand that "when I say 'yes' to everything, those are opportunities that are not being given to other folks within the space."[104] Many years now into this cisgender straight male athlete mobilization, allies have been learning—sometimes with substantial missteps and painful confrontations along the way—to use their platform in more nuanced and thoughtful ways. The work is *always* in progress and is never easy or uncontested.

TAKING A STAND IN A CULTURE WAR

The connection between politics and entertainment is not new by any means. Historian Steven J. Ross recounts that it was the US government itself that first mobilized Hollywood celebs, enlisting movie stars like Charlie Chaplin and Douglas Fairbanks to raise money for World War I by asking fans to buy war bonds. By 1918 J. Edgar Hoover had the FBI watching over those Hollywood stars who might radicalize Americans. This fear of the power of the Hollywood Left drove Cold War investigations, too, Ross writes—though he is clear to note that the Hollywood *Right* actually has had a *lot* of power and influence over the decades.[105]

Celebrities do have the power of platform. They can draw attention, and their opinions can carry weight. This is how using your platform can contribute to social change—and can help to win a culture war. Celebrities can raise interest in a way that almost no one else is positioned to do. They have a wide reach. They also have a kind of emotional relationship with fans that traditional politicians tend not to have.[106] The celebrity platform is complicated and limited, but it is clear that celebrities can be serious and informed political actors. They—and their audiences—can also exercise a lot more agency than many experts give them credit for.[107] Many culture workers who are politically active make a life of thoughtful engagement with the world and are both realistic and optimistic about the role they can play in social change. They are constrained by their business, and their political engagement may come with political risks. Yet they are savvy and self-aware in the way they move within it.[108] Celebrities who use their platforms are rarely the frivolous, inauthentic, self-serving know-nothings that is the caricature.

When it comes to use of artistic, commercial, and personal platforms, I have come to believe that the perfect is the enemy of the good. If we are waiting for corporations or individual celebrities or storytellers to be pristine in the way that they conduct themselves as political actors, we will always be disappointed and will always only understand their work in a cynical way. Professional athletics and Hollywood are *businesses* that are not set up, primarily, to serve social justice. Yet those who work within these industries can meaningfully work in the service of change. When they use their platforms in this way, they have a reach that is undeniable.

3. CHANGE YOUR WORKPLACE

Hollywood is a mess right now because, above all else, Hollywood is a business. The entertainment industry does not exist to change hearts and minds. It does not exist for cultural and political change. It does not exist to be a kind of public service for marginalized people and their allies. This is widely understood by insiders. They don't *expect* any different as they go about their work of making art and entertaining fans. The people I interviewed know they are fully engaged with the project of commerce, its demands, and its artistic and political limitations. And they know that they navigate a fraught and complicated workplace, just like any worker does.[1]

This chapter focuses on the conditions of cultural workplaces, particularly Hollywood, as experienced by insiders.[2] I did not set out to study the business side of Hollywood or elite sports. But the people I spoke with talked forcefully about how they see the relationship between their workplaces and LGBTQ+ social change. They understand that making room in the culture for more LGBTQ+ visibility and belonging would necessarily include changing their workplace.[3]

Many outside of Hollywood lament that Hollywood is a business, first and foremost, and that this gets in the way of pop culture's service to social change.[4] But how does this business actually work? Here I explore the mechanisms of the workplace for queer workers, as people talked with me about them. I do not find it interesting or useful to simply criticize television, film, or sports for what they are *not* doing to contribute to social justice. Yes, Hollywood and elite sports *are*, primarily, businesses that will always be driven by bottom lines. But they are also in the business of selling stories and emotional connections. And, in this way, they impact—or have the capacity to impact—politics and culture. Also, in this way, we can identify and strive for workplace changes that do allow these businesses to challenge and change the broader culture.

UNSTABLE HOLLYWOOD

Just a few years ago, I might have said that the streaming revolution was straightforwardly *good* for diversity, inclusion, and belonging. What I was hearing in my interviews then was echoed by analysts. There was a lot of optimism that recent technological and structural shifts had created more space for marginalized people and voices in Hollywood—and that this diversity in programming was good for business for the streamers.[5] This is echoed by academics who study the business. Communication scholar Aymar Jean Christian points out that the large "corporate" or "networked" streamers embraced "diversity to attract 'buzz' and awards" and understood the "brand value" of diversity and intersectionality. There was also space in the market for "independent TV channels" that marketed to smaller audiences and often distributed their content via the larger platforms like YouTube.[6] Katherine Sender—also a communications scholar who is a must-read on LGBTQ+ media and markets—writes that ascendant streamers embraced LGBTQ+ content and that "queer, intersectional shows were not incidental to the streamers' business models but were fundamental to their expansion into producing original content in order to build and retain their subscriber base."[7]

In my earlier interviews, I heard a lot of hope about the new ways that stories were delivered. Streaming platforms could produce prestige and niche shows that win awards and inspire lots of watercooler chatter and critical acclaim but do not necessarily draw in millions of viewers. This could create opportunity for more kinds of storytelling.

In the early years of streaming, there was an 85 percent jump in original scripted series, just from 2011 to 2018, when that number reached 495—and this number jumped to 599 by 2022.[8]

Nisha Ganatra, the writer/producer/director/actor we met in the previous chapter, is an example of a creator who experienced the early years of streaming services as providing opportunities for her to tell the stories she wanted to tell. When I spoke with Ganatra in the summer of 2017, streaming platforms needed to fill content and bring in new viewers. She felt that this business imperative made room for different kinds of storytelling that did not center on traditional White characters or heteronormative stories but allowed for more narrative diversity. This had not been her experience with trying to pitch her work in the past, when she was being pushed, she felt, to tell her stories but with a White leading character or in a way that was comfortable for straight people. That shifted with the early years of streaming. "Now it's not like that. Everyone is asking me, 'What do you have that's Indian?' Or suggesting: 'Why don't you make that character gay?'" at the writing stage.[9]

For their part during these years, web spaces, like YouTube and TikTok, allowed creators to produce their own work and just upload them directly. This "reduces the barrier to entry" to storytellers who might not land network or streamer deals, as Jen Richards noted of the Emmy-nominated YouTube series she co-created and acted in, in 2015–16.[10]

These early years of optimism could not survive COVID-19. The global pandemic immeasurably exacerbated a period of instability in the business that had already begun with the Hollywood "tech-over."[11] COVID shut down film and television sets and emptied movie theaters—and those theaters still have not fully bounced back.[12] Demand for in-home viewing rose, from the earliest *Tiger King* days of the pandemic (who could forget that March 2020 queer icon?). At the same time, there was a backlog of unpurchased and unproduced work that it was not safe to make. For movies, US box office revenue hit a forty-year low in 2020, while Netflix added 26 million new subscribers in the first half of that year. By August 2021, more than 81 percent of households in the country had "at least one TV-connected device," up from 72 percent in August 2019.[13]

This boon for streamers was short-lived. "The streaming gold rush . . . is over," wrote one analyst in the spring of 2024.[14] Netflix made headlines in the spring of 2022 by losing subscribers two quarters in a row and tanking on Wall Street. "Everything changed after that," Jen Richards told me in early 2024. "It sent a chill through the industry, and everyone stopped buying then." Whereas, in the early days of streaming, "every platform was incentivized to gather as much content as they could, and they didn't have to make money on it," Richards explained. "All the streamers now have realized that they have to make money in order to stay afloat, and none of them knows how to do it yet."[15]

The people I interviewed in the past few years have been acutely feeling the uncertainty of this current moment in Hollywood. One television producer I spoke with at the end of 2021 felt that there was a small window in the mid-2010s when television writers and other creatives "were king." They had ample opportunity to sell their shows to booming streamers, which included a lot of creative freedom. This resulted in a glut of content and a lot of instability. This producer described the current business as "chaotic."[16] Three others during this time, just as the business was emerging from the COVID shutdown, all independently said that Hollywood was like the "Wild West."

As one example, writer Gianna Sobol described the emergence of the writers' "mini room" as a product of the past few years.[17] In this unstable working arrangement, streamers do not yet commit to picking up a show but want to see a few scripts first. So they hire writers for ten weeks or even fewer to produce scripts for a show that they may or may not buy.[18] Streamers, too, now buy shows with fewer episodes per season (even as few as six per season, or eight or ten). These models introduce new job insecurity for writers, who now must look to work on multiple shows each year. There is also a sense among writers and producers that streamers are less likely to give a show due time to find an audience, to succeed a bit more slowly. They feel that they have to create hits almost immediately—creating more job uncertainty and an overall sense of anxiety about the current way the business works.

The extended writers' and actors' union strikes that virtually shut down Hollywood in 2023 educated the public on the extent to which the streamers' model exploits their workers. As actors' union president Fran Drescher summarized in the midst of the strike: "The digital age is cannibalizing us."[19] These challenges by the Writers Guild of America and the performers' SAG-AFTRA threw into sharp relief the extent to which Hollywood *is* a workplace that is in the midst of a massive and destabilizing shift as streamers adjust their creative and economic models and as generative artificial intelligence threatens the jobs of creative workers.

In the summer of 2025, when I did another round of interviews, the words I heard over and over again to describe the industry were *contraction* and *constriction*. The business is getting smaller, especially in Los Angeles proper, where less and less of the work of making TV shows and films is taking place. As a result, lots of people in all aspects of the business, from talent to crews, are out of work. *And* whoever is left with a job is being asked to do the same work with smaller budgets.[20] There is just less opportunity now for storytellers and everyone working around them. In this environment, the current instability of the business may end up simply replicating and perpetuating marginalization of those people and stories that already had been largely excluded from mainstream television and film.[21] Many I interviewed in recent years expressed genuine enthusiasm for the opportunities that streamers could present. But they understood and worried that the current way in which storytelling is delivered means that the common cultural experience of network television and epic films has been all but lost to small, more niche spaces.[22]

Writer/actor/producer/director Brittani Nichols, who identifies as Black and queer, spoke with me in April 2022 and worried about the marginalizing effect of the way that stories are told now. Over the course of her career, Nichols has written and/or acted in series and films on a range of platforms, from a web series, to streaming, to independent film. She then became a writer on the recent network award-winning hit show *Abbott Elementary* (on ABC), a show created in 2021 by a Black woman, Quinta Brunson, about a group of teachers and their school, featuring a predominantly Black lead cast. I spoke with Nichols after her first season on *Abbott*, and she expressed concern about the way that storytelling was being marginalized through streamers. She said that pitches from queer people and people of color are often automatically understood as being for streamers:

> So now you've just created a box where you think these stories belong, and you're still missing the point of these stories should be across *all* platforms and be on all mediums. And it's like, if we're supposed to be using this art in this medium to broaden people's minds and to show people things that they might not have seen before, characters and identities and people and situations, you're just serving that to the people that already like those things or feel that way, and it's not doing what it's supposed to do.[23]

For some, the larger reach of network television can be appealing and important.[24]

Even within these streaming spaces, with the instability of the past few years, there is a sense that opportunities are constricting for newer stories and storytellers: "The last things in are the first things out in this system," said Jen Richards in early 2024. "So a lot of us who had come in during streaming, when it was a little easier to get in, when the doors were cracked up, we were the first ones shoved out and have the doors closed." Peter Paige (who is in his fifties and White) agreed, in the summer of 2025: "There is still progress that has been made and is being sustained. *But* there's less of it *for sure*. For sure! So, women, people of color, queer people, are all getting a little bit of a shove-off right now." He continued, "When economics get tight, marginalized people get screwed. It's just that simple. They just recenter, they just recenter."[25]

These recent conversations have led me to conclude that it is not as simple as more creative outlets translates to more inclusion. In the aftermath of the industry's streaming and COVID precarity, marginalization in storytelling is simply being replicated through current innovations in television and film. New risk aversion also seems to lead to the pulling back of Hollywood's still-new and ever-precarious commitments to diversity in storytelling.[26]

HOW ANTI-QUEERNESS WORKS IN HOLLYWOOD NOW

White cisgender straight male youth supremacy in Hollywood has been alive and well throughout the massive changes of recent years. These entrenched and structural inequalities and exclusions have been documented by observers of the industry and have been fought against, for example, by the #OscarsSoWhite and the "me too"[27] and Time's Up movements.[28] They also have been experienced and reported by many people I spoke with over the years.

How *do* LGBTQ+ people experience this Hollywood workplace? We still know too little. One study co-sponsored by the SAG-AFTRA union was published in 2013 and reported overall progress in the industry. But it found that SAG-AFTRA members still faced workplace homophobia and transphobia and perceived anti-LGBTQ+ bias.[29] An update to this study, that could look in a broad and quantitative way at the industry, is sorely needed. LGBTQ+ data is not collected in a systematic way in Hollywood.[30] This makes it difficult to track bias, and it works against affirmative efforts on the part of networks, studios, and shows to hire LGBTQ+ people. There are several complex ways that the entertainment business now excludes, marginalizes, and discriminates against LGBTQ+ actors and other creatives—alongside everyday microaggression and workplace culture challenges, which have not gone away. Some of these mechanisms seem explicitly anti-queer. Some seem gender- or sexuality-neutral on their face, but they're not. The three mechanisms that I focus on here are severe risk aversion in the business, presumptions about audience, and typecasting and pigeonholing.

RISK AVERSION

"Institutional risk aversion" is central to the way that Hollywood does business.[31] Producing television shows and, especially, feature films is expensive. Potential profit is substantial, so the gambles are high. Risk aversion in the business leads to sidelining people who are not White cisgender men, including LGBTQ+ people and their stories. It also silences people who might speak up for change in their workplace, and this prevents progress in the industry. This has always been the case. However, COVID-19 and the streamer instability of the past few years have raised new insecurities and uncertainties. Any creative risks that Hollywood decision-makers were willing to take when streamers were new are long gone. The chaos of the past few years has created a high-anxiety time in Hollywood, where there is substantial lack of clarity about what content will succeed.

Risk aversion might sound race-, gender-, and sexuality-neutral, but it absolutely is not. Many people I interviewed felt that straight White cisgender men were given a lot of leeway to experiment and to fail and were not seen as gambles by networks or studios.[32] Anyone who was *not* them, however, felt that they were being treated as too risky to hire, even if they had ample and irrefutable work experience. Here, risk aversion closes Hollywood off to new work, storytelling, and people. It frames "merit" in a narrow way for hiring. The way that people I spoke with understand this is that straight cis White guys in Hollywood have a freedom to fail, to be mediocre, to take risks. Anyone else does not.

Many I interviewed felt that these mainstream White guys are not just seen as talented good investments, but they are also seen as either safe bets or as *good* risks who are granted a certain amount of benefit of the doubt.[33] This provides them the relative space to take chances and the freedom to fail, and fail as *individuals* rather than as representatives of their entire group.[34] Jamie Babbit, one of Hollywood's most successful working television directors, feels she has been called upon to prove herself over and over again in her career, to men who do not see her as a director type who can coordinate and command a set full of creative and technical people.[35] She finds that there is still a mystique that favors these mainstream men and opens doors for them: “You know, a mediocre dude walks in who did a commercial, and there’s this mythology of like ‘Oh, he’s a genius.’” Brittani Nichols echoed this. “People think that straight cis White dudes are inherently competent. They sort of trust that they can handle things—or just figure things out.” There is an institutional *comfort* with these men. For anyone else, there is a sense that it’s too *risky* to hire them, especially if they are unknown to the mostly White straight cis male decision-makers in Hollywood.[36] “They consider marginalized voices a risk,” Peter Paige added in the summer of 2025. “And whereas ten years ago, being a marginalized voice was *interesting* and *exciting*, now it is a detriment to a pitch.”

Another kind of Hollywood risk aversion that works against institutional change is its orientation toward workers who are vocal about their politics or speak up against bias and other problematic conditions in their workplace. This can extend to global and national politics, as was the case in the fall of 2024, when members of a number of Hollywood unions called for a ceasefire in Gaza while expressing anger and fear about “our industry’s McCarthyist repression of members who acknowledge Palestinian suffering.”[37] Several people talked with me about the consequences they perceived of speaking up, about their fear in taking individual risks of this kind.

This is a kind of risk aversion that is institutionally created by the norms of the business. And it presents a barrier to changing the workplace. Working in Hollywood is an unstable career, yet a lifelong dream, for most people in the industry. Creatives from actors to directors have no job security and are constantly hustling to find and keep work. This is even more the case at this current moment of extreme instability and austerity in the industry. There is also a widespread perception that you are only as good as your last job. So even those who have been wildly successful on one project do not feel that they can rest on their laurels and assume that they will be able to make a lifelong living at their craft.[38] Hollywood is also a buyers' market: there are lots of willing and eager people waiting in the wings for any job, so there is a hefty "reserve army," to use Karl Marx's term, of replacement workers who can keep working creatives in line by their very existence.[39]

Hollywood feels like a small town, and there is a widespread sense among people I interviewed that it is easy to develop a bad reputation. So being the squeaky wheel, being *difficult* (a word I heard many times[40])—or, even worse, being litigious—would endanger an already-precarious career. This setup can breed caution and silence in the face of injustice or illegal discrimination in the workplace.[41] There was some sense that the "me too" movement might have changed this just a little bit, in that it opened some space to report workplace abuse. But there was still a lot of fear about the ramifications of this. Trying to make it in a business with little job security or longevity, and with a nagging and real sense that you are replaceable, does not make for conditions where individuals in the industry can readily fight for workplace change. "I think Hollywood sort of operates on fear," said an actor in 2018 who was quite politically active. "Most people—because everyone in this town [feels] so replaceable, because 'there's ten people for every job'—most people operate from a position of: don't rock the boat."[42]

PRESUMPTIONS ABOUT AUDIENCES

In this "riskiest business," the bottom line is always front of mind, and there is little reliable or truly predictive data about what "imagined audiences" actually want.[43] As a result, decision-making in Hollywood happens with a set of narrow presumptions about what audiences will accept and be drawn to.[44] Conservative, risk-averse decision-making can lead to underestimating audiences' ability to connect with LGBTQ+ characters and storylines—not to mention stories centered on BIPOC stories and characters, LGBTQ+ and otherwise. This results in a lack of adequate diversity and inclusion in casting and storytelling.

Fans and audiences can help drive change in Hollywood, but industry presumptions about them often get in the way of that change.[45]

Hollywood decision-makers generally understand themselves to be coastal liberals. But they orient their decisions to an archetypical audience in the Midwest of the United States, and they presume that this audience is narrow-minded in its tastes.[46] This coastal exceptionalism drives decision-making around race, gender, and sexuality.[47] Jen Richards said in early 2024 that she had been hearing that executives want "purple content" that is "aiming for the middle" and is ostensibly apolitical. They "don't want to risk alienating anyone."[48] A *New York Times* piece in the summer of 2024, through an analysis of the summer hit about tornadoes, *Twisters*, echoed this: That in the post-COVID instability of the film business, Hollywood is toning down film's politically progressive messaging, following presumptions about what would appeal to a broader audience. "Put bluntly," the piece noted, "it amounts to an attempt by Hollywood to bend to red state audiences."[49] Others I spoke with in mid-2025 reiterated that they felt Hollywood was looking to make stories for "the flyover states" or, as one writer put it, "much more sort of broad appeal, much less political, much less niche stories."[50]

In recent decades, Hollywood decision-makers also draw on "industry lore"[51] and make presumptions about international audiences and orient themselves toward explicit demands of international markets and censors.[52] The economic logic underlying this is undeniable now. In film, revenue from international sources (in presale deals to distribute a film before it is completed and in projected ticket sales) are substantially factored into the budgeting of Hollywood film production. International entertainment markets are growing substantially more quickly than US markets. In 2021, for instance, international film ticket sales (all non-US and non-Canada box office sales) made up 79 percent of the total market. China did not have much of an outside market until the mid-1990s. But now, since 2020 it is the largest movie market in the world. Streaming services, too, are becoming massively more globalized, featuring hit content from around the world and near-worldwide access. Netflix is in at least 190 (almost all!) countries, and more than 60 percent of its subscribers come from outside of the United States (though it is not available in China).[53] This alignment with international markets can drive casting choices, to bring in actors who play well to large international markets.[54] It can also impact the kinds of stories that are made and the way those stories are told on large and small screens.[55] This global orientation absolutely impacts the inclusion of LGBTQ+ content in versions of films or television/streaming shows that air in international markets.[56]

And yet presumptions about audience are often wrong. For instance, the conventional Hollywood wisdom is that films with Black leads of any gender are "unbankable,"[57] especially internationally. However, *Black Panther* (2018) broke domestic records and was released to strong showings in many countries around the world.[58] And Ryan Coogler's *Sinners* (2025), also starring Michael B. Jordan, was a massive success. It was the biggest box office draw on its opening weekend, and it brought in ticket sales that hadn't been seen for a debut of an original movie since another Black-led film six years earlier, Jordan Peele's *Us*.[59] Conventional wisdom also holds that films with women leads of any racial background will not do well at the box office either, especially the international ones. Yet one 2018 study found that movies with leads who are women outperform those without—not just in the United States but worldwide. And the blockbuster of the summer of 2023, *Barbie*, had worldwide ticket sales of almost $1.3 billion by the end of August 2023, making it one of the top twenty highest-grossing movies of all time.[60]

The elusive "audience" is also not historically fixed. People I interviewed *did* recognize a change here: that when it came to LGBTQ+ storylines and content, there *has* been a substantial shift in what they were able to put on-screen. Max Mutchnick, the co-creator of *Will & Grace*, which first aired on NBC in 1998, summed up these earlier perceived audience concerns with a memorable story. The night before the pilot was to be shot on Stage 17 at Radford Studios in Studio City, Mutchnick had dinner at the home of a very well-known (gay) director.

This director told Mutchnick that the show had the best chance of success if it abided by the following rule: "When they're watching *Will & Grace*, don't ever let America think about butt fucking." Mutchnick insists this is a direct quote. Over time the writers started to use a catchall phrase to bring their attention to a scene or storyline that possibly lived too close to the edge. When there was an episode with a strong sexual component or any idiosyncratic gay culture, the writers would ask themselves, "Is it too butt-fucky?" Not making anything "too butt-fucky" came easily to the gay writers on the show. "We were using the same mechanism we used the first time we went home to see family after coming out of the closet," Mutchnick said to me. "They were cool with the gay thing as long as you didn't make them think or talk about it. Holding back your truth was frustrating at home and it was frustrating writing the show. However, I understood the delicate balance I had to strike to keep my seat at the table. It was the same balance we used to keep the show on the air."[61]

Even in the past few years, creatives in Hollywood have internalized the message they feel they have received that decision-making plays to the middle of the country and what people there presumably will tolerate or want. I did not talk primarily with studio or network heads, so I do not have their perspective to share on this point. But those I spoke with extensively—actors, writers, directors, producers, and showrunners—felt that presumptions about audience drove decision-making for their projects. And they feel that the decision-makers at networks and studios *underestimate* audiences in this way. Nisha Ganatra said to me in 2017 that the relationship to audiences could be different—and that these audiences have shown that they *are* open to broader content:

> The networks are interesting right now because streaming culture has pushed everyone narratively, I think. The idea used to be that networks only want shows that appeal to "Middle America," and now we have more data and proof (sort of) to show that this whole idea of "Middle America" was a flawed perception to begin with. There

> are successful shows that are perceived as not a traditional network show—and those successes allow creators to follow in their footsteps and take some more risks on a network show. But I am also aware that there were shows that refused to be homophobic and had diverse content (before it was a thing called diverse content), like *Grey's Anatomy* was the first time I saw a hospital show with three main characters that were Black doctors and they weren't related to each other and an Asian doctor and it was all on the same show—and also *Glee* did that, right? I'm sure most traditional network worries were "that's never going to work on a network." And guess what? "Middle America," whatever that is, loved those shows!

And Brittani Nichols said to me of network television: "It's a bunch of people in LA assuming that they know what people in the Midwest want." They make assumptions, she said, that "people in the Midwest won't care about queer characters or characters of color and then you don't give them the opportunity to affirm or deny that." This underestimation of audiences can have quite a chilling effect on LGBTQ+ inclusion and storytelling, and diversity on-screen more broadly.

TYPECASTING AND PIGEONHOLING

Before there is an audience, there are storytellers. But the Hollywood workplace builds professional and artistic roadblocks for LGBTQ+ storytellers, especially actors, through a complex process of typecasting and pigeonholing. Here I highlight the ways that queer actors feel they have been typecast into similar roles over and over again and pigeonholed into a narrow set of roles. Getting cast for a project is already tough. Casting is not just a creative decision; it is also a business one that involves the input and ultimate sign-off from network or studio executives. And, of course, casting is a subjective process that involves assessing people on many superficial qualities and physical ascribed attributes that they have little to no control over—a practice that at least one insider described to me as "brutal."[62] When actors are typecast and pigeonholed, this limits their professional range and reach.

It is a common experience for actors to have a constrained set of choices in the roles they audition for and, ultimately, book. This can take many forms. Women over a certain (youngish!) age move overnight from young romantic leads to "mom purgatory."[63] Actors who are billed as "plus sized" (the industry term) find themselves at audition after audition reading for comedic rather than romantic roles.[64] Actors who have played one kind of archetype get stuck playing that type over and over again. Or actors who have had the good fortune to land a culture-penetrating "indelible" role,[65] like one of the *Friends* friends, often have a tough time getting out from under these roles, where they become sort of culturally melded with their character.

Typecasting and pigeonholing tend to disproportionately limit the experience and advancement of minoritized people in the Hollywood workplace. There has been an increasingly robust public conversation about the role of race and racism in casting. A 2021 study, for instance, found that Black talent was "pigeonholed and funneled into race-related content, which often plays into stereotypes" and narrow opportunities.[66] On a panel of South Asian and Southeast Asian actors hosted by the Casting Society of America in the spring of 2021, prolific actor Rizwan Manji talked poignantly about his limited opportunities for advancement as a South Asian actor. "Nothing is written for me. Nothing is," he said, yet "White people can play everything."[67] With race, as with other forms of identity, the way that casting practices constrain actors of color ranges from very direct to quite coded.

I heard from many actors about the ways that they experienced racism and colorism in their casting experiences and choices and the trade-offs they felt they had to confront in their careers. "I never wanted to play terrorists, and it was kind of off the table, and so I would play kind of terrorist-adjacent kinds of roles"—like a CIA informant gone rogue, said Amin El Gamal, the Egyptian American and Muslim actor whom we met in previous chapters. He feels that he has been pigeonholed because of his ethnicity. "No matter how queer I might be or how American I might be, I'm seen as my ethnicity," he said in our first conversation in 2018. In our second interview in 2022, El Gamal felt that actors who shared his background as Middle Eastern and North African (MENA) were often "pitted against each other as tokens." As a result, El Gamal feels that he sometimes has to make career choices that involve creative and political compromises. "I *would* like my values to align in my work and I don't think that's happened yet."[68]

For queer actors of all racial/ethnic backgrounds, there is an active and ever-changing public conversation about casting. There is evidence—though it is a bit dated now, and there has not been, to my knowledge, an updated study—that some LGBTQ+ actors feel disadvantaged in the casting process.[69] I spoke with many gay, lesbian, and bisexual actors over the years who had a lot to say about navigating the casting process. Several publicly out actors spoke with me about auditioning and the way that they felt their sexuality or perceived sexuality impacted their experiences. For queer actors of color, many I spoke with felt that options were so limited even for *straight* actors of color, and that their sexuality constrained their opportunities even further. El Gamal said his embodied self was policed during auditions, reporting that he had received the feedback that he should "butch it up."[70] When I spoke with El Gamal in 2022, they said that while progress has been made in queer representation and opportunity in Hollywood, they believe that "we're still afraid of what queerness really is." Much of the mainstream storytelling is quite "heteronormative" and "assimilationist" and is stuck in a certain kind of storytelling about queer lives (like difficult coming-out or disclosure stories). This, then, limits options for queer actors.

Actors reported that it was rarely that they were told *directly* they were not right for a part because they were out as lesbian, gay, or bisexual. But there was coded language and subtlety to the audition process that telegraphed to them that their sexuality was in play in casting decisions. They heard, "You're just not right for the role" or "He's too on the nose" or "the obvious choice" for gay roles. Slightly less coded, actors heard that they were "too flamboyant" or "a little light" for the part. And, even more direct, they heard: "We're not going gay with this."

Many actors I spoke with felt they *had* been typecast and that being publicly out had impacted their career and the opportunities they were afforded. Michael Urie, who identifies as queer and has played lots of high-profile and celebrated gay parts, talked with me extensively about casting and sexuality. He revealed that early in his career, especially after he played the role of Marc St. James on the ABC hit *Ugly Betty* (2006–10), he was counseled by many people not to accept any more gay roles so that he would avoid typecasting: "I know if I had said this, that I'm not going to play any more gay parts—if I had made the choice to say this—I wouldn't work, I wouldn't do anything." He believes, though, that there are now a wider range of less-tropey gay roles so that he has been able to play a *range* of gay characters that are more nuanced, less one-note and monolithic.[71] This was a goal that was expressed by other actors I spoke with as well: that at least there was some diversity and complexity to the gay roles they booked.

These narrow casting decisions and problematic dynamics are often chalked up to the pervasive risk aversion in the industry.[72] Casting professionals are not free to make their own casting decisions because they are beholden to network/studio executives of media conglomerates seeking the widest possible audience and the largest possible financial return on their investment. Actors understand that casting directors answer to executives and do not have full leeway—and that casting gay actors *might be* the riskier choice: "Everyone in the business is afraid for their jobs" and under a lot of scrutiny, actor/writer/producer/director Peter Paige said to me. "There's ten billion actors out there who could do this part. Why am I going to bring somebody in and set myself up for a slap on the wrist? That could ultimately cost me my job and my livelihood?"[73] This logic was not even understood to come solely from straight casting directors. A number of actors said they felt that even *gay* casting directors seem to give in to the risk aversion and, according to interviews, their internalized homophobia to deny LGB actors roles.

Risk logic came up in my conversations particularly around the question of whether publicly out LGB actors could play *straight* roles, especially leading roles.[74] Mostly this has been a conversation about men. Women's work is still devalued in Hollywood, and it is still common wisdom that it is leading men who sell a movie to audiences. So their value to a project is overestimated. And there are, quite simply, *more* leading men—and just more men, period—than women in films.[75] The "leading man" role, especially in film, drives a lot of the metric for success for male actors in Hollywood, and this goal still seems to be elusive for publicly out gay actors. These actors *have* made progress but have not yet fully broken this barrier of success, especially as leading men in action movies or as straight romantic leads.[76] Jonathan Bailey—an out gay actor who plays gay roles but also stars as a hot, straight Viscount in the *Bridgerton* Netflix series and as Prince Fiyero in the 2024 and 2025 *Wicked* films, and was named *People* magazine's Sexiest Man Alive in 2025—is an interesting example to watch.[77] But many people I spoke with still feel this is a bridge too far for most audiences, especially when stakes are high with an expensive movie.[78] Despite the fact that audiences *know* that actors are *not* the role they inhabit, there is *something* about the suspension of disbelief about sexuality that seems, in this logic, to be too much for audiences. Embedded in this leading man conversation is an understanding that movie stars must have very broad appeal—and concern that they would not if they were publicly out as gay. This is not a new conversation.[79] Yet this vigorous casting conversation has continued in various iterations in recent decades.[80]

The conversation, on the other hand, about casting questions for *straight*-identified actors who play gay, lesbian, or bisexual roles, has shifted over time. For a long time, in the earlier years of LGB stories and leading roles, straight actors playing gay roles might be able to count on praise and award buzz.[81] In this slightly earlier era, especially, they also confronted the concern that they might be pigeonholed into gay roles in perpetuity—especially for those in long-standing TV series. Several people, for instance, raised with me the example of actor Eric McCormack, the straight actor who played gay Will Truman on *Will &*

Grace, who might be both typecast for playing a long-standing, popular role *and* also for playing a gay lead. This was not a concern that McCormack, himself, shared, either in his interview with me or in public comments on this specific casting concern. And in fact, he's gone on to a variety of straight lead roles in several series, including *Travelers* and *Perception*.[82] Eric Stonestreet, too, in his conversation with me, brushed away this concern about his career after *Modern Family*'s Cam.

In the past ten or fifteen years, there has been a shift to a focus on so-called "authentic casting" with respect to many forms of identity: a focus on ensuring that an actor shares core identities with the characters they play. This has tended to mean that when straight actors play gay characters, this is understood by many as a form of cultural appropriation and career opportunism, even if their hearts are in the right place.[83] There is also now a recognition that the casting of straight actors in gay roles takes potential jobs away from gay actors who may have more limited options, especially if their sexual identity intersects with other marginalized identities. These critiques have only gotten more emphatic in the past decade, and high-profile straight actors differ in their views of whether they should continue to play queer roles.[84]

This call for "authentic" casting does not necessarily translate to actual casting practices. Calling casting directors "some of the most narrow-minded people that exist in the industry," Brittani Nichols believes that casting professionals could be *much* more proactive about finding queer actors, and much more open to giving audiences credit for what they are willing to watch. She talked about casting for one of her shows, for a lesbian character, and working with casting directors who kept bringing in presumably straight actors for the role: "It's them bringing in all of these straight women who are now putting on their lesbian cosplay, and I'm like 'This is fucking offensive—I've seen ten straight women in a row with a beanie and plaid on, and I'm offended by this experience.'"

When I asked Peter Paige in 2021 about the current state of the casting conversation, he, himself, brought up the question of authentic casting and said that he *did* believe that LGBTQ+ roles should go to LGBTQ+ actors: "I actually really think that the best performances of queerness are played by queer actors, people who intrinsically understand the experience." He acknowledged that this was controversial and that there are exceptions, but "if I see one more straight guy mincing and lisping around a screen doing what I call 'gay face,' I'm going to lose my mind. That affect that many, many queer men have adopted through the ages or intrinsically have, it comes at a price, it comes with a responsibility. It is not put on like a shirt. It's not a costume. And I think that that's so lost."[85]

There is also increasing public intolerance for cisgender actors of any gender playing trans and nonbinary characters. The award buzz for cisgender actors playing transgender characters even a few years ago has given way to more and more criticism of this casting practice and high-profile refusal of these actors to accept these roles. There is also a push in Hollywood to bring more trans and nonbinary actors into the business and to move away from pigeonholing them in trans and nonbinary roles, especially given that there are still a near-infinitesimal number of trans and nonbinary roles in television and film, and a decreasing number of LGBTQ+ characters in both TV and film.[86]

In 2014 *Time* magazine featured trans actress Laverne Cox, of Netflix's *Orange Is the New Black* (2013–19), on its cover and declared that there was a "transgender tipping point" in both popular visibility and politics.[87] There was a turning point around this time, as well, in the casting conversation, in part due to the intense public debate about two high-profile trans women's roles going to cisgender men in the Amazon hit *Transparent* (2014–19) and the award-winning film *Dallas Buyers Club* (2013). The public critique of this casting practice grew particularly pointed when Jared Leto, who played transgender woman Rayon in *Dallas Buyers Club*, gave an insulting speech as he was accepting the Golden Globe Award for the role (he then went on to win an Academy Award two months later). In addition, Jeffrey Tambor, who played Maura Pfefferman on *Transparent*, went on to face accusations of sexual harassment of two trans women connected to the show, from which he was fired in early 2018.[88] So the public critique was not simply about casting cis men in trans women's roles. It was also about the fact that sometimes these actors don't seem to learn any empathy or sense of responsibility after inhabiting these roles. Despite the intensity of this critique, this was not the end of the practice of casting cis male stars in high-profile trans women roles. Eddie Redmayne played the lead role in *The Danish Girl* in 2015 and was nominated for both an Academy Award and Golden Globe, along with many other awards.[89]

A few years after *The Danish Girl*, Jen Richards wrote a poignant critique of the 2017 film *Anything*, which cast cisgender man Matt Bomer as a trans woman. She argued that it is still the case that most people do not believe that they know any trans people, so their impressions of trans experiences come from popular culture. Casting cis men to play trans women, then, contributes to the dangerous trope that trans women are not "real women" and are covering up a secret identity. She wrote: "Every time a cis man gets applauded for bravely portraying a transgender woman on screen, every time he picks up an award for it while sporting a tuxedo, we're reinforcing the belief that at the end of the day, a trans woman is still really a man."[90]

When I spoke with Richards in 2018, she truly felt that this argument about how these casting practices endangered real-life trans women had changed the casting conversation forever: "I think that's the argument that horrified Hollywood, to the point where they changed their mind on this issue." She continued, "I don't think Hollywood's going to make that mistake again." She said that she would not rule out the possibility that cis actors could play trans roles, but "right now, in this cultural context, when a man plays a trans woman, it leads to violence. That's it. If trans women weren't being killed, I wouldn't care as much."[91] Writer and producer Shadi Petosky confirmed in 2021 how powerful this argument had been. She attributed a true change in casting practice to years of work by trans advocates and artists (gaining steam in 2014), increasing public pressure of cisgender actors not to take trans roles, and to Richards's public response to Bomer's casting: "A cis person will not play a trans person on screen, from that moment forward."[92]

Casting conversations and decisions, then, have changed a lot as a result of successful engagement and activism by individuals and advocacy organizations.[93] In 2018 Scarlett Johansson withdrew from a role as a trans man after her casting had been announced to vigorous criticism, citing that she understood and appreciated the argument that the part should go to a trans actor.[94] And just in the past few years, especially in television and streaming, there have been many acclaimed representations of trans and nonbinary characters played by trans and nonbinary actors.[95] This includes a number of animated series that particularly have been a space for nonbinary representation (and opportunity for nonbinary actors).[96] There also has been more intentionality and affirmative attention, and more informed practice, to hiring trans and nonbinary actors.

And yet this progress is certainly not inevitable or linear. In early 2024, Richards identified a "backslide" in the opportunities for trans creatives. With the risk aversion and "aiming for the middle" of the past couple of years, and the horrible anti-trans politics of the political Right, "the simple act of being trans is considered political" these days. By the summer of 2025, Richards's assessment was even more dire: "The careers of trans people in Hollywood have largely been decimated. There was a moment when it was cool to include us, it felt like a way for series to signal that they were on the right side of an emerging civil rights issue, and of course there are a lot of creatives who genuinely care about trans people and their dignity. Ever since the Bud Light fiasco, however, those opportunities dried up. The mere inclusion of a trans person on-screen is now considered a politically 'woke' act, no matter who that character is or what they do. And with the studios becoming increasingly risk averse, we who were last in are first out."[97] Shakina Nayfack, a writer/director/actress and trans activist, echoed this in the fall of 2025: "In my opinion, TV and mainstream film are, I'll say, on hiatus for us. . . . Producers, investors are afraid of walking themselves into a culture war. So we and our narratives suffer."[98]

So, too, the "authenticity" imperative could have a problematic side. It can and should result in more opportunities for queer actors, and it *could* be LGBTQ+ positive and affirming. It could *also* further pigeonhole queer actors into an already very small number of queer roles.[99] This is a concern that cisgender LGB actors and writers expressed to me. It is also one that trans and nonbinary actors and writers express. Trans and nonbinary talent noted that there are still so few out trans and nonbinary working professionals. And because there is new demand for authentic representation, they feel they could be easily tokenized or brought into a project only to check a box. They also worry that they will only be considered for trans and nonbinary parts or jobs. This both limits their opportunities and pits them against each other in auditions for a very small number of roles.

The authenticity imperative also asks a lot of actors. Almost by definition, it requires actors to fit into neatly labeled, legible boxes so that their identities as *people* fit seamlessly into the identities of *characters* they might portray on-screen. If not done with care, as talent agent Deven Hartley pointed out to me, it also has the potential to result in invasive and possibly illegal disclosure for actors about their identities, their bodies, or their medical history.[100] A call for authenticity in a casting breakdown cannot, legally, result in asking an actor directly about how they identify and relies on self-identification instead. But this still may result in actors feeling pressure to come out at work—and to *have* a clear label that defines them. It can also lead to a casting competition among a small number of publicly out queer actors in a way that potentially pits these actors against each other.

It is also worth noting that these complicated casting questions come as a result of the fact that there *are* now a number of publicly out actors and that there is increased visibility for queer talent. Pigeonholing, typecasting, and the limitations that out actors face now could be understood as a complicated consequence of visibility. When actors were closeted, they could play all roles, including romantic leads (like Rock Hudson, for example). As Michael Urie said to me: “I mean, before anyone was out, there were plenty of gay leading men.” Reflecting on his own career, he said, “Forty years ago, there were no out gay actors in show business. It wasn’t a thing then. I probably would have worked more forty years ago—from inside the closet."[101]

HOLLYWOOD'S PROGRESS: PARTIAL AND PRECARIOUS

Hollywood *has* changed—but slowly, partially, and not in a linear way. And it is unclear to what extent those changes will survive the current political moment. Efforts toward diversity, equity, inclusion, and belonging (DEIB)[102] have not come easily to Hollywood. In recent years, the industry has responded to broader US politics and social movements, like anger over Trump's first term, the "me too" movement, and the Black Lives Matter movement's activism in the wake of the police murder of George Floyd in May 2020. It also has responded to pressure from civil rights groups targeted directly at the industry[103] and to demands inside the industry, like recent union activism for better working conditions.[104] *Audiences* also change Hollywood. Audiences make it clear that they are eager for more diversity in storytelling and storytellers, and they do this through their easy and immediate access to Hollywood creatives through social media. (As one production company exec said to me in 2021: "The feedback loop is constant!")[105] Institutional change in Hollywood has primarily come from below and from outside the industry, rather than being driven by independent insider elite initiatives. But this *has* resulted in initiatives at the top that are really having an impact on the business, its leadership, and its culture and consciousness.[106]

Not all of these DEIB initiatives are new to the past few years. Some date back decades and are also the result of responses to social movement critiques and action.[107] But many DEIB efforts gained new momentum and public attention in recent years. These are institutional projects introduced by individuals with authority in the industry and are designed—through research, training, and mandates—to diversify many aspects of the business.[108] Casting practices have been one substantial target of change, as I have discussed here. And some of these practices are institutionalized through new LGBTQ+-focused initiatives.[109] Beyond casting, there has been additional attention to *storytelling*, as Hollywood confronts new questions about which stories can and should be told and by whom. Just as there is new concern for authentic casting, there is a new sensitivity to and scrutiny of who is writing what stories and how connected the writers' room is to the story they're telling—of who gets to tell which stories.

As with other changes in the business, new understandings of and commitments to diversity in storytelling come in large part as a response to the social movements of the past few years. When I asked Fawzia Mirza—an actor/writer/director who identifies as South Asian, Muslim, and queer—about the timing and impetus of the changes that she says have been real over the past few years, they answered:

> I would say, since 2017 a lot *has* changed. The #MeToo movement led to a more mainstream awareness of systemic misogyny. The Muslim ban forced us to reckon with extreme Islamophobia. In 2018 *Crazy Rich Asians* premiered, which showed Hollywood that Asian community turns out. And during the COVID-19 pandemic, a social justice revolution centering Black and Indigenous communities impacted education, culture, and storytelling tremendously. Ideally, these historic moments should have led to doors opening for diverse filmmakers and artists. And they did. Even though profitability and capitalism are always at the center, there are most definitely more films centering our community, made by our community.[110]

Newer mentorship and training programs have focused on writers, showrunners, and directors, in particular, to correct for the fact that, typically, these roles have been filled by straight cisgender young to middle-aged White men, even as there has been some substantial progress in the past fifteen years or so.[111] Many of the largest media companies and the networks started mentorship, training/shadowing, and pipeline programs or "bootcamps."[112] So, too, the unions have run programs focused on increasing opportunity for underrepresented creatives. And some of the most high-profile storytellers with clout in the business—often Black women like Shonda Rhimes, Ava DuVernay, and Issa Rae—have their own initiatives to nurture underrepresented talent in storytelling.[113]

Among people I interviewed in the past few years, there is broad agreement that some things *have* changed in the Hollywood workplace, and that there is least some celebration of diversity and some inclination to do better in casting, storytelling, and creating a workplace environment that centers and supports many people and experiences. Yet most people I spoke with also were not overly sanguine about the pace or extent of these changes—especially now in the early days of Trump 2.0. Even in the years right before Trump retook office, they understood that structural and systemic change was hard and took time and that there was not always the will or patience for it. I heard two related areas of concern about where more sustained and systemic change needed to be focused but was not yet: workplace culture and industry leadership.

Andria Wilson Mirza—the then-director of ReFrame, an initiative of the Sundance Institute and Women In Film that supports gender representation and equity in the entertainment industry—was clear that changing the Hollywood workplace is not just about opening doors. There is, instead, a need for a broad and sustained cultural shift: "We can't just advocate for hiring equity without also advocating for a workplace that is free of harassment and abuse," she said. "Because why would I push you to hire inclusively, to bring a queer woman of color to your set, if she's going to be abused? That is a *horrifying* thing to think about. And yet it is so common in our industry." She assessed that in Hollywood there is interest in window-dressing-like shallow change yet "a real resistance to deep work which threatens the underlying power structure." She surmised that this had to do with leadership: "Hollywood is not run by a liberal elite. There's, in fact, large corporations that drive all of the work that we do."[114]

At the top, there is still a substantial lack of diversity, which hinders broader, systemwide workplace change. For instance, the Writers Guild of America West found that there have been significant gains at the lower-level staff positions for writers of color in recent years.

But this does not translate to upper-level, decision-making roles like television executive producer (EP) or showrunner. For these, for instance, White men were still 45.9 percent and 46.2 percent of EP and showrunner roles, respectively, in 2023–24.[115]

Many people I have spoken with over the past few years who had been optimistic about the DEIB-related changes they were seeing in their business still believe—correctly—that straight White cisgender men are disproportionately in decision-making roles as, for instance, senior writers, showrunners, and network or studio execs. Diversity initiatives, meanwhile, have been aimed at junior and mid-level positions, and it remains to be seen if these newer hires will be given the opportunity to advance in their careers or grow into roles as decision-makers who can make change. Many I spoke with felt that while there *had been* some new commitment to diversity in storytelling and representation in recent years, the same old decision-makers were making the same old decisions, green-lighting stories that centered on cisgender straight White men and even actively fighting back against storytelling that did not. A more wholesale change would take self-awareness and hard work, rather than a self-congratulatory approach to the work. As Brittani Nichols observed about the broad uniformity and lack of diversity and self-awareness of the executives: "How do you all not look around and realize that four of you are wearing the same pair of glasses?!"

It is also very unclear if and to what extent these newer DEIB-focused initiatives will survive Trump's presidency and his assault on diversity. Hollywood, like other workplaces, tends to have a short memory, little patience, and risk aversion when it comes to workplace corrections toward greater inclusion and belonging. Its short-lived response to the "me too" movement and to Black Lives Matter mobilizations in the years right around 2020 had already begun a rollback before Trump 2.0. This has only accelerated since January 2025.[116]

TRANS-EXCLUSIONARY POLITICS IN SPORTS

While this chapter has focused primarily on Hollywood as a workplace, I want to say a bit about sports. Many of my earlier interviews focused on what it would mean to sports and the broader culture to have more publicly out LGB elite athletes. Among those I interviewed, there was a sense that the workplace of elite athletics was at least getting a bit better for lesbian, gay, and bisexual athletes. There were new legal protections in place in collective bargaining agreements—even in leagues with conservative reputations like the National Football League.[117] And normative culture was bending, at the very least, toward acceptance of LGB players and intolerance of homophobia. Commentator Cyd Zeigler (who is gay) said to me way back in 2011 about these changing norms, "I think it's easier to be homosexual in sports today than it is to be homophobic."[118]

In recent years, the focus has shifted to politics and policies of transgender and nonbinary athlete participation—in large part in response to the increased and vitriolic, bad-faith political and cultural attacks on these athletes. The political and religious Right have set their sights on trans sports participation, at all levels of play, as a wedge issue to rally their base. They have targeted basic civil and human rights for trans and nonbinary people,[119] and they have brought their bigotry to fights over sports and pop culture.[120]

There is a *workplace* aspect of this attack, and LGBTQ+ people and their allies are fighting to change a workplace that seems intractable or hostile to change—or even just to hold on to changes they have won in recent decades. To be sure, elite sports is a big business, as is Hollywood. It is also a business, like Hollywood, with precarious, episodic, contingent jobs that people have often dreamed of and worked hard for their entire lives. But in the current moment, it is both the business exigencies *and* the political ones that are most impacting the way that LGBTQ+ athletes—especially those who identify as trans or nonbinary—are able to access and experience their work.[121] This workplace attack in sports also has broader meaning and resonance, because sports are so central to American culture. "If they can paint trans people as dangerous on the court or the field," Chris Mosier said to me in the summer of 2025, "they can say that we are a threat everywhere else. And that, I think, is the big pull-out idea. That is the whole reason that they attack sports: if they can say that we're dangerous on a basketball court or in the locker room, they can say that we are a threat to your child in the bathroom in Walmart."[122]

It is not necessarily obvious why sports would become such a primary target for the political Right. Yet if we look to history, we can understand that sports in the United States have been wrapped up in concerns with normative and narrow conceptions of gender, especially masculinity, at least since the late 1800s.[123] We can trace the *current* anti-trans efforts to the immediate anti-LGBTQ+ and anti-trans stance of the Trump administration and to the state-level so-called "bathroom bills" of the mid-2010s that were designed to restrict public accommodations for trans and nonbinary people.

States led by right-wing governors and legislatures have now passed laws or enacted policies to ban transgender athletes—especially girls, but sometimes including boys—in twenty-nine states.[124] Trump issued an executive order on February 5, 2025, that threw the weight of the federal government behind banning trans girls and women from sports participation and from women's locker rooms. Disingenuously framing the action in the name of "safety, fairness, dignity, and truth," the order threatened to pull funding from schools that did not comply.[125] A number of high-profile sport-governing bodies fell in line. The NCAA amended its policies to ban trans women athletes almost immediately after Trump's order. The US Olympic & Paralympic Committee followed suit in July 2025 and the IOC in March 2026.[126]

Many of these trans-exclusionary policy actions rely on a false and bad-faith argument that trans girls and women at all levels of play have a competitive physical advantage and are pushing "real" girls and women out of sports.[127] These bills are disingenuously called things like the "Protection of Women and Girls in Sports Act," as a federal bill that passed through the House of Representatives in January 2025 has been named.[128] LGBTQ+ sports activists recognize that this tactic pits cisgender women and girls against transgender women and girls. Danne Diamond, former director of policy and programs for the sports advocacy organization Athlete Ally, said they felt that the "protecting women" frame was a particularly successful one for the political Right, even though the bills did not do anything to address the documented challenges women and girls face in sports. They said that this was a honed strategy after the "bathroom bills" failed to pass, in some cases, and resonate more broadly. Yet the framing is the same in the sports case. "When trans women and girls are in public spaces," Diamond said of this narrative, "they are somehow a danger or threat to cis women and girls. It's the same underlying concept, just now moved to a sports frame."[129]

Of course, these anti-trans laws impact athletes' ability to do their work and to do it safely.[130] And these laws remain in place without strong intervention or adequate protections from institutional allies. In the early 2010s, the National Collegiate Athletic Association (the NCAA) took a surprising lead role in trans athlete inclusion. The organization has rightfully enraged many with its unjust exploitation of and refusal to duly compensate college athletes, many of whom are Black, for the profit-generating work they do.[131] Yet the NCAA was an early leader and institutional ally, developing and promoting a policy for transgender athlete participation in 2011 that was more inclusive than what had come before it in elite sports. The NCAA also initially used its considerable clout to protest anti-LGBTQ+ state laws. For example, it pulled a number of championship games from the state of North Carolina after the state passed a high-profile, horrendous anti-LGBTQ+ law, HB2, in 2016.[132]

However, the NCAA has disappointed many sports advocates in recent years when it has passed up the opportunity to take a stronger stand.[133] It has declined to use its substantial power by, for example, removing lucrative games and tournaments from states that have passed recent anti-trans athlete policies. And it dragged its feet on responding to advocates' calls to update its trans inclusion policy, especially to include nonbinary athletes. It finally created a hasty, decentralized, and confusing revision in January 2022 and then stalled in announcing additional policy updates until its outright ban on trans women's participation in response to Trump's executive order in early 2025.[134] Mosier has been especially critical, saying to me in the fall of 2021: "The NCAA, for having been such a leader a decade ago, has really relinquished that position and is now one of the organizations dragging behind." Mosier felt that the NCAA could also be blamed for the passage of some of the early state-level anti-trans laws. "The NCAA has an incredible platform," he noted. "I believe they could have stopped *several* of these bills" if they had used that platform to pull tournaments and championships out of anti-trans states.

These regressive politics and the failure of institutional players like the NCAA to adequately respond leave sports advocates playing defense: working to combat policies that simply shut athletes out of their sport. This does not leave adequate room to have a more progressive and fundamental conversation about how to include a more expansive understanding of a workplace that has been so binarily divided by gender. LGBTQ+ sports advocates have been working to expand sports' politics and policies to include nonbinary athletes and the complex conversation about what it means to participate in a space that is almost entirely organized and divided by binary gender. Mosier says that the sport of running is a leader here, in that many races and racing organizations have created nonbinary divisions.[135] And, inspired by a few high-profile nonbinary athletes who have also become advocates and activists, like WNBA basketball player Layshia Clarendon, this important conversation about gender and inclusion in sports has gained some attention and some policy traction by employers like pro leagues.[136] Yet sports is so caught up in electoral politics now, brought into this fray by the cynical and transphobic Right. LGBTQ+ athletes and advocates are having to work hard to hold on to hard-won prior gains, rather than having the opportunity to move forward on full inclusion and equity.

CHANGE YOUR WORKPLACE, CHANGE THE CULTURE

There is an idea that comes from Critical Race Theory called *interest convergence*. Law scholar and co-founder of this legal tradition, Derrick Bell, introduced this in his written work in 1980. The idea is that the majority (and Bell was writing specifically about race and White people here) will only change in ways that might benefit a minority if the majority feels it is in their interest to do so. In other words, when there is a convergence of interest between a majority and a minority, a majority might allow or even push for a mutually beneficial change. Applied in this case, we could say that Corporate Hollywood, as one scholar dubbed the business's decision-makers, would only really make change for those who are typically marginalized in Creative Hollywood when they would see that it's in their interest to do so.[137]

There is some strong evidence that there is an interest convergence at play in the business of popular culture: that what is good for social change is also good for business. Racial diversity in casting brings in *more* viewers and is, ultimately, better for the bottom line for television and film. One 2021 study found that Hollywood is costing itself *billions* of dollars each year by not being better than it is at racial inclusion and equity in TV and film.[138] And when it comes to LGBTQ+ change in pop culture, there are many examples of the ways in which this is specifically true: that the good politics of LGBTQ+ equity and inclusion aligns with good business and with producing excellent work (e.g., squeezing in a *Heated Rivalry* reference, post-production!). On the one hand, homophobia and transphobia can cost a lot of money and moral capital. Corporate America has affirmed that it believes "discrimination is bad for business" and it may make business decisions that negatively impact states that have considered or enacted anti-LGBTQ+ laws.[139] On the other hand, being LGBTQ+-inclusive by catering to queer and ally audiences and fans can simply be good for business, pure and simple. This can take the form of marketing and programming to a new fan base, as the WNBA did when it discovered that it had a sizable lesbian following, or expanding programming to capture new audiences or build a "brand" as cutting-edge and inclusive.[140]

Hollywood changes slowly and reluctantly, which might seem counterintuitive, since it was made by and still attracts outsiders in so many ways. There are many aspects of the work that maintain the status quo. But, we have seen, Hollywood does respond to social movements and to both creative and market pressures. The resolution to the writers' strike in the fall of 2023, in a way that was favorable to writers' needs and demands, is another example of this and cause for hope.[141] Hollywood seems to follow social change rather than lead it.[142] But it *has* followed when it is in its interest. For LGBTQ+ creatives, they have worked hard to make institutional changes in their workplaces, and their work has paid off—not because of the altruism of the business, or because it has a mission to contribute to social change, but because it is in the *interest* of cultural decision-makers in Hollywood and in elite sports to *be* more inclusive in their workplaces and in the stories and images they contribute to the world.

There are now a number of examples where companies have made the calculation that what is good for business is to roll back their commitment to equity and inclusion. They are either pre-complying with Trump's threats and legally dubious executive orders, or they are reading the fact that Trump is president again as a sign of what American consumers *want* in their culture, or they are currying favor when they want or need something from him. Hollywood is not immune to this corporate calculus, and this has consequences for both what we see on-screen and who gets to tell on-screen stories (see the Paramount-Skydance merger of the summer of 2025).[143] To be sure, we are at a moment of extreme precarity in already-precarious creative professions. That insecurity extends to LGBTQ+ civil rights, where the anti-queer politics of the past few years are fueling a backtracking in risk-averse Hollywood casting, hiring, and storytelling. This could be a moment of entrenchment, when what is "good for business" is reconsidered in a way that is truly devastating to queer people.[144] But it could also be an opportunity for profound and lasting change. "We don't destroy, we reclaim," said Shadi Petosky about queer people throughout history. In this case, that fight to claim the cultural workplace has been succeeding and will continue to succeed in changing the culture.

4. OVERACHIEVE

Mediocrity is a perk and a privilege. Two Black women commentators on race and gender remind us that the demand of exceptionalism is aimed only at minoritized people, and that it is a double bind. Ijeoma Oluo writes, "I have been exceptional, and I shouldn't have to be exceptional to be just barely getting by." Brittney Cooper notes that the burden of exceptionalism comes with a cost: "When you are twice as good, white folks will resent you for being better."[1] It shouldn't be the responsibility of those who are marginalized to have to overachieve to make a mark on their profession or their culture. But it often is.

As we have heard from Hollywood insiders, the business builds barriers to the entry, success, and longevity of marginalized workers. It also holds them to unfairly high standards. At the same time, when they *do* excel, they can change their world. In sports and in Hollywood, excellence can lend itself to industry change and to broader cultural change. Those who *overachieve* in their cultural work have a platform. They also have a lot of creative freedom and are given wide latitude to take risks. In Hollywood, this helps diversify creative content and brings sidelined stories into the mainstream. This success also earns a seat at the table, an entry to the room to influence decision-making. From this spot, successful people can influence culture. Some actors told me about speaking up when they felt that a role was too stereotypical or was not true to life. Others told me of ways they draw on their clout or success to push the envelope on LGBTQ+ inclusion and storytelling. Excelling at work means that many people I interviewed have been professionally situated to effectively change LGBTQ+ visibility, representation, and storytelling.

To be clear, this is not the explicit primary professional goal of most of the artists and athletes I interviewed. I talked with some who have intentionally mobilized the thing they are good at to make explicit political change. But most people I spoke with were very thoughtful about their professional choices and were adamant that they do their work for art, entertainment, or sport success and *not* for education or politics. They believe in the power of their professional work first and foremost. They want to entertain. They want to make people laugh or feel something. They want to win games. They want to make art for art's sake, tell stories for the stories' sake, play well for the sake of play. Many, in my conversations, rejected the idea that they make creative or other professional choices for political ends or that their work has overt educational or political aims. They consider any educational or political gains of this work to be a welcomed but secondary collateral benefit.[2] Yet people who excel at their cultural work can and do impact LGBTQ+ social change in a number of ways.

TELL POWERFUL STORIES

It makes sense that many of the storytellers I spoke with could easily recall stories that had nurtured and transformed them. This feels authentically true about stories for me, as well. It is why I love television, movies, and reading so much—and why I was initially drawn to this project and to the opportunity to talk with some of the best storytellers of our time.

Stories can make us feel, teach us about who we are, bind us to others in community, and even change us. But do they make a real difference? Author Jonathan Gottschall, in his book *The Storytelling Animal*, writes that we *do* know that stories—especially fictional ones—have an impact. "Research results have been consistent and robust: fiction *does* mold our minds. Story—whether delivered through films, books, or video games—teaches us facts about the world; influences our moral logic; and marks us with fears, hopes, and anxieties that alter our behavior, perhaps even our personalities."[3] Stories, in the way they can make their recipients *feel*, can also be a call to action that can bring change in the world. Stories can spark the emotions and empathy that are at the foundation of movements for social change. "That's what good art does: It opens your heart and then it places something in it," actor and activist Wilson Cruz said to me.[4] This kind of transformation of emotion has a long history in LGBTQ+ movements and others that have been led by queer people, like the AIDS movement.[5]

It is not surprising that the storytellers I spoke with believe, too, that stories *matter*, and that they are thoughtful about what it means to them to put stories out into the world. Even those who did identify as politically engaged and who did believe that entertainment could be politically powerful were certain that overly preachy storytelling would be bad art. They were clear that they did not want to overtly proselytize. They wanted, instead, to tell stories that audiences would feel moved or amused by, connected to, or embraced by. "Anybody can smell an agenda in the way that you're writing a character, and they'll call bullshit on it," said writer and actor Dan Bucatinsky.[6] Writing "on the nose" messaging is going to turn viewers off, said writer Laura Zak: "As soon as an audience member can pick up on that, you've lost them. They're going to feel patronized and talked down to."[7]

Several writers I spoke with wanted to tell stories that had not been told before—often *theirs*. These stories had not been green-lit because they featured people of color, queer people, and women. Writers and actors talked with me about not seeing themselves in the professional opportunities they were being presented. As a corrective, they went about making their own work instead—both in the service of art/entertainment and for the purpose of change. For actors, sometimes this meant learning new skills as producers and screenwriters and being self-reflective about their own contribution to Hollywood storytelling. Actor Amin El Gamal said to me, in our second conversation in January 2022, that they were starting to do this new kind of work: "If I want to be in a position to make a story the way I want to, then I just have to do it. It's on me," they said. "No one is responsible for my creative fulfillment. What a ridiculous, privileged thing to expect. So I have taken accountability for it."[8] Actor Ellen D. Williams took a break from acting a few years ago because, while she was grateful for the opportunity to work, she "got tired of telling other people's stories." She identifies as gay and biracial and Filipino/American and said, "Someone that looks like me, I don't see in lead roles." So she turned to writing and asked herself, "Okay, so, then, what story do you want to tell?"[9]

Storytellers I spoke with expressed that they felt their work had the capacity to connect people across lines of difference. This has been made even more possible through the extensive reach and popularity of some of the groundbreaking work in LGBTQ+ storytelling. A gay longtime writer for *Modern Family*, for instance, told me a story of encountering a worker on set who he described as a "big, burly guy from Jersey." Abraham Higginbotham said the guy struck up a conversation about *Modern Family*, which he said he loved. He recounted that the man brought up the gay couple on the show, Mitch and Cam, and said that he and his girlfriend or wife joke about which one of them is the Cam in their relationship. "That's exactly what this show is doing in a way that is rare and special. I mean, I was listening to this guy thinking: 'You are identifying with Cam! That's your guy! That's the one in your mind that is your favorite character, and you think you're like him sometimes and you're a big, burly straight guy!'"[10]

Storytelling can feature these fictional characters that fans fall in love with, identify with, and learn from.[11] It can also be powerful and *nonfictional*. Coming out publicly as LGBTQ+ can be a form of this storytelling that can build connection and community.[12] This tactic is not new to the LGBTQ+ movement.[13] This is what public coming-out stories often are—and Outsports has been doing this storytelling work for decades. One of the earliest institutions of the LGBTQ+ sports movement, Outsports.com was a website founded by two White cisgender gay men in 1999.[14] Since then, it has raised visibility and built community for LGBTQ+ athletes at all levels, from youth sports to the pros. It relies on the reach of the Internet to create a place for athletes to tell their stories and to find each other. The site has been involved in high-profile professional stories. For example, Outsports ran the first big story on former NBA player John Amaechi's coming out in 2007.[15] It also publishes a wide range of stories and first-person narratives of young and unknown athletes who are coming out for the first time, and there is a section of the website dedicated to this purpose called "Coming Out Stories."[16] Outsports works to build interactive community through these stories, often including direct contact information, like email addresses, for the subjects of their features, and coaching these athletes that they are likely to garner more attention than they could possibly imagine once their stories are published.[17]

These coming-out stories often do resonate widely. For example, when Outsports ran a feature on gay former college football captain Brian Sims in the spring of 2009,[18] Sims reported that within weeks he had received three hundred positive emails from around the world. This included an email from a high school wrestler who came out to his teammates by forwarding Sims's Outsports profile to them. It included another email from the best friend of a twenty-seven-year-old former football player who was in the process of coming out. "This article," the friend wrote, "showed [the athlete] how there is no stereotype, for jocks or gays, and it just made him break down and cry, he was so relieved that he wasn't alone."[19]

I spoke with Sims, who became a Pennsylvania state legislator and served five terms until he ran for Pennsylvania's lieutenant governor in 2022. He spoke with me about the power and reach of his Outsports coming-out story—and the personally transformative impact it had on him. I interviewed him in the fall of 2012, and he said by that point he had received and responded to thousands of emails about the story—hundreds of emails each day in the months that followed the initial story—not one of them negative. In fact, just by virtue of telling his story publicly, Sims was being asked by strangers to give advice about gay athletes they knew and cared about. He was also being asked to mentor young athletes who had just come out or were thinking about coming out to the adults in their lives.[20]

On the other side of storytelling, I heard from a gay former lacrosse player, Andrew Goldstein, who encountered an athlete's public coming-out story at a personally meaningful time for him. Goldstein told me that when he was in high school, a high school football player, Corey Johnson, came out publicly and made national news. This story was a "heart opener" that "planted a seed." It did not immediately prompt Goldstein to come out to his family or teammates, but it "created a possibility" that was transformative for him.[21]

MAKE PEOPLE LAUGH

Queer Australian comedian Hannah Gadsby's 2018 Netflix stand-up special, *Nanette*, was a cultural phenomenon.[22] In this first special, Gadsby was clearly incredibly talented and brave in sharing their stories of being the target of violence, misogyny, and homophobia. They also offered something else that was new and thought-provoking: a take on their profession of comedy, its role, and its limits. Their critique of comedy related to the architecture and the individual and collective functions of jokes. They explained that successful jokes necessarily require two things: first a setup, then a punch line, and that in between these two things must be *tension* that is then relieved with a laugh. But the act of creating and then relieving tension for Gadsby was traumatic and exhausting. The requirements of a joke mean that, for instance, in Gadsby's story about their own coming out, "I froze an incredibly formative experience at its trauma point and I sealed it off into jokes." To tell a good joke, Gadsby surmised, "punch lines need trauma because punch lines . . . need tension, and tension feeds trauma." In addition, the need for a punch line does not leave room for full storytelling: "I feel like, in a comedy show, there's no room for the best part of the story . . . which is the ending." Instead, Gadsby told their audience, they needed to be a *storyteller*. "It took me ten years to understand I was allowed to take up space in the world." And now, "I need to tell my story properly." In their ending bit, they offered this challenge to their audience to *connect* to and through their storytelling:

> Laughter is not our medicine. Stories hold our cure. . . . I don't want to unite you with laughter or anger. I just needed my story heard, my story felt and understood by individuals with minds of their own. . . . I just don't have the strength to take care of my story anymore. . . . All I can ask is just please help me take care of my story.[23]

Gadsby ties together storytelling and comedy here. They also raise challenges for what comedy has been and potentially could be to social change.

Comedy comes in many forms these days.[24] In its various iterations, comedy has always been connected to survival, community building, and social change. Of course, comedy has also always been quite problematic, used in a way that "punches down at the powerless."[25] But it has also always served as a "route to cultural citizenship and identity for groups and people who are traditionally marginalized."[26] As one commentator said in an article on comedians as public intellectuals: "The point of comedy has always been, on some level, a kind of productive subversion."[27] At its core, comedy can be this effective form of resistance: a response to oppression and a way to build community strength and cohesion.

Many of the people I interviewed loved and chose comedy for these reasons. "Especially now, when we're talking about joy and resilience, and resistance, I think that comedy is the way forward, it's how queer people have survived," said D'Lo, who identifies as a queer/transgender Tamil-Sri Lankan-American actor, writer, and comic. He said that he had used comedy in the past as "the razzle-dazzle front so that nobody would out me."[28] Actor, writer, and director Fawzia Mirza said that for her "comedy was always a survival tool" and a way to feel safe. When I asked what comedy meant to her, Mirza explained that growing up as a queer, Muslim Pakistani in a small rural White fishing town in Canada, then in Indiana in the United States, they felt like an outsider. They said they learned from an early age that comedy "was a way to find a sense of community and help people laugh *with* me instead of *at* me."[29]

Many of the comedic performers and comedy writers I spoke with have a theory of their comedy. They are clear that entertainment delivered to a broad audience is their primary goal.[30] But, if they also have something to convey beyond the story, comedy is an effective, accessible, and broadly appealing delivery mechanism. Actor Alec Mapa called comedy "the ultimate Trojan horse" that can build rapport and help a serious message go down more easily.[31] A few people described comedy as this kind of soothing "spoonful of sugar."[32] They also described comedy as a safe way to build connections across difference with audiences. "The laugh is the way in," said writer/actor Bucatinsky. "People take in information they don't realize they're taking in when they're laughing," writer Higginbotham noted, especially if they can connect with funny, flawed, and charming characters. This intimate form of storytelling helps to create a sense of empathy and familiarity and trust with an audience that has let their guard down because they are laughing.[33]

Comedians can build this connection by inviting an audience to laugh *with* them, demonstrating that they trust the audience not to laugh *at* them or the characters they create. Mirza explained, "It's like you build up a lot of currency with an audience. You get them to laugh, to trust you, through connecting. That connection fosters so much good will that a new door opens, to begin to really talk to your audience and have a serious conversation." And, as actor Harvey Guillén said to me about the way he felt this mechanism worked for him in storytelling: "When you present it with comedy, you're almost letting me in your house and your comfort zone." He continued, "People like to be around people who make them feel comfortable and drop their guard and feel like they're with friends. And I feel that comedy does that. It makes you feel comfortable. It makes you feel like you're around somebody you can joke around with."[34]

Eric Stonestreet, the actor who played Cam on *Modern Family*, had a lot to say to me about the role of comedy in changing how people think and feel. He stressed several times that his primary job as an actor was to *be an actor* and that the first aim of his show was to entertain through comedy. We, at the show, "just want to make people laugh," he said, "and let people sit back, relax, and know that they're in the hands of talented and good people that love to do what they do."[35] He said that he regularly made it clear in interviews that the "show's agenda" was not to "shove a gay agenda down anyone's throat." At the same time, he recognized that "social change and change in people individually comes from opening your hearts and minds. And there's no better way to open people's hearts and minds than with laughter. So, when people are sitting there watching Cam and watching Mitch and they're laughing and enjoying them, there's no doubt that something is *changing* in them." Stonestreet gave an example of hearing from a fan while he was doing a call-in radio show, a woman with a thick Southern accent, who told him that her husband, a truck driver who was on the road for work a lot, wanted her to wait until he is home so that they could watch and laugh together at *Modern Family*. "You single-handedly have shown him that gays aren't just after his be-hind!" Stonestreet recounted that this caller said to him. "That boils it right down," said Stonestreet. "You have to meet people where they are. For me to go and knock on that guy's door and say, 'You're a fucking idiot! You're stupid! You need to accept gay people!' will never work! But he sits down, with his wife, and realizes through laughter and a TV show" that he held a flawed and problematic view of gay men.

In the context of the artistic work itself, which clearly came absolutely *first* for the creatives I spoke with, comedian and actor Lea DeLaria summed up the theory of comedy that I heard over and over again: "If you can make people laugh, you can teach them anything."[36]

BE IN THE ROOM

If you're not in the room or at the table, you can't make change. Of course, there are significant barriers to entry to marginalized people. But their presence, and the work they do once they have found a way in, creates change. For those in a position to hire, they use their place in a room to bring other underrepresented people into the work.[37] For actors, being at the table in a way that can impact cultural change means turning down roles that perpetuate stereotypes or speaking up when they feel they are being asked to deliver an inauthentic portrayal. For writers, being in the room—a room that is tough to access and often has its own closed-door mystique[38]—means creating complex stories and bringing historically absent experiences to the table while rejecting problematic portrayals. This is not an *easy* spot to be in: being an *only* or one of only a few in a room, and then working to use your position to move the room in a new or different direction. It is a vulnerable and precarious position that often demands a lot of people. And the people in these roles often feel that they are replaceable in a highly competitive job market. Or, as one writer said to me, they are junior hires who feel tokenized as "the diversity voice" in the room but then often feel that their voices are not taken seriously.

Many of the people in Hollywood I spoke with shared their view that their presence has helped to bring authenticity (a word I heard a lot) in storytelling. And they provide a viewpoint that others in the room might not be able to bring. Several actors of color, for instance, shared the ways in which their contributions in the room have successfully corrected for mistakes or advocated for a shift toward authenticity. They talked about bringing their own cultural knowledge into storytelling in places where that insider knowledge seemed to be lacking. For the actors I spoke with, this could take the form of requesting that characters have accurate or authentic names or pronunciations of names.[39] They also talked about using their position in the room to *refuse* some representation and storytelling.[40] LGBTQ+ culture workers who are in the room also intervene to correct what they viewed as inaccuracies, refuse certain content, and bring in new storylines from their own experiences. One lesbian writer/producer/director talked about conferring with the director for a project she was working on in which she felt that the sex scene between two cisgender women was implausible and would be instantly recognized as such by lesbian viewers. Another lesbian writer intervened when she felt that a lesbian hookup had been written as a "male fantasy" and did not ring true. "That is not what would happen with this lesbian endeavor," she recounted. She was successful in getting this scenario removed. Other queer creatives and executives have intercepted negative storytelling. For example, actors have refused to say lines they have found offensive in their portrayal of queer people.[41]

And queer creatives understand their value in being in the room, drawing on their own experience and bringing their own stories to the table. I interviewed two gay writers on the hit network show *Modern Family*, and they both talked about the importance of being in their writers' room, especially to write for the gay couple on the show, and of the importance of not being the *only* gay writer in the room, so that they could bring some diversity of opinion and experience to the storytelling. They wrote and got in jokes that they felt had insider meaning, they spoke up when they felt that other writers presented trope-y or tired dialogue or portrayals, and they became a resource in the room to test out material.[42] Being in the room in these ways has not always been an easy experience, especially for those who hold multiple marginalized identities, when the business is more precarious and not as open for them. One lesbian writer recounted pitching a queer storyline, and the showrunner "joked" about this writer's "gay agenda" in a way that really silenced her for the remainder of the job.

USE CLOUT

"Celebrity gets shit made," one actor shorthanded it for me.[43] The people who are best situated in Hollywood to use their place in the room to make change are those with clout, critical acclaim, and a reputation that allows them more creative freedom. They have the freedom to "dictate the terms of their art."[44] Good reputations and the capital that comes with them must be earned and has a short shelf life in Hollywood. However, with this precarious clout can come the ability to both prevent change and to make it.

One way that clout can accomplish change in Hollywood is through at least a modicum of freedom from constant, anxious creative interference. This is a business where there is a lot of involvement in the creative process by non-creatives.[45] So having latitude to do their creative thing is one critical way that high-powered LGBTQ+ people and allies have made changes in storytelling. Television creators described the hyper-scrutinization and micromanagement they felt they had endured on their shows by network executives, who they described as giving notes on script and casting and feedback on set during shooting. Yet, successful people and their work are left *relatively* alone. As *Modern Family* writer Higginbotham summed it up: "If your show makes good money, you are scrutinized less. And if your show doesn't make good money yet, you're scrutinized like you can't even fucking imagine." Successful people who are marginalized and underrepresented in the industry also report that they have been able to use their position in the room more effectively and freely to advocate for creative changes when they can draw on their clout.

Academy Award–winning film producer Dan Jinks, known especially for *American Beauty* (1999) and *Milk* (2008), told me he felt that groundbreaking LGBTQ+ work in television could be attributed to the fact that its creators already had some capital in Hollywood: "If Joe Schmo went to a studio and said, 'This is what we want to do,' who's going to listen? But it's because these writers were successful enough that they were able to use their clout and their talent and say, 'This is the story we want to tell on TV, and we're going to tell it really well,' that there's now a lot of this on TV."[46] This reliance on clout and proven talent is not an altruistic move on the part of networks or studios. It is, rather, what is perceived to be good for business.[47]

In the early years of my interviews, before streaming services had fully taken off, I heard the names of *several* show creators and showrunners who were considered successful enough to have creative freedom. However, in the past few years, there is a sense in the business that this is changing: that there are just a rare few who are afforded this privilege. Now, even most proven successes are more constrained than they used to be. In other words, for most people, clout may not be buying the same kind of freedom that it used to. Adrienne Erickson, a production company executive, said to me in November 2021 that it used to be the case that a history of success granted a certain amount of creative freedom. However, streamers now have to compete with movies, so they are pouring so much money into producing television shows that the stakes are very high for successes. The result, then, is that "Oscar winners get network notes, just like everybody else."[48]

In recent years, Shonda Rhimes and Ryan Murphy are the two television/streaming icons with this level of clout who are most frequently mentioned in the press and in my conversations.[49] And they are two superstar television creators who have used their authority to diversify storytelling and storytellers and to change the industry. Murphy introduced his Half Initiative in 2016 to ensure that his projects have more inclusive hiring practices than is typical in Hollywood. And GLAAD found in its 2020 study of LGBTQ representation on the television shows of the previous year that just four "power players," including Murphy and Rhimes, "account for 14 percent of all LGBTQ representation across their 22 shows." The other two are Greg Berlanti and Lena Waithe, both LGBTQ+-identified Hollywood superstars, as well.[50] In my view, this statistic is just one of many indications that Hollywood creatives with true clout are genuinely changing the business and the stories it tells—and that they are the people now best positioned with the freedom and authority to do so.

ACTIVATE SOCIAL NETWORKS

Hollywood is a business that runs on networks, relationships, and the relational resource that sociologists call *social capital*.[51] Observers have long understood that Hollywood is and always has been a closed and tight-knit community. Sociologist Todd Gitlin cynically assessed that "the creators of the culture that blankets America, and much of the rest of the earth, make up a little society at one with itself" and that these "old-boy networks bind this savage business together against its own ignorance and against its centrifugal whirl."[52]

Queer social networks and social capital operate in the context of the general norms of Hollywood. Sometimes derisively dubbed the "Gay Mafia" of Hollywood,[53] queer social capital has anecdotally worked to advance the careers of LGBTQ+ creatives. The people I interviewed fully understand the extent to which Hollywood runs on relationships. To them, the business often feels like a small, insular world in which people hire people they know or are already connected to. These days, queer social capital in Hollywood serves a number of functions. It provides the opportunity for networking and advocacy for LGBTQ+-identified creatives. It also, like some of the Hollywood unions' LGBTQ+-specific committees, provides protections in the industry. And, like GLAAD, it mobilizes the existing strength, visibility, and clout of the LGBTQ+ community. These examples institutionalize the more informal social capital, helping to turn it into work opportunities and community strength.[54]

In addition, individual queer networks allow for queer people to hire and support each other in the creative process. As director Jamie Babbit described, "It's so much of an underground whisper network to get any job"[55] that having any affinity provides a boost. Babbit described women's social capital and queer social capital working as kind of an alternative and corrective form of opportunity for those who are less likely to find themselves making deals in traditional spaces dominated by wealthy straight White cis men. "You know what?" she said. "I don't play golf. And if I fucking played golf and belonged to the Bel-Air golf club, that's like 80 percent of directors where they're making their fucking deals. So I'm not getting jobs by hanging out at the Bel-Air." So, she said, she was grateful to have encountered people in the industry who especially looked out for people who were not at these clubs and affirmatively wanted to hire them.

Social and professional networks are critical for hiring and advancement in a relationship-based business like Hollywood. Social networks are also instrumental to increasing visibility for LGBTQ+

people. One fundamental way is that they can facilitate the public coming-out process for high-profile culture workers. We have seen this in recent years in elite sports, where the relatively small network of LGBTQ+ athletes and their allies, and the advocacy and media organizations they have built, have been central to orchestrating the public coming out of elite athletes. I talked a bit about this in chapter 1, where I introduced publicist Howard Bragman and the professional services he provided to athletes, musicians, and actors who wanted to come out publicly. I also noted that there have been some pathbreaking athletes, like football player Michael Sam and college basketball player Derrick Gordon, who have had well-documented public coming-out processes that have reportedly involved the active guidance of networks of other gay athletes and advocates in the LGBTQ+ sports movement.[56] The importance of this—and the relative *newness* of it—cannot be underestimated. The community of publicly out LGBTQ+ athletes could still be larger, and there are likely many athletes who have not come out in their personal lives or in public yet. But there is still a relatively new active and organized community such that athletes no longer have to navigate the coming-out process alone.[57] These athletes can turn to others who share their strong *athlete* identity and this fairly unusual circumstance to provide mentorship and support as they navigate the experience of being a pathbreaker.[58] These activated networks allow for more athletes to come out publicly, increasing LGBTQ+ cultural visibility.

These kinds of social networks can be celebrated for what they accomplish both professionally and for the world. It is also critical to understand their limitations and the harm they can perpetuate in these cultural industries. These pop cultural social and professional networks are not power neutral. The tend to be homogenous in many ways, and this then "produces a set of players who are markedly homogenous" in the Hollywood workplace and beyond.[59] This is true for queer social networks, as well. Queer social capital can work to maintain existing power relationships in several ways. First, the Gay Mafia narrative that a group of powerful gays run the industry is a trope that can keep institutional homophobia in place by celebrating a few high-powered LGBTQ+ success stories while keeping broader systems of exclusion and marginalization in place.[60] Queer social capital itself can also reproduce intersectional forms of privilege by keeping professional opportunities within networks of queer-identified people who, by virtue of broader racism, sexism, and cisnormativity in the industry, tend to be White, economically well-off gay cisgender men.[61] "We haven't been picked for pipelines, and we haven't *had* the professional development, in the numbers that we really needed to," said actor and writer Scott Turner Schofield, speaking of trans, particularly trans masculine, talent.[62] This, too, mirrors the dynamics of the broader business.

THE PARADOXES OF EXCELLENCE

Succeeding while being mediocre is a privilege usually only reserved for White—mostly straight, cisgender, wealthy, and able-bodied—men.[63] By contrast, everyone else has to be exceptional in order to succeed in competitive and risk-averse businesses like Hollywood and elite sports. The necessity to *overachieve* at work in order to make institutional or cultural change is one of many undue weights placed on queer people, people of color, and people marginalized by gender, among others. It can come with a personal price. An overachievement imperative can also come with a community question, and one that I will explore in the next chapter: Is excelling in mainstream ways worth it? Is succeeding in the mainstream, even when this success comes with the secondary benefit of cultural and political change, too much of a sacrifice of identity and community? Queer theorist Michael Warner rejects this trade-off. He argues that celebrating this kind of "place at the table" orientation undermines queer movements and change.[64]

To be quite clear, cultural change was *not* the primary goal of the work of many of the artists, culture workers, and athletes I interviewed. Many were adamant about the fact that their work was primarily about the work itself. But marginalized people who *excel* at their work *are* positioned to contribute to cultural change. When they have proven themselves through their work to earn a modicum of creative freedom, they often take that freedom to tell new stories and bring in new storytellers. And when they have a public story to tell, they do so in transformational ways. They use their storytelling talents, especially through humor, to make connections across lines of difference in ways that teach and build empathy. When they gain entry to rooms where creative decisions are made, they do the often difficult and vulnerable work of speaking up for creative change. They find ways to build networks of people who *also* have this kind of access and who can collectively contribute to community visibility and strength. Once these culture workers are successful, it can burdensome, vulnerable, and exhausting to use their success to make institutional and social change. And yet they do.

5. BECOME NORMAL *and* STAY QUEER

Are LGBTQ+ people "just like everyone else," or do they have a distinct culture that should be celebrated and preserved? This may sound like an academic question, but it is absolutely one that has structured LBGTQ+ politics since the beginning of the modern movement in the 1950s.[1] This debate has especially flared up in key moments, like when marriage was a key focus of the LGBTQ+ civil rights movement.[2] It is part of an active and contentious discussion of what is gained and given up by assimilation into mainstream values, family structures, gender expression, local communities, and politics.

There have been periods in American history when there has been an active, organized effort to frame queer people as threatening to the country. After World War II, the US government moved to deny gay Americans the opportunity to serve as federal employees, urging that "those who engage in overt acts of perversion lack the emotional stability of normal persons" and have a weak "moral fiber" and predatory nature.[3] A generation later, the public coverage of the devastating AIDS epidemic again portrayed gay men as, in one historian's words, "dangerous outsiders who threatened the nation."[4] We are living through another one of those periods right now, too, well into the twenty-first century.[5]

The prospect of "becoming normal" for gay Americans seems radical by contrast—and perhaps unattainable.[6] Yet this word—*normal*—has been at the center of gay scholarship, politics, and culture for decades. Activist and writer Larry Kramer named his Tony Award–winning play *The Normal Heart* in 1985. In the 1990s, writing about gay/queer politics of the time, Andrew Sullivan and Michael Warner, from very different political places, titled their books *Virtually Normal* and *The Trouble with Normal*, respectively. And *The New Normal* was the name of a short-lived TV show in 2012–13, which centered around a gay couple and their quest to become parents through surrogacy. At the same time, the term *queer* has been central to LGBTQ+ politics and pop culture since the early 1990s. It has even made its way to mainstream television through shows like *Queer as Folk* and *Queer Eye* that celebrate distinctive communities, friendships, love, sex, and cultures. These very terms, *normal* and *queer*, have defined a political distinction in LGBTQ+ social change efforts. But what do they mean? Law scholar Kenji Yoshino offers one helpful explanation: "By *normals*, I mean openly gay individuals who embrace a politics of assimilation. . . . By *queers*, I mean gays who emphasize their difference from the mainstream."[7] Pop culture has played a central role in defining and maintaining the mainstream and the margins—the normal and the queer—around gender and sexuality.[8]

Many LGBTQ+ culture workers I have spoken with over the years have found pop culture *essential* for their own individual and community exploration. One young trans actor, Syd Diaz, said it succinctly: "I don't think I knew who I was until I saw myself onscreen."[9] Culture workers also, though, have applauded the fact that pop culture has the power to make LGBTQ+ people *normal* for everyone else. Pop culture can create familiarity and a sense of empathy and connection, and this has been celebrated by people who create this culture. Some of the most successful mainstream television shows have shown the ways in which LGBTQ+ people—and especially White cisgender gay men, who are particularly represented in these shows and broader pop culture[10]—are just the neighbors on the block, coworkers at the watercooler, and parents in the carpool line. Of course, this is limited representation. But many people I spoke with have felt that there is a lot to be gained in the normalization through pop culture of LGBTQ+ people, identity, desire, relationships, and family.

Just as normal matters for many, *queer* is celebrated in both the creation of art and in the personal biographies of many who become pop cultural activists for LGBTQ+ social change. I interviewed many culture workers who talked about how their own marginality and sense of difference led to their ability to be successful creative people and to be political people. They self-monitored and observed their peers so closely as closeted young people that they were able to become astute writers of fictional characters. Or they were both athletes and theater majors, and this helped them to develop a critical approach to normative masculinity. Or they identified as straight but grew up adopted or in a multiracial home and developed a visceral connection to a more expansive definition of family. These public people then have been able to *leverage the queer* in their own biography: they have put their own experiences to work for speaking out, using their platform, or creating content that moves the needle on LGBTQ+ social change.

For some, then, embracing the normal—joining the center—has always been the aspiration and the tactic. For others, staying queer—or maintaining the margins—has been more important. No matter what, pop culture is at the heart of these strategies.

BECOMING *NORMAL* THROUGH POP CULTURE

In March 2015, Shonda Rhimes accepted the Human Rights Campaign's Ally for Equality Award. In her speech, she revealed how much writing and storytelling had meant to her as a socially and racially isolated, lonely kid and how much she believes in the power of storytelling. She explained that her television shows, which have been notable for their diversity of all kinds in casting, are about something else: "I really hate the word 'diversity.' It suggests something other. As if it is something special. Or rare." She said, instead, that she is doing something else with her work. "I have a different word: NORMALIZING. I'm normalizing TV." She continued by explaining why this was important to her:

> You should get to turn on the TV and see your tribe. And your tribe can be any kind of person, any one you identify with, anyone who feels like you, who feels like home, who feels like truth. . . . The goal is that everyone should get to turn on the TV and see someone who looks like them and loves like them. And just as important, everyone should turn on the TV and see someone who *doesn't* look like them and love like them. Because, perhaps then, they will learn from them. Perhaps then, they will not isolate them. Marginalize them. Erase them. Perhaps they will even come to recognize themselves in them. Perhaps they will even learn to love them.[11]

In this way, one of the most successful storytellers in television provided an argument for the ways that pop culture has the power to define *normal*.

Many of the people I interviewed remembered growing up without seeing their reflections on television and film. They have come to feel that this erasure has been replaced with at least some LGBTQ+ pop cultural representation. Through their professional experiences, they could feel the wide reach that is possible with today's mainstream storytelling. They truly have come to believe in the power of their work to build understanding and connection across difference, introduce new familiarities, and nurture empathy. They believe that pop culture confers a kind of positive valence to those who are included in it. This helps to familiarize viewers, fans, and consumers with LGBTQ+ people and lives and win them over.[12] This brings LGBTQ+ people out of the margins and into the mainstream. They point to the power of television, especially. In this format, viewers come to know their favorite TV characters over years. Viewers invite these characters into their homes, while they are in their pajamas or eating meals, on their couches or in their beds. This is one of the reasons why TV resonates so deeply for many viewers.[13]

The actual word *normal* came up a *lot* in my conversations, sometimes with air quotes, sometimes with a sense of distaste, and sometimes with a sense of pride and accomplishment.[14] Culture workers take note of the ways that storytelling now normalizes some LGBTQ+ lives by nurturing a casual familiarity with LGBTQ+ characters and storylines. LGBTQ+ people in mainstream stories are next-door neighbors now who are accessible and relatable and "just like you" in a kind of mundane way. They have the same problems with their teens making curfew, the same work frustrations, the same relationship malaise. "We're just, like, fricking normal people," said lesbian screenwriter and actor Guinevere Turner of queer storytelling and its mission: "These are our regular old lives. We have stupid, petty relationship drama and animals and jobs and parent drama!"[15]

The "lovable gay neighbor"—a funny sidekick best friend who is tangential to the storyline—is a bit of a trope of representation of the past generation.[16] The just-like-you, inside-the-home, main character LGBTQ+ friend or family member is *newer*, especially in the realm of mainstream television, where it can be particularly effective at building sustained and intimate connections.[17] On some of the biggest television hits of the past two decades, there have been gay and lesbian next-door neighbors and family members—and, again, it is important to stress the limitation here that these hits mostly feature White cisgender gay, economically privileged men as the queer people who get to live this close. *Desperate Housewives*, which ran from 2004 to 2012 on ABC, had a gay couple who were neighbors on suburban Wisteria Lane. *Will & Grace*, on NBC from 1998 to 2006, then again from 2017 to 2020, featured two gay leads, Jack as a literal neighbor, and Will, who lived with his straight roommate and best friend, Grace. *Modern Family*, on ABC from 2009 to 2020, included a gay couple, Mitch and Cam, who were also parents. These were three shows that were massive mainstream hits (famously drawing a bipartisan fan base in the case of *Modern Family*[18]) and award winners in their time. And the gay people and couples in these shows were fully integrated into their communities and extended families.[19] This is even true now in the most mainstream of mainstream pop culture: the Hallmark movie, which has begun to embrace the gay neighbor and beloved community member as a protagonist also deserving of a saccharine and formulaic love story.[20]

Some of the LGBTQ+ television writers and actors I spoke with emphasized just how different this mainstream representation was from the pathologized and isolated portrayals of the past.[21] They stressed just how much it mattered that these gay characters now were just part of the fabric of their worlds in a way that inspired connection to mainstream audiences.[22] Jen Richards, who was not professionally associated with any of these shows, said that they had a "*Will & Grace* effect": "a seismic effect on Americans' perception of gay people by inviting them into their living rooms every night, and getting them to laugh along *with* them rather than just *at* them. I've said this a million times, and I'm not the only one: My little Southern Republican grandmother loved *Will & Grace*. That makes a huge difference."[23] In a later interview, in the summer of 2025, Richards added that this kind of storytelling could be a way to fight back against the politics of the moment: "At this point in my life, I'm ready for the fight. I am. If that's what it comes to. I hope it doesn't. I genuinely hope it doesn't. And until that day comes, I'm going to fight with words and stories and try to show other Americans that trans people are not scary, they are regular people, and they're going through these same kind of things as everybody else, and that their stories provide opportunities for everyone else to learn and self-reflect about what gender means and how we relate to each other, that it makes us *all* better when we have those stories included."[24]

Abraham Higginbotham, who worked on both *Will & Grace* and, for a long time, *Modern Family*, said that these shows educated and familiarized and made possible new conversations among a broad set of viewers. Of the gay characters on *Will & Grace*, he said, "Will and Jack, they were everybody's friends. People let them into their homes, and people started to go, 'Oh, I see how gay people actually care about each other, how they take care of each other and other people.'" Of the impact of *Modern Family* and the gay couple on the show, Higginbotham said, "Mitch and Cam are winning Emmys. . . . And kids are growing up in a world where they're like 'Oh, yeah, gay families are a thing. And they're a normal thing. They have full lives. They love one another and navigate all the same day-to-day joys and challenges that our family does.'"[25]

While these mainstream television shows are not created *for* the purpose of education or politics, they do have the collateral benefit of providing a shared vocabulary, understanding, and familiarity with LGBTQ+ people and lives.[26] This provides a normalizing kind of education for community outsiders. As director Jamie Babbit said of television's role with respect to LGB identity, in our 2012 interview: "It makes it normal. . . . Because now kids who are in high school, they already know gay characters, and they know them intimately because they see them every week on their televisions. So when the kid comes out in Texas—'Oh, I know that kid! It was on my TV!'"[27]

Of course, these three network television successes are nowhere near the only on-screen hits where LGBTQ+ characters are central to the storytelling. Many newer films and TV shows, too, represent more diversity and inclusion of BIPOC, trans and nonbinary, and young characters. Teens and young adults are at the center, and queer young people are right there alongside their straight and cisgender friends, sometimes living the joy and exhilaration of being young and sometimes worried about school performance, crushes and loves, fights with parents, making ends meet, and first jobs and apartments. These mainstream TV shows and films are also, importantly, about identification for queer audiences, community building, and reflecting the broad range of youth current experiences and possibilities. But they also work to normalize and integrate LGBTQ+ people, lives, and stories. A groundbreaker here was *Glee* (2009–15). After *Glee*, more recent examples include the hit film *Love, Simon* (2018), then its related television show, *Love, Victor* (2020–22), and the TV/streamer shows *Sex Education* (2019–23), *Euphoria* (2019–), *The Fosters* spin-off *Good Trouble* (2019–24), *Never Have I Ever* (2020–23), *Generation* (2021), *With Love* (2021–23), *The Sex Lives of College Girls* (2021–25), *Ginny & Georgia* (2021–), *Heartstopper* (2022–24), *The Summer I Turned Pretty* (2022–25), and *Heated Rivalry* (2025–).

These newer projects geared toward young people are too numerous to name, and this limited list should also include all manner of soap opera and reality television shows that feature queer people and storylines, and television and films that mostly focus on queer worlds, like *Pose* (2018–21) and *The L Word: Generation Q* (2019–23) reboot and the mainstream 2022 rom-com *Bros*. It also should include other central forms of normalizing pop culture, especially for young people, like TikTok and other social media, video games, and a wide range of LGBTQ+ young adult literature and fan fiction. We can also see other pop cultural ways that media represents LGBTQ+ people and families in parallel ways to straight and/or cisgender people, like in the television commercials that actors and spouses David Monahan and Larry Sullivan have done with their son;[28] in recent commercial campaigns with trans spokespeople that have come under attack by anti-trans conservatives;[29] or in the tabloids, which have featured the gossip on same-sex celebrity couples and weddings since before same-sex marriage was even legal everywhere in the United States.[30]

The people I spoke with about this pop cultural inclusion understand the potentially transformative impact of falling in love with, becoming family with, letting LGBTQ+ people into your homes and hearts, whether in real life or through pop culture. They also have come to believe that this kind of normalization creates new allies and advocates. As a gay sportswriter said to me as a way to explain rapid social change on gay and lesbian social acceptance, "everyone's got a lesbian sister."[31] This is a great shorthand. Visibility of real people and of fictional characters can create "lesbian sisters" for a broad public, and this can effect real change. Social science research supports the assertion that "what may have once been seen as unconventional or taboo can become normalized through long-term media portrayals," and that this new normalization and familiarity can favorably change hearts and minds.[32] In pop culture, it is the *reach* and extent of that work itself—to mainstream audiences, over and over again—that makes it possible to have this impact.[33] And in real life, it is visibility and proximity that seem to matter—actually *being* the next-door neighbors, the relatives and friends, the community service providers.[34] This theory has always informed the movement's focus on *coming out* as a key strategy for LGBTQ+ social change.[35] There is strong evidence that reporting to *know* someone who is LGBTQ+ increases support for LGBTQ+ people and civil rights. This support has increased quickly and considerably in the past couple of decades as more and more people report knowing someone who identifies as LGBTQ+.[36]

"We are in everyone's family," gay actor and activist Rory O'Malley said, "and that's what has accelerated everything."[37] By January 2025, GLAAD found that 63 percent of adults who do not identify as LGBTQ+ report personally knowing someone who identifies as gay and lesbian. Only 34 percent report knowing someone who identifies as bisexual, 22 percent personally know someone who is transgender, and 11 percent know someone who is nonbinary.[38] Views on LGBTQ+ inclusion and civil rights protections are substantially impacted by knowing someone who identifies as LGBTQ+. According to a Data for Progress report, which polled US adults in March 2025, "In general, Americans who know a transgender person are significantly more supportive of policies to protect their rights."[39]

Familial connection and love can also inspire an impulse for LGBTQ+ advocacy. For people who are positioned to have a platform in pop culture, having "lesbian sisters" helps them play a role in normalizing LGBTQ+ identity and inclusion.[40] Patrick Burke, whom we met in chapter 1, and his prominent hockey family became advocates for LGBTQ+ inclusion in sports after his young hockey player brother, Brendan, came out as gay and then tragically was killed in a car accident soon after. Burke poignantly explained to me:

> I've never been able to understand people who say, "Look, I love you, I care about you, you're my best friend, you're my son, you're my brother, you're a huge part of my life, I trust you with all my secrets, I'll tell you anything, I'll always be there for you as long you like women." I've never understood how someone could have a close relationship with somebody and then throw it all away just because they come out.

He continued:

> Right from day one our family said, look, we're going to be in Brendan's corner and hopefully he has an easy life and that he never has any trouble, and no one ever picks on him and there's never any drama related to his sexual orientation. But when there is that drama, then we're going to be there and we're going to have his back no matter what. . . . I always thought one of my jobs as the older brother was to fight for him and make his life as easy as possible. And I don't think that role changed just because he's gone. I think now my role is to carry on his legacy and fight his fights for him, and to make life easier for the next generation of Brendans. . . . That's my job as Brendan's brother.[41]

For Burke, becoming a public advocate for LGBTQ+ equality and inclusion in sports was about fulfilling his role as a protective and unconditionally loving older brother.

Burke has not been alone in the way he has embraced his familial role. In the past decade or so, there have been a number of high-profile people in sports who have been compelled to LGBTQ+ advocacy through their love of an LGBTQ+ family member, notably a number of star Black athletes.[42] Former basketball star, Dwyane Wade has been a vocal and steadfast advocate since early 2020, when he publicly announced that his twelve-year-old daughter had come out as trans. In an interview on *The Ellen DeGeneres Show*, Wade said: "We are proud parents of a child in the LGBTQ+ community and we're proud allies as well. And we take our roles and our responsibilities as parents very seriously."[43] Wade and his wife, actor Gabrielle Union, also have spoken out publicly about moving their family from Florida to California, in part because of the hostile political environment in the Sunshine State. Union said in an interview with *Parents* in the summer of 2023: "When you have the kind of rhetoric that is being espoused in Florida and adopted into law, that's not an option if my child isn't safe there."[44]

Despite the incredible work of these celebrity allies and the integration of LGBTQ+ characters and storylines into the most mainstream of television shows and films, familiarity with LGBTQ+ people is not, on its own, a solution to institutionalized homophobia and transphobia.[45] It is clear that most people now know someone who identifies as LGBTQ+, and this has not eliminated anti-gay and anti-trans violence or put a stop to the anti-LGBTQ+ politics of the past few years. Similarly, there are now so many LGBTQ+ culture workers who, by their own celebrity or by the stories they create, have a central place in the culture and lend their talents to LGBTQ+ normalization. Yet, as writer Michael Bronski observed back in 1998, this role has not eliminated LGBTQ+ vulnerability:

> In contemporary Western culture, homosexuals are granted the roles of "artists" and "creators of culture." . . . While these roles or functions make *social* space for the obvious or "out" homosexual to exist in mainstream culture, the do not create a safe *physical* space for homosexuals to live in.[46]

Visibility, in this way, presents both an incomplete and a potentially dangerous strategy.[47] At the same time, something *is* happening when LGBTQ+ people become neighbors and sisters now, in mass-mediated form and in real-life communities and families. Their proximity and intimacy nurtures new empathy and connection and motivates advocacy. When LGBTQ+ people *become normal*, they inspire and accomplish social change.

STAYING AND LEVERAGING QUEER

Normal is not without its detractors, even when that normal is fictional. Many writers, actors, and show creators talked with me about the fact that their work was criticized from within the LGBTQ+ community for portraying LGBTQ+ people in ways that were "too normal" or accommodating to mainstream/straight/cisgender audiences. Once these characters and stories moved away from the caricatures and tropes of previous generations, they were quickly criticized for being *too* much like straight and cisgender people. There is, of course, no one way in which "the community" receives work by and about itself. Disagreement among LGBTQ+ people about their representation speaks both to the broad diversity of the community and to how high stakes representation can feel when there are still so few authentic images and stories.[48] Yet, even acknowledging this diversity and the fact that no single representation of a community can please everyone, community critique feels particularly painful to many of the culture workers I spoke with.

Some LGBTQ+ creatives feel that community insiders could be especially critical of their work. This has been frustrating and hurtful to them, as they have been trying earnestly to make authentic and complicated stories. They have felt they were in a bind. They have been criticized for creating stereotypical or caricatured characters, *or* characters that aired community dirty laundry and showed queer people in a negative light to a broader public, *or* characters that were too much like straight or cisgender people. The mainstream pathbreakers have been massive targets, operating under both what one television critic called "the burden of sole representation"[49] and the burden of their success. As writer Higginbotham explained: "Our community feels starved for representation, and then when it happens, we often rise up in anger because the representation isn't perfect, or how the people *we* know exist in the world."[50] *Will & Grace* faced criticism that Jack was a walking gay stereotype while lawyer Will was the embodiment of respectability politics and was basically straight and in a sexless but codependent relationship with Grace.[51] *Modern Family* took a huge hit along the same lines: presenting gay characters in Mitch and Cam, who were criticized for being both too caricatured *and* too normal. This appraisal landed particularly on the assertion that Mitch and Cam were desexualized and never showed physical affection and that this was a capitulation to mainstream straight audiences that might be uncomfortable with gay sex[52] (and the show responded head-on with an episode called "The Kiss" in season 2).

These critiques of mainstream LGBTQ+ representation were not just focused on TV shows. When *Love, Simon* became the first big-studio gay teen rom-com in 2018,[53] actor and writer Jacob Tobia identified the bargain struck in the movie in the way it upheld normative masculinity while allowing some expansion of love for a mainstream rom-com. Of their own experience as a college student, Tobia wrote in *The New York Times*:

> I was *that* flamboyant gay kid who made everyone else look bad by association. Many gay men on campus were so unsettled by me, so vicariously ashamed of my gender expression, that they'd avoid eye contact, wouldn't even talk to me. The irony is that these very gay men were allowed to be "normal" because I was the campus freak. My unabashed femininity was what paved the way for gay men in, say, fraternities to come out without jeopardizing their masculinity. I was the shameful femme foil to their butch pride. At the same time as they disavowed me, they profited from my existence.

Of the film, Tobia argued that the main character, Simon, who was White, was able to be out, gay, and popular because of his conformity to masculine gender norms, and he existed in contradistinction to Ethan, "a black, femme gay guy who wears ascots and keeps his hair long and straightened. . . . He is the gender-nonconforming queer kid who blazed the trail and bears the brunt of the bullying and harassment because of it."[54]

These critiques of fictional representation are, in part, a recognition of the importance of this kind of storytelling: the stakes are high, so the critique is worth making. Here the concern is that mainstream representation of LGBTQ+ lives and stories has become *too* normal. There *is* now a kind of *homonormative* LGBTQ+ person who can exist sympathetically in public, but that kind of person must be mainstream and privileged in other ways.[55] Indeed, the critique is that some LGBTQ+ people "become normal" as a result of the further marginalization of others. They trade normalcy for the possibility of a more expansive range of intimate, sexual, familial relationships and gender identities and expressions. This critique of representation is accompanied by a fear that assimilation into the mainstream will come with a loss of distinction and community. This draws on long-standing sociological, artistic, and political insight that outsideness and marginality can be productive and can confer a kind of uniquely insightful view of and knowledge about the center.[56]

The idea that margins can be productive spaces of sight and insight is not specific to queer theory or to this century. We can look back to one of the founding fathers of sociology, W. E. B. Du Bois, in his analysis of the impact on Black Americans of enduring centuries of racism and White supremacy. In 1903 Du Bois wrote in *The Souls of Black Folk* of the experience of the color line: that to be Black in the United States meant to be "a sort of seventh son, born with a veil, and gifted with second-sight in this American world." He argued that this position provided "double-consciousness, this sense of always looking at one's self through the eyes of others, of measuring one's soul by the tape of the world that looks on in amused contempt and pity."[57] Racial marginality, in Du Bois's view, furnished African Americans with a deep knowledge of the *center*—White Americans—because their survival depended on it.

Half a century later, in the wake of the US social movements of the 1960s and 1970s, Black feminists took up this view to understand the impact of the intersection of racial and gendered marginality. bell hooks, in the preface to *Feminist Theory: From Margin to Center*, described the "particular way of seeing reality" that develops from the margins and is unique to them. Of her experience growing up Black in small-town Kentucky, hooks wrote of the ways in which this understanding from the margins provided both for survival and community strength:

> We focused our attention on the center as well as on the margin. We understood both. . . . Our survival depended on an ongoing public awareness of the separation between margin and center and an

> ongoing private acknowledgment that we were a necessary, vital part of that whole.[58]

Many others, especially intersectionality theorists, have since taken up these themes of the "creative tension of outsider within status."[59]

In the context of queer theory, the recognition of the standpoint and power of the margins builds upon the race and gender analyses that have come before it. It also highlights an assertion that creativity, artistic expression, and contributions to mainstream culture are also born of marginality—and that these are *gifts* to the broader culture. With a loss of the margins—with assimilation—will be a loss of this gift, some assert.[60] A number of queer writers and activists in recent years have worried about the cultural impact of LGBTQ+ *normalization* and assimilation. And they have celebrated the extent to which queer people, from their standpoint outside of the center, have gifted that center with art, culture, and the energy for and commitment to cultural and political change.[61] As writer and activist Sarah Schulman said to me: "I don't think America changes from the center. I think it only changes from the margins."[62]

In the context of my conversations with culture workers, I have come to think of this creative power of the margins as a kind of *leveraging the queer* for the purpose of creating culture and for advocating for LGBTQ+ social change.[63] Straight, cisgender, and LGBTQ+ people I interviewed have relied on their own biographies to give them artistic and political sensibilities that allow them to succeed in various ways in their creative work and their advocacy.

Many straight cisgender people I spoke with had something they have drawn on in their own biography that has helped them become effective creatives or advocates for LGBTQ+ social change. For many people, artistic and political commitments do not come out of nowhere or even from loving a queer family member or friend, but from some outsider experience that they could leverage for empathy and dedication. Among the people I spoke with, this was a powerful and varied list of experiences that included growing up bookish and nerdy, loving magic, loving fashion, loving video games, facing perceived homophobia and other bullying as a child, losing a close loved one, majoring in theater in college, having mixed-race parents or a minoritized racial or religious identity, and being adopted.

Drawing on outsiderness might not be what we would expect from athletes in sports with such traditional masculine capital as football, wrestling, hockey, and rugby. But so many of the straight cisgender men in these sports who were public advocates for LGBTQ+ social justice had something in their biography that they leveraged to connect them to and fuel their commitment to LGBTQ+ social change. We met many of these athletes in chapter 2. For example, Hudson Taylor, of Athlete Ally, was a star college wrestler who took women's studies and theater classes as a student at the University of Maryland, where he began to question what he had learned growing up evangelical Christian. He also picked up magic as a kid and has been devoted to it ever since.[64]

Three retired pro football players I interviewed similarly have leveraged their family experiences for LGBTQ+ advocacy. Former linebacker Scott Fujita, a very early public ally of marriage equality, has drawn on his family background as an adopted child—and a White child with a formerly interned Japanese American father. When I asked him about his LGBTQ+ politics, he located his commitment in his family's story:

> I don't think I grew up as a gay rights advocate or anything. I think I just grew up having a sense that I wanted to fight for the little guy. . . . My dad was born in a Japanese internment camp during World War II. Growing up, I always had kind of a deep resentment that it was never talked about in school . . . it wasn't a part of the curriculum. So I was always sort of affected and had a chip on my shoulder first of all that no one stood up for my dad and his family back in the '40s and then, in the '80s, no one was talking about it in class. So I kind of made that my champion issue. . . . I don't know if that's the mindset that sort of carried me through and made me feel that I should advocate

> for other topics that were important to me, or where I saw someone who I perceived to be a minority or an underdog being mistreated, persecuted against.[65]

Another Super Bowl winner, Brendon Ayanbadejo, has been a long-time committed public ally for LGBTQ+ justice and marriage equality. He, too, has drawn on his family history and his parents' interracial relationship, and the fact that he felt that he "never really fit in" with respect to his racial identity.[66] Chris Kluwe, another NFL veteran and committed public LGBTQ+ ally, has drawn on his parents' embrace of education and active engagement with the world and his own video-game playing, musician bookishness in his commitment to politics and LGBTQ+ justice. *Beautifully Unique Sparkleponies* is the title of his book of essays, and in it he writes about how he was both "the nerdy kid with thick glasses" who "always had my head in a book" and "the best player on my soccer and baseball teams," concluding: "Never be ashamed of who you are. I'm a nerd who plays football. It doesn't matter to me what other people think about that, because they're not the ones living my life."[67]

Of course, being a cisgender straight man jock who reads or does magic or takes women's studies classes is not the same as living in a homophobic and transphobic world as an LGBTQ+ person. But, in these cases, having something that makes you somewhat of an outsider in your community or having an experience that gives you a bit of additional empathy or a will to fight can be leveraged for social change.

LGBTQ+ creatives, too, talked with me about how they have drawn on their marginality to make them better artists. One of the mechanisms here has been the *closet*, which several people said makes their inhabitants into experts in human behavior. Growing up closeted meant feeling the need to navigate the world in an exceedingly careful way, hyper-attuned to the responses of others. Many felt this made them experts at observing humanity and also award-worthy actors in their own lives. When they had to *act straight* in their lives, they could then channel the skills that they had picked up in the closet into their creative work.[68] As Abraham Higginbotham said of his particular line of work and the way he has parlayed his past pain into his talent: "I had to suffer, so now I'm funny." He expanded a bit on how this might have worked—through observation and commentary. "Built into the defense mechanism that we had to use for many, many, many, many years to get through life is the ability to figure out how to be funny, to insult others before they insult you, to be verbal, to push away, to stand outside and judge rather than get in the middle of the room and do the goddamn Macarena with all the people not trying to hide who they are."

Artists, too, who were bullied or who otherwise felt like outsiders as kids—whether they were closeted or not—also drew on their outsiderness in their work, for compassion, community building, and creativity. Lesbian writer and producer Bridget McManus recounted:

> As a kid, I was body shamed for being overweight, so I never fit in and didn't really have any friends. In fact, my classmates used to play "don't sit with Bridget" at lunch in elementary school. It was painful at the time, but it ended up being a great blessing in my life. Because no one would talk to me, I became a good listener, which has made me a better writer and performer. And it was with other writers and performers that I eventually found community and a sense of belonging.[69]

Performing also provided a place of belonging, safety, and praise for many. This was true for contribution to sports, too. Former professional basketball player John Amaechi, who is six feet ten inches tall, said to me about finding his sport:

> I walked in and it was the first time that I didn't feel like a monster. I felt like this is a place where I fit, and people looked at me for the first time like a commodity, and I could see my own potential in other people's eyes, and I thought that was amazing. The first time I had experienced people saying "I want you on my team" ever. And that's why I did it.[70]

Still others felt that they could compensate for the horrible feeling of being a target of bullies or simply of feeling weird and socially marginal or queer by being high achievers, by cultivating ambition, drive, and determination for excellence in their work. This was then rewarded by their workplace.[71] In all of these ways, culture workers could leverage queerness to make art and culture. Hopefully it is clear, from the previous chapters, that these queer creatives also leverage their queerness in the ways that they make themselves publicly visible, through their advocacy, and in their creative/athletic contributions to their workplaces and to culture.

This individual contribution to culture also has institutional counterparts. For example, with the New Queer Cinema movement that began in the early 1990s as a response—from anger, pain, and fear—to the AIDS crisis and to the conservative US politics of the time. A retrospective look at New Queer Cinema on its thirtieth anniversary made it clear that the films and activist filmmakers who founded and located their work in the movement were not interested in bringing audiences along gently and comfortably. Writer-director Todd Haynes, who was part of the movement from the start, was quoted in *The New York Times*' retrospective as saying that the films associated with New Queer Cinema were "acts of protest and rebellion" that had a "spirit of challenging normalcy and heteronormativity and identifying with criminality."[72] This creative movement was born of necessity out of structural oppression. It then leveraged queer identity and activism to make films that were explicitly political, identity affirming, and community building.

THE NORMAL-QUEER BIND

The normal-queer, center-margin dichotomy has structured the LGBTQ+ movement since its very beginning and has informed and divided the politics of so many minoritized groups in the United States. The margins exist because of structural violence and injustice. They have also become reclaimed and celebrated spaces of solidarity, art, insight, and strength. These marginal spaces have nurtured community, distinctive identity, and contribution to center culture—but at a substantial cost. On the other hand, normalization, or a place at the center, has accomplished the changing of hearts and minds, cultural understanding, and expanded civil rights gains. It is still, to this day, an absolute achievement with vicious and dangerous detractors.[73] Yet this mainstreaming, assimilation, and becoming normal can come with trade-offs. It can come with a loss of distinctive identity and community and a possible dulling of sensibilities that lend themselves to creativity. It can force a bargaining of one kind of acceptance for other kinds of continued marginalization. And it can trade mainstream approval for a narrowed range of relationship models or expressions of self.

The margin and the center are always in a complex relationship to each other. With the designation of a *normal* definitionally comes an *abnormal* or pathological,[74] and who *gets* to be normal is limited and informed by structural privilege. Becoming normal, then, comes sometimes at the expense of distinctiveness, community, diversity, intersectional identities, authenticity, and creativity. Similarly, sometimes the margins are leveraged for a normalization project, so that the margins become a creative space in the service of erasing the margins.[75] This duality of margin and center, normal and queer, sounds theoretical, but it absolutely connects to one of the key debates in many social movements by and for minoritized people: whether maintaining margins and distinctive culture is vital or whether joining the center and assimilation into mainstream culture offer the best chance for full cultural and civic belonging.

When it comes to LGBTQ+ social change, there is an impossible demand here: that to change the culture so that marginalized groups belong and have full and equal access to civil protections, those groups have to both join the center and maintain the margins. They have to become normal *and* stay queer. This is a cultural and political demand that is made of many minoritized groups, and LGBTQ+ people are no different. Requiring a marginalized group to be *extraordinary* just to be able to enter and succeed in mainstream American institutions places an undue burden on them. So, too, does the condition that marginalized groups must completely renounce their distinctiveness if they hope to access the rights and privileges of the center. This impossible bind has not yet, in US history, had a resolution.

As a community outsider, it is not for me to say whether and how the strategies of becoming normal and staying queer should inform the fight for LGBTQ+ social justice. Hopefully I present and do justice here to the complexity of this conversation as I have learned it from community insiders. From my interviews and what I have learned from scholars and activists, I believe that the conversation has shifted and could continue to shift to a focus on freedom for *authenticity* as a goal: that joining the center does not have to mean being a perfect individual or community member, living and loving and having sex in a narrowly proscribed way. Perhaps with authenticity, mainstream visibility might not have to push out queer possibility and community, and mainstreaming would not have to be a loss. There is little historical evidence that the center allows anyone at the margins to be their authentic selves. But the shifting of the frame from a focus on *assimilation and sameness* to *authenticity* has been an important one in popular culture and art.[76]

Marginalized groups in the United States all stand in this place of straddling margin and center. They contribute to the culture and then are both celebrated for the work that their marginality helps to produce *and* are resented for their successes. There is an unattainable needle threading of normal/queer here—and the need to be exceptional to succeed is an unfair burden, of course. Within this bind are true differences in the theory of change about how a culture war around gender and sexuality can be won.

CONCLUSION

From the very first minutes of his new presidency in January 2025, Trump made it a priority to try to disappear LGBTQ+ people, especially trans and nonbinary people. He recruited all of his authoritarian tendencies to seize control over culture and identity. In his inauguration speech, he imperiously decreed that "as of today, it will henceforth be the official policy of the United States government that there are only two genders: male and female." He then moved to reinstate his ban on transgender service members. He passed another bad-faith executive order banning gender-affirming medical care in young people—in the name of "protecting children." He required federal agencies to remove words, research, and resources that he said displayed "gender ideology"—even, in one example from the State Department, removing a reference to trans and queer travelers from a previous post to now just serve as a travel resource for "LGB Travelers."[1] This horror show has set the tone for the way that this emboldened Trump 2.0 has governed.

And all of this is the rotten cherry on top of the past couple of years, when the Right has cynically decided that an all-out strategy of transphobic lawmaking offers them the best chance of political success.[2] In the 2024 election cycle, all told, Republicans spent $222 million on anti-LGBTQ+, anti-trans political ads,[3] even though polling suggests that this is near the very bottom of voters' priorities.[4]

For those of us who are dedicated to LGBTQ+ social justice, it feels like we have *lost* the battle at this particular moment. But, to belabor a metaphor, the culture *war* continues.

Culture wars are, fundamentally, fights about who gets to *belong*—in private spaces and in public ones, in families and communities, in and through institutions, and in state policy and law. Truly winning a culture war means winning a right to belong, but not by agreeing to assimilate and bargain away what is personally and collectively distinctive. Truly winning a culture war means being able to participate as authentic selves in public and private life.[5] And expanding the culture in this way—making it more participatory, open, and diverse—is good for *everyone*, even though the framing of a culture war as having winners also implies that it has losers.[6]

Popular culture in late-stage capitalism is not perfect and never will be. It runs on self-interest. It is a business—a huge, inequitable collection of businesses.[7] Popular culture will always be a commodified and constrained space—a "commercial public sphere"[8]—driven by bottom-line decision-making. And it will be risk averse to a fault, often following rather than leading social change.

And yet, and yet, I admit: I am in love with television and movies (and will happily trade sleep for TV any night of the week); I feel so connected to and grateful to sports through my son, who is a baseball player; and music saves my life on a daily basis. I admire and have so much respect for the culture workers in the pages of this book and so many others like them. They make the choice to work in ways that truly change our culture. They step into the spotlight and onto the field as their true selves. They speak up from their places of influence, standing next to their queer family members and truly embracing them. They intervene in their workplaces when they know their stories are being mistold. They give beauty and grace to the world. They make us laugh. They create characters whom we are compelled to root for and come to see as integral parts of our lives.

I cannot help but go back to one of my favorite quotes from writer and activist Audre Lorde.[9] She reminds us that silence is not an option, that "the weight of that silence will choke us." She implores: "there are so many silences to be broken."[10] Art and popular culture are ways of breaking silences. They bring joy, community, and emotional resonance. They are ways to speak back, make noise, and simply exist in public. And they endure.[11] This is no small feat. The politics of our current time are truly regressive and terrifying, and pop culture cannot act alone to counteract them. Trump and his Republican Party truly want to erase and silence queer people. And the anti-democratic nature of our imperfect democracy amplifies and disproportionately strengthens the voices and voting power of an anti-LGBTQ+ minority.[12] Yet, despite this, pop culture keeps moving ahead with queer leadership and storytelling.

People do this work—with agency, bravery, humor, humility or not—confronting the cultural and structural obstacles that have always been in their way. They are savvy, strategic, hardworking, and talented. And this takes a toll and presents serious paradoxes. Visibility comes with vulnerability. Advocacy comes with personal and professional risk. Speaking up at work comes with precarity. Overachievement comes with burden. Joining the center and maintaining the margins come with losses and trade-offs.

Many are quite critical and dismissive of the fact that pop culture has commodified LGBTQ+ identity and representation for its own self-interested, revenue-generating purposes, and that, for this reason, pop culture can never really serve social change. This is *not* my primary take. I have, instead, what I consider to be a complex and ultimately hopeful look at the limits and possibilities of pop culture. Ultimately, my analysis comes down on the side of seeing mainstream popular cultural engagement and celebrity advocacy as contributing in a net *positive* way to LGBTQ+ social justice. Despite all its limitations and paradoxes, despite the partial and fragile nature of any progress, pop culture is a central actor in the LGBTQ+ movement. Art and popular culture have *always* been part of movements for cultural and structural social change. They have always been part of winning the culture wars of their historical moments.[13] This is true even though, for many culture workers, the social change they may be responsible for is a collateral benefit of the artistic or athletic work they do rather than their primary goal.

Of course, pop culture is just one front in the culture war, and there are so many like-minded heroes and activists fighting in the ways that they know best, through electoral politics, collective action, legal battles, and health care struggles.[14] The imperatives that provide the titles of the chapters in this book are not meant to imply that it is only through pop culture that LGBTQ+ social justice can and will be won.[15] This is not the case. With these imperatives, I also do not mean to put the weight of social change solely on the shoulders of queer people themselves and/or on culture workers. It should not be the responsibility of marginalized people to change the culture around them. Yet, in this world, especially right now, we all still need them and their work. As Tony Kushner wrote, at the very end of his epic play *Angels in America: A Gay Fantasia on National Themes*, "The world only spins forward. We will be citizens. The time has come."[16]

ACKNOWLEDGMENTS

Two a.m. is my time for devouring stories. I love this time of night, when it is quiet and I can turn all of my attention to the beauty, drama, emotion, and humor of fictional lives. When I was little, I consumed books under blankets, via flashlight. Now, thankfully, I can be out in the open, drinking tea and eating chocolate chips at my kitchen counter while I watch TV or point my nose toward my book. I engage with these stories as any nerdy sociologist would, googling actors and characters as I watch; checking in on social media to see if TV viewers felt as I did about the latest episode of something; extending my viewing pleasure by immediately reading *Vulture* recaps so that I don't have to stop thinking about the characters of a show that, mercilessly, only drops once a week; telling myself I'll just read one more chapter and knowing it's a total lie. I love stories and I love putting myself in stories in this way, and I have so much admiration and awe for storytellers. How do they even *do* this beautiful thing?

My first thanks goes to all of the incredible artists, athletes, and those who support them, who put such beauty into the world and were willing to talk with me about it. I feel truly grateful that I was able to speak with so many smart, creative, committed people who gave me their time and trust. I didn't always navigate the culture of Hollywood or elite sports like a pro, but people overwhelmingly treated me with generosity and grace. The words of many of these amazing people appear in the pages of this book. But to *everyone* I interviewed, even if your words or stories do not appear here, please know that I learned so much from each and every one of you over the years.

There are two people without whom this book would not exist. First, thank you to my incredible editor at the University of Chicago Press, Elizabeth Branch Dyson. She graciously began talking with me about this project when it was in its *very* early stages, and she generously made time for me to update her, year after year, over coffee and lunches at all the usual spots in Hyde Park. I cannot imagine anyone smarter, savvier, or more patient. To the extent that this project has a bold take, it is because Elizabeth encouraged me to take it. Thank you, Elizabeth, for all of your years of support, enthusiasm, and guidance. You are, simply, the absolute best.

Second, this book would be nothing without Bryan Rosenberg. Bryan was a PhD student in my program at NYU when this project began, and he conducted all interviews with me through 2018. We prepped and strategized for each of these early conversations together; we navigated our LA trips together, finding the perfect coffee spot, vegan meal, or end-of-day run/hike; talked endlessly about the shape of the project; and became true, trusted friends. There are no words to express my gratitude to you, Bryan.

In addition, my cousin Ian Stulberg and his husband, Bob Berman, provided a beautiful home research base in Los Angeles and lovingly curated "my" room there. Thank you for that, and for pumpkin chocolate chip cake every visit, for transcription help, for all of the noodging about when the book would be done, for so many wonderful questions and dinners, and for being receptive to all of the many nicknames I gave you both along the way.

There are *so* many people I want to thank for generously helping me to recruit interview participants, offering advice about navigating Hollywood when I asked, and enthusiastically and patiently listening to me talk about this project for so many years. These include friends, family, students, colleagues, and many people I interviewed who took an interest in the project and were, so incredibly, willing to help. I truly apologize for anyone I am forgetting here, but I want to make sure to mention: Bob Berman and Ian Stulberg, Josh Burstein, Tony Chen, Wendy Chen, Sebastian Cherng, Jackie Cruz, Aidan Dowell, Dave Fleischer, Chanda Hall (also for amazing photography!), Jessica Herthel, Ted Hong, David Hornik, Lauri Hornik, Jessy Hsieh, John King and Melissa King, Melissa Klurman, Reggi Levin, Hilary Lustick, Nina Mauceri, Charlton McIlwain, Cori Flam Meltzer and Brad Meltzer, Chris Mosier, John (Yanni) Palella, Vikash Reddy, Joe Salvatore, Lis Howard Shea, Erin Sircy, Debbie Stulberg, Mark Stulberg, Madhavi Sunder, Russell Wetanson, Patti Wolf-Schwaiger, Chris Woods—and super-connectors who also were awesome at answering *so* many of my questions along the way: Amin El Gamal, Brian Ellner, Dave Monahan and Larry Sullivan, and Gianna Sobol. There are so many others, as well, who I interviewed who then generously connected me with other people in their networks, allowing me access that I never would have had otherwise. I can't thank you enough. And, of course, to the whole Stulberg/Stulberg-adjacent crew, I couldn't do *any* of my life without you.

I am grateful, too, that I had the chance to present versions of this work not only at conferences, but also at the Qualitative Methods Group at the Community College Research Center, Teachers College, Columbia University (thank you, Maggie Fay), and Patrick Egan and Daphna Harel's Queer Empirical Research Seminar at New York University. Thanks, too, to my NYU department's research funding support at critical points in the project.

I must also thank David R. Craig at USC Annenberg for suggesting the title of this book during our interview in 2014. I retain a love-hate relationship with the title, but also think it's a perfect challenge and am so grateful for this suggestion.

For editing and transcription support, I could not have managed the sheer number of *words* in this project without Jackie Cruz, the late Bill Sell and his team at The Last Word, Ian Stulberg, and patient and brilliant editors Meghan Drury and Laura Portwood-Stacer.

At University of Chicago Press, thanks so much to Mollie McFee, Erin DeWitt, Rae Ganci Hammers, Levens Herbert, and Olivia Aguilar for all of their careful and generous support and for always and patiently receiving and responding to my many, many questions. Thank you to June Sawyers for the index. I also must thank the anonymous reviewers in both rounds of review—and the faculty board at Chicago—for their incredible input. You have all made the book so much stronger—but, of course, all shortcomings are mine.

And, finally, to my partners in the Core Four, thank you for the best life I could ever hope for: Also, thank you, Avery, for being my late-night TV and tea buddy with an amazing sociological eye and the best TV theme song choreography. Thank you, Eli, for allowing me to fall in love again with baseball through your journey—and for patiently answering my gazillion questions about the game. Thank you, Evan, for valuing laughter as much as I do—and for always going to sleep before me so that I can settle in to late-night storytelling. Of all the stories I love so much, I love our family's the most.

APPENDIX A. STUDYING POP CULTURE

There are a few rich production studies that examine the connection between pop culture and LGBTQ+ social change that have really informed my research.[1] In general, however, few academics or other analysts of popular culture study the production side.[2] Many studies tend to focus on the representations and images themselves through *content* analysis or on the broader sociopolitical context.[3] My work is in the tradition of these various kinds of projects, in that it grapples with the complexities of LGBTQ+ visibility, pop cultural production, and celebrity. But my interviews allow me to examine the connection between popular culture and social change from the *production* side, and my work updates a set of studies that primarily were conducted after a period of significant change in LGBTQ+ pop cultural representation in the 1990s and early 2000s.

I was not necessarily the obvious person to do this project. I was an outsider to Hollywood and to LGBTQ+ identities. As a sociologist, I have studied social movements and their connection to educational institutions for decades. Before I pursued a PhD in sociology, I got a master's degree in cultural studies, and I absolutely believe that popular culture is one of the central educational institutions of our time. I also believe in its capacity to contribute to social change. On a more visceral level, I truly believe in *stories* and their ability to save us. Fiction has always been a way for me to embed myself in new worlds and find a home there. I have always been drawn to the artists and storytellers who make their work out of a sense of their own outsiderness and marginality.

My initial idea for this project was simple. Step one: Learn how to use Twitter. Step two: Tweet at Lady Gaga and have her respond enthusiastically that she would be honored to do an interview for an academic book. Step three: Interview her and all of her celebrity friends. On a family vacation in 2011, I had my much-younger brother teach me how to use Twitter. We crafted a tweet and sent it around to several A-list celebrities who either played high-profile LGBTQ+ characters on TV or in film or who were outspoken advocates for LGBTQ+ equality. It should come as little surprise that I got no responses. I then changed course. I found one "in" in Hollywood through a friend of a friend. He was kind, supportive, and generous and lined up my first set of interviews in Los Angeles and then connected me with a number of people after that.

In the end, between the fall of 2011 and the fall of 2025, I interviewed 170 people (all but forty-four of whom I met with in person at least once). This group included television, film, and theater actors; TV and movie producers, directors, and writers; television show creators; others in the entertainment industry (like casting directors, publicists, entertainment lawyers, and studio executives); musicians; athletes; political and sports writers; and activists—among others. I recruited from what I called my *wish list* of people who have contributed to the recent pop cultural portrayal and visibility of LGBTQ+ people, experiences, issues, and politics, as well as people in the entertainment or sports industries who have been advocates or activists for LGBTQ+ social justice. I expanded the initial list through the suggestions of people I interviewed, and I never said no to anyone who offered to put me in touch with a friend or a colleague who might be willing to sit for an interview. I supplemented this incredible list of interviewees by cold-contacting people through their publicists or through Facebook, Twitter, Instagram, and publicly available email addresses. Though this did not initially work with Lady Gaga, it did work for some. Overall, this truly has been an experiment in the power of social networks and social media, and I was so fortunate to gain access to and the trust of a wide range of culture workers.[4]

Several interviewees described Hollywood as an insular club in which connections are everything. I found that people were quite open to offering to connect me to their colleagues, clients, and friends, or using their names to help. This is how I gained most of my access—often with enthusiastic and frequent follow-up from me. I came to call this recruitment method—drawing on a term used by social scientists—*assertive snowball sampling*. I was also surprised by just how open people were to our conversations and the time they spent with me in such an uninterrupted way. They were almost never on their phones, they regularly went over the time we had allotted, and they willingly gave their time to a stranger like me in the middle of their workdays. They generally completely defied the stereotype of Hollywood that I had acquired from the frenetic, self-involved, brash Ari Gold character on the HBO show *Entourage*. I guess I should not have been surprised that people were willing to talk with me about the work they love and believe in.

Of course, accessing a world that was not my own was a challenge, and I did not always navigate it perfectly. But I found more openness than I had expected.[5] I have learned a lot from anthropologist Sherry B. Ortner, whose ethnographic study of the independent film industry in the United States also prompted her helpful methodological reflections on Hollywood access. She wrote that the dearth of academic studies of Hollywood—especially, I would underscore, production studies—can be attributed to access challenges in this relatively closed community: "In the case of Hollywood, the problem of 'access' seems to be particularly acute, and has bedeviled most outsiders." Ortner argues, though, that interviewing Hollywood creatives is a form of "studying sideways" for academics, and this can be to our benefit: we often draw on a shared educational and class privilege and status that can help with access and rapport building.[6] She also writes that we are more likely to have success with access if our potential interviewees share a sense of interest in our work, which I definitely found to be the case as I was recruiting.

I made some methodological choices along the way that I hope might be instructive to anyone reading this in a qualitative methods class or considering their own study of culture industries. Some of these, I think, helped with my access and helped build trust. I have already talked a bit about how I accessed and relied on social networks and, quite frankly, deliberate name-dropping[7] (with permission) to access interviewees. For trust, once I began to hear from people that they had been misquoted and felt mistreated by journalists, I promised to check everyone's quotes with them before I published them. I also promised to check again about using participants' real names in connection with their quotes. I worried about this a *lot* over the years. It truly kept me up at night. How random would it seem to an athlete or Hollywood insider to hear from this academic that they had talked with *years* before? Would it call the legitimacy of my project into question if I contacted someone ten years after our initial conversation? What if no one got back to me and I couldn't use any of their great quotes? In the early years of my interviews, I sent a few updates on the project, so participants knew I was still working on it. And, with some, I stayed in regular touch, sometimes asking for follow-up interviews and sometimes asking for help connecting me with a potential interviewee. Then, once I had a full first draft, I reached out to the approximately ninety people I wanted to quote, and I hoped for the best! Almost all of them eventually allowed me to use their quotes, many offering small modifications or updates, as I had promised they could make. I also asked people to amend anything that seemed out-of-date. A few people asked that I make it clear what year I had interviewed them, so their quote would be in historical context. But most stuck with what they had said. Many thanked me, both when we initially talked and in my email communication with them at the end of the project, for giving them a chance to check and revise quotes. I am absolutely sure that my promise here and my follow-up helped both with trust building and with ensuring that my research remained current, despite how many years these interviews took me to complete. Checking quotes like this is not standard practice in qualitative sociology, and I would not recommend it for all projects, especially with anonymized participants. But this felt critical for this project and like the right thing to do. I'm so grateful that almost everyone I contacted was so responsive.

There is so much to be written, always, about how a researcher's complicated mix of identities impacts their data collection and analysis. I am a White, Jewish, economically privileged Gen Xer. I identify as a straight cisgender woman—albeit with a lifelong complicated relationship to my gender and my body that has had real, sometimes quite painful, consequences in my life. And both out of political commitment and out of love for so many people in my life, I am devoted, in the strongest possible terms, to LGBTQ+ social justice. It seems presumptuous of me to write a book that sounds, from its title, to be prescribing steps to social change for LGBTQ+ people, and I hope I have approached this project with the humility that it deserves.

Most people I interviewed did not ask me about my gender and sexual identities. Of course, when they did, I was completely honest and open about my own identity and experience and the stake I feel I have in this project. I published a *Huffington Post* piece about my identity during the project,[8] in part so that if potential interviewees did google me, they might come across the piece and learn a bit more about how I think about myself and my experience as it relates to this work. I thought constantly about how to approach my own identity throughout this project, and I talked about this with trusted friends and colleagues throughout the project. My outsiderness is not something I ever took lightly, though readers can certainly disagree about whether I can legitimately do this work and add my voice to this conversation.

I also learned a lot about framing my work from a study that I encountered as I was revising the book manuscript: sociologist Michèle Lamont's *Seeing Others: How Recognition Works—And How It Can Heal a Divided World.* Lamont also interviewed "change agents" from a broad range of industries, including Hollywood and comedy/stand-up, about "how they conceive of their work and its impact."[9] Lamont argues that a central question of American history and politics is "*who matters*." The "search for recognition," she writes, "calls for an entirely new frame of understanding our social world," a new way of conceiving of the role of culture. She found that the artists and culture workers she spoke with often strove to do the work of "broadening our definition of 'who matters.'"[10] Methodologically, it was helpful to see Lamont's choice—like mine—to name her participants (when they agreed, which they mostly did), and to see the great access that she had with the same kinds of Hollywood artists I did, in front of and behind the camera.

Of course, even after almost fifteen years with this project, there are limitations to what I could do and what, ultimately, I did in my study. There are important cultural spaces, especially for young people, that I was not able to cover but that are central to LGBTQ+ social change. These include young adult (YA) literature and graphic novels; social media influencers and communities on YouTube, TikTok, and Instagram; and video games/gamers.[11] I also would have loved to be able to study music in more depth. While I do have a bit to say about these aspects of pop culture, I did not learn nearly enough. And while it is true that social media is a primary source of pop cultural engagement for young people, I do think that pop culture is more transgenerational now, especially thanks to streaming services and the availability of almost anything online. I see this with my own Gen Z kids, who are just hitting their twenties. My daughter is just as likely to fire up old episodes of *New Girl* or *Gilmore Girls* as to scroll through TikTok, and her music taste spans decades. My son is just as likely to endlessly rewatch old episodes of *The Office* or *Modern Family* and to watch all the broadcast games of football in real time on a Sunday afternoon (and then listen to recaps on broadcast sports radio) as he is to watch gamers play Xbox sports games on Twitch or YouTube. They love and need good stories, just like I do. So it is true that a lot about pop culture has changed for young people in the past decade. But I truly believe that they do also have access to, engagement with, and an appreciation for the culture of previous generations—and the products from these periods often still mean something to them. I can't wait to read future studies on all the aspects of pop culture and LGBTQ+ social change that I do not sufficiently cover here.

APPENDIX B. INTERVIEWS CONDUCTED

NAME	RELEVANT PROFESSIONAL ROLE (FORMER OR CURRENT)*	DATE(S) INTERVIEWED
Anna Aagenes	College athlete (track & field) and sports advocate	April 11, 2014 (in person)
Kye Allums	College athlete (basketball) and sports advocate	March 12, 2013 (in person)
John Amaechi	NBA athlete and author, psychologist	April 26, 2014 (in person)
Brendon Ayanbadejo	NFL athlete, advocate, writer	May 31, 2012 (by phone)
Jamie Babbit	Television and film director Known for: *But I'm a Cheerleader*; *Looking*; *The L Word*	July 27, 2012 (in person) January 10, 2018 (in person)
Alan Ball	Television and film writer, producer Known for: *American Beauty*; *Six Feet Under*; *True Blood*	January 18, 2012 (in person)
Kristin Bauer	Actor Known for: *True Blood*	June 12, 2014 (in person)
Ben Baur	Actor Known for: *Hunting Season*; *Something Like Summer*	June 12, 2013 (in person)
Paris Barclay	Television director, writer, and producer Known for: President of the Directors Guild of America; *Glee*	April 27, 2012 (in person)
Josh Barro	Political writer and commentator	April 23, 2013 (in person)

Billy Bean	MLB athlete, writer, sports advocate	December 7, 2012 (in person)
Kathy Behrens	NBA league executive	October 3, 2013 (in person)
Elizabeth Berger	Writer and showrunner Known for: *Love, Simon*; *Love, Victor*	April 26, 2019 (in person)
Trish Bendix	Writer and editor	July 24, 2017 (in person)
Adam Bouska	Photographer and nonprofit co-founder Known for: NOH8 Campaign	July 25, 2012 (in person)
danah boyd	Writer and scholar	October 24, 2012 (in person)
Howard Bragman	Publicist and writer	January 20, 2012 (in person)
Belle Brockhoff	Olympic athlete (snowboarding)	May 5, 2014 (by Skype)
Dan Bucatinsky	Actor, writer, producer Known for: *Scandal*; *It Got Better*; *Hacks*; *Does This Baby Make Me Look Straight?*	July 27, 2012 (in person) July 25, 2017 (in person)
Steve Buckley	Sports writer	April 5, 2013 (in person)
Nick Burd	YA writer Known for: *The Vast Fields of Ordinary*	March 21, 2012 (in person)
Patrick Burke	NHL league executive and sports advocate	September 17, 2012 (by phone)
Gabrielle Burton	Writer, director, filmmaker Known for: *Kings, Queens, & In-Betweens*	June 24, 2014 (by phone)
Ursula Burton	Actor, writer, director, producer Known for: *Kings, Queens, & In-Betweens*; *The Happiest Day of His Life*	June 13, 2014 (in person)
Nevin Caple	College athlete (basketball), sports advocate, nonprofit founder	October 8, 2013 (in person)
Aymar Jean Escoffery (formerly known as Aymar Jean Christian)	Academic	October 11, 2022 (by Zoom)

Bob Cooper	Television and film executive Known for: HBO president, *And the Band Played On*	July 25, 2012 (in person)
Ron Cowen	Television and theater writer and producer Known for: *An Early Frost*; *Queer as Folk*	April 18, 2012 (in person)
Duncan Crabtree-Ireland	SAG-AFTRA executive	May 31, 2012 (by phone)
David Craig	Television and film producer and executive, advocate, academic	June 11, 2014 (in person)
Wilson Cruz	Actor and activist Known for: *My So-Called Life*; *Rent*; *Noah's Arc*; *Star Trek: Discovery*; GLAAD	December 7, 2012 (in person)
Chuck Culpepper	Sportswriter	April 25, 2013 (in person)
Wade Davis	NFL athlete and sports advocate	July 20, 2012 (in person)
Lea DeLaria	Actor, comedian, musician Known for: *Orange Is the New Black*; *One Life to Live*	September 19, 2014 (in person)
Danielle Pretsfelder Demchick	Casting director	April 26, 2022 (by Zoom)
Danne Diamond	Athlete and advocate	November 5, 2021 (by Zoom) March 14, 2024 (by phone)
Syd Diaz	Actor Known for: *Genera+ion*; *Ghostbusters: Afterlife*	November 4, 2022 (by Zoom)
D'Lo	Writer, actor, comic Known for: *Looking*; *Transparent*; *Sense8*	July 30, 2025 (by Zoom)
Zackary Drucker	Artist, photographer, filmmaker Known for: *Enigma*; *The Lady and the Dale*; *Transparent*	August 4, 2025 (by Zoom)
Jamie Duneier	Television writer Known for: *Proxy*; *Parenthood*	June 11, 2014 (in person)

Alexander D. Eadie	Actor Known for: *Legacies*	October 24, 2022 (by Zoom)
Taylor Edelmann	College athlete (volleyball)	October 14, 2013 (in person)
Amin El Gamal	Actor Known for: *The Newsroom*; *Transparent*; *Good Trouble*; *Breaking Fast*	January 12, 2018 (in person) January 13, 2022 (by Zoom) July 16, 2025 (in person)
Brian Ellner	Communications and political strategist and advocate	February 27, 2012 (in person) July 23, 2013 (in person) August 5, 2014 (in person) November 3, 2021 (by phone)
Adrienne Erickson	Production company executive	November 10, 2021 (by Zoom)
Samy Nour Younes Figaredo	Actor and activist Known for: *The Other Two*; *Transparent*	September 27, 2022 (in person)
Dave Fleischer	Activist and organizer	January 19, 2012 (in person)
Scott Fujita	NFL athlete and advocate	September 26, 2013 (by phone)
Nisha Ganatra	Television director, producer, writer Known for: *Chutney Popcorn*; *Transparent*; *Better Things*	July 24, 2017 (in person)
Janina Gavankar	Actor Known for: *The L Word*; *True Blood*; *The Morning Show*	April 27, 2012 (in person)
Scott Genkinger	Casting agent Known for: *Desperate Housewives*; *The Fosters*; *Good Trouble*	November 15, 2011 (by phone)
Andrew Germek	College athlete (crew)	October 4, 2012 (in person)
Andrew Goldstein	College and professional athlete (lacrosse)	June 11, 2014 (in person)
Steven Goldstein	Activist and nonprofit founder	November 14, 2014 (in person)

LZ Granderson	Sports and politics writer and journalist	April 22, 2013 (by phone)
Christopher Griffin	Social media influencer and educator Known for: @plantkween	April 19, 2022 (by Zoom)
Pat Griffin	Academic and sports advocate	June 28, 2012 (by phone) January 9, 2014 (in person)
Larry Gross	Academic	July 26, 2012 (in person)
Harvey Guillén	Actor Known for: *Huge*; *What We Do in the Shadows*	March 20, 2015 (by phone)
Bill Harrison	Publicist	November 16, 2011 (by phone) July 24, 2017 (in person)
Deven Hartley	Talent agent	July 12, 2022 (by Zoom)
Abraham Higginbotham	Television writer, producer Known for: *Modern Family*; *Will & Grace*; *Ugly Betty*; *Uncoupled*	April 26, 2012 (in person)
Mel Hinkle	Actor and talent agent	August 5, 2022 (by Zoom)
Mark Indelicato	Actor Known for: *Ugly Betty*; *With Love*; *Hacks*	February 19, 2013 (in person) September 30, 2021 (by Zoom)
Sean James	NFL athlete and activist	June 6, 2012 (in person)
Dan Jinks	Film writer and producer Known for: *American Beauty*; *Milk*	October 20, 2011 (in person)
Avan Jogia	Actor and writer Known for: *Victorious*; *Twisted*; *Straight but Not Narrow*	July 25, 2012 (in person)
JJ Jones	Music executive Known for: ASCAP	July 31, 2013 (in person)
Chase Joynt	Nonfiction filmmaker and writer Known for: *No Ordinary Man*; *Framing Agnes*; *Vantage Points*	July 24, 2025 (by Zoom)
Jenny Kanelos	Nonprofit co-founder Known for: Broadway Impact	January 9, 2013 (in person)

Dave Karger	Entertainment magazine writer and journalist Known for: *Entertainment Weekly*	April 9, 2012 (by phone)
Michael A. Kerker	Music executive Known for: VP ASCAP Musical Theatre	June 11, 2013 (in person)
Carole Kirschner	Television executive and mentoring/ training program leader	October 12, 2021 (by Zoom)
Alan Klein	Activist and public relations Known for: ACT UP; Queer Nation	November 15, 2012 (in person)
Chris Kluwe	NFL athlete, advocate, author	November 15, 2012 (by phone)
Alex Kondracke	Television writer, producer Known for: *D.E.B.S.*; *The L Word*	July 26, 2012 (in person)
Larry Kramer	Activist and writer Known for: Gay Men's Health Crisis; ACT UP; *The Normal Heart*	March 7, 2012 (in person)
Scott Lazes	Documentary filmmaker	October 8, 2012 (in person)
Erin Levy	Television writer, producer Known for: *Mad Men*; *Counterpart*	July 24, 2017 (in person)
Eli Lieb	Musician Known for: "Young Love," "Safe in My Hands"	June 10, 2014 (in person)
Caroline Liem	Casting director	March 17, 2022 (by Zoom)
Daniel Lipman	Television and theater writer and producer Known for: *An Early Frost*; *Queer as Folk*	April 18, 2012 (in person)
Michael Lombardo	Television executive Known for: HBO	January 19, 2012 (in person)
Greg Louganis	Olympic athlete (diver), activist, author	December 6, 2012 (in person)
Scott Lowell	Actor Known for: *Queer as Folk*	February 8, 2012 (by phone)
Alec Mapa	Actor, comedian, writer Known for: *Ugly Betty*; *Desperate Housewives*	July 25, 2017 (by email)

Paul Marchegiani	Entertainment lawyer	February 15, 2012 (by phone)
Sam Marchiano	Sports journalist and sports advocate	September 10, 2013 (in person)
James Duke Mason	Writer, activist, and city official	October 21, 2011 (in person)
Eric McCormack	Actor Known for: *Will & Grace*	March 16, 2012 (by email)
Dave McKeown	Talent manager	August 5, 2022 (by Zoom)
Bridget McManus	Comedian, actor, writer Known for: *Transparent*; *The Queen Latifah Show*	March 14, 2023 (by Zoom)
Aaron McQuade	Advocate Known for: GLAAD	February 25, 2013 (in person)
Andria Wilson Mirza	Nonprofit director and advocate	March 8, 2022 (by Zoom)
Fawzia Mirza	Writer and director Known for: *Signature Move*; *The Red Line*	March 2, 2022 (by Zoom)
David Monahan	Actor and television writer Known for: *Dawson's Creek*; *Big Little Lies*; *Ginny & Georgia*	April 27, 2012 (in person) July 23, 2017 (in person)
Chris Mosier	Athlete (All-American duathlete) and sports advocate Known for: Team USA; Nike; *ESPN Body Issue*	June 7, 2013 (in person) October 12, 2021 (by Zoom) April 17, 2024 (by Zoom) July 29, 2025 (by Zoom)
Christina Munger-Rivera	College athletic administrator	December 6, 2012 (in person)
Max Mutchnick	Television writer and producer Known for: *Will & Grace*; *Partners*; *Mid-Century Modern*	January 18, 2012 (in person)
Shakina Nayfack	Performer, writer, director, activist Known for: *Difficult People*, *Connecting*, *Quantum Leap*	September 22, 2025 (by Zoom)
Brittani Nichols	Actor, writer, producer, director Known for: *Abbott Elementary*; *Suicide Kale*; *Transparent*	April 14, 2022 (by Zoom)

Ann Northrop	Activist and journalist Known for: ACT UP; *CBS Morning News*; GAY USA	June 28, 2012 (in person)
Denis O'Hare	Actor Known for: *Milk*; *True Blood*; *American Horror Story*; *Dallas Buyers Club*; *The Normal Heart*	December 14, 2011 (in person)
Rory O'Malley	Actor and nonprofit co-founder Known for: *The Book of Mormon*; 8; *Hamilton*; Broadway Impact	April 30, 2013 (in person)
Peter Paige	Actor, television writer, producer, director Known for: *Queer as Folk*; *The Fosters*; *Good Trouble*	February 13, 2012 (by phone) June 11, 2014 (in person) November 18, 2021 (by Zoom) July 31, 2025 (by Zoom)
Ernie Palmieri	College/athletic administrator	February 10, 2014 (in person)
Jeff Parshley	Photographer and nonprofit co-founder Known for: NOH8 Campaign	July 25, 2012 (in person)
Shadi Petosky	Writer, animator, producer Known for: *Danger & Eggs*; *Twelve Forever*	June 12, 2014 (in person) October 14, 2021 (by Zoom)
Alan Poul	Television writer, producer, director Known for: *Tales of the City*; *My So-Called Life*; *Six Feet Under*	April 26, 2012 (in person) October 7, 2021 (by Zoom)
Sue Rankin	Academic and sports advocate	May 2, 2014 (in person)
Amy Ray	Musician and activist Known for: Indigo Girls	June 20, 2013 (in person)
Cathy Renna	Publicist and media relations expert	October 2, 2014 (in person)
Jen Richards	Actor, writer, activist Known for: *Her Story*; *Nashville*; *Tales of the City*; *Mrs. Fletcher*; *Better Things*; *Mayfair Witches*	January 11, 2018 (in person) February 20, 2024 (by phone) July 24, 2025 (by Zoom)

Jeffrey Richman	Television writer and producer Known for: *Frasier*; *Desperate Housewives*; *Modern Family*; *Uncoupled*	April 16, 2013 (in person)
Angela Robinson	TV/film writer, director, producer Known for: *D.E.B.S.*; *The L Word*; *True Blood*; *Professor Marston & the Wonder Woman*	July 25, 2012 (in person)
Daphne Rubin-Vega	Actor Known for: *Rent*; *Smash*; *Tales of the City*	June 4, 2013 (in person)
Emily Saliers	Musician and activist Known for: Indigo Girls	June 20, 2013 (in person)
Dan Savage	Writer and activist Known for: The It Gets Better Project; *Savage Love*	January 26, 2012 (in person)
Kirsten Schaffer	Film advocate and nonprofit leader Known for: Outfest	January 18, 2012 (in person)
James Schamus	Film executive, producer, academic Known for: Focus Features; *Brokeback Mountain*	April 9, 2012 (in person)
Scott Turner Schofield	Actor, creative producer, activist Known for: *The Bold and the Beautiful*, *Studio City*, *The Conductor*	October 10, 2025 (by Zoom)
Sarah Schulman	Activist, writer, academic Known for: ACT UP; Lesbian Avengers; *People in Trouble*; *The Cosmopolitans*	May 3, 2013 (in person)
Mark Schuster	Academic, college administrator, sports advocate	June 8, 2012 (in person)
Jake Shears	Musician and author Known for: Scissor Sisters; *Boys Keep Swinging*	October 29, 2013 (in person)
Brian Sims	College athlete (football), elected official, activist Known for: PA House of Representatives	October 25, 2012 (in person)
Michael Skolnik		June 6, 2014 (in person)

Gianna Sobol	Television writer Known for: *True Blood*; *Counterpart*	July 24, 2017 (in person) October 14, 2021 (by Zoom) July 7, 2025 (by phone)
Richard Socarides	Writer and media and political strategist Known for: White House adviser to President Bill Clinton	January 20, 2012 (in person)
Eric Stonestreet	Actor Known for: *Modern Family*	June 14, 2012 (by phone)
Larry Sullivan	Actor Known for: *Will & Grace*; *Modern Family*; *Big Little Lies*; *Trinkets*	April 27, 2012 (in person) July 23, 2017 (in person)
Amir Talai	Actor Known for: *What to Expect When You're Expecting*; *LA to Vegas*	January 10, 2018 (in person)
Meredith Talusan	Writer and editor	October 10, 2017 (in person)
Hudson Taylor	College athlete (wrestling) and sports advocate Known for: Athlete Ally	September 20, 2012 (in person) September 27, 2017 (in person) February 16, 2022 (by Zoom)
Rose Troche	Television and film producer, director, writer Known for: *Go Fish*; *The Safety of Objects*; *The L Word*	May 31, 2012 (in person)
Guinevere Turner	Actor, writer, director Known for: *Go Fish*; *The Watermelon Woman*; *The L Word*; *The Owls*	December 7, 2012 (in person)
Michael Urie	Actor Known for: *Ugly Betty*; *Partners*; *The Temperamentals*; *Buyer & Cellar*; *Torch Song*; *Shrinking*	March 5, 2013 (in person)
Carly Usdin	Director and writer Known for: *Suicide Kale*; *The Syd + TP Show*	February 3, 2022 (by Zoom)

Kirk Walker	College coach (softball)	December 7, 2012 (in person)
Rutina Wesley	Actor Known for: *True Blood*; *Queen Sugar*; *The Last of Us*	September 24, 2013 (by phone)
Russell Wetanson	Entertainment lawyer and executive	October 20, 2011 (in person)
Ellen D. Williams	Actor Known for: *How I Met Your Mother*; *Baskets*	February 15, 2022 (by Zoom)
Judd Winick	Writer, artist, reality television cast member Known for: *The Real World: San Francisco*; *Pedro and Me*	May 15, 2012 (by phone)
Kenji Yoshino	Academic and legal scholar	April 23, 2012 (in person)
Laura Zak	Writer, actor, producer, activist Known for: *Her Story*; *Danger & Eggs*	January 11, 2018 (in person)
Cyd Zeigler	Sports writer and advocate Known for: Outsports.com	October 21, 2011 (in person) December 6, 2012 (in person)
Dave Zirin	Sports and politics writer Known for: *The Nation*; *A People's History of Sports in the United States*; *Game Over*	July 16, 2013 (in person)
Anonymous	Television executive	November 8, 2011 (in person)
Anonymous	Writer and producer	November 21, 2011 (in person)
Anonymous	Rep (publicist, agent, or manager)	January 12, 2012 (in person)
Anonymous	athlete	March 29, 2012 (in person)
Anonymous	Entertainment magazine editor	April 3, 2012 (in person)
Anonymous	Actor	April 26, 2012 (in person)
Anonymous	Television writer	April 26, 2012 (in person)
Anonymous	Actor	April 27, 2012 (in person)
Anonymous	Talent manager	May 15, 2012 (by phone)

Anonymous	Nonprofit leader	October 3, 2012 (in person)
Anonymous	Television producer and executive	October 9, 2012 (in person)
Anonymous	Athlete and sports advocate	October 11, 2012 (in person)
Anonymous	Nonprofit leader	June 18, 2013 (in person)
Anonymous	Nonprofit leader	June 18, 2013 (in person)
Anonymous	Film production executive	July 25, 2013 (in person)
Anonymous	Music executive	July 31, 2013 (in person)
Anonymous	college sports executive	February 21, 2014 (in person)
Anonymous	college sports executive	February 21, 2014 (in person)
Anonymous	Professional sports league executive	March 21, 2014 (in person)
Anonymous	Professional sports league executive	March 21, 2014 (in person)
Anonymous	Professional sports league executive	March 27, 2014 (in person)
Anonymous	Professional sports league executive	July 2, 2014 (in person)
Anonymous	Actor and activist	September 13, 2022 (by Zoom)
Anonymous	Actor	October 3, 2022 (by Zoom)

Note: "Known for" is selective and incomplete here, and includes projects that are most relevant for this book. Anonymous participants either asked not to be named or I was unable to reach them to ask them if they wanted to opt out of being named. They are arranged by the date they were interviewed.

NOTES

PREFACE

1. No identity labels are perfect or perfectly inclusive, and conventions change quite quickly. I have chosen to use "LGBTQ+," primarily, because I feel it best reflects the politics and history of the social movement story I tell and reflects a widely used umbrella term in the US movement now. I also use "queer" as a broad term for people who have been minoritized due to their sexuality and/or gender identity or expression. Throughout the book, I use the terminology of the people and publications I am citing throughout, which means that sometimes my language varies.
2. I owe the title to one of the people I interviewed for this book: David Craig, a Hollywood producer, LGBTQ+ activist, and University of Southern California scholar (David Craig, interview with author, June 11, 2014).

INTRODUCTION

1. Romano, "The Cruel Truth"; *The New York Times' The Daily* podcast episode "25 Days to Go"; Simmons-Duffin, "Trans Health Care."
2. Harrison, "On Football Saturdays and Sundays."
3. One version of the commercial can be found here: https://youtu.be/VVU7pYq3WHw?si=uGkN1EGrzFsXMA_W.
4. Demirjian, "Federal Workers Ordered."
5. Wilson, "Trump Says."
6. Hunter, *Culture Wars*, 50.
7. Bronski, *The Pleasure Principle*, 8.
8. On belonging, see powell and Menendian, *Belonging Without Othering*. They write of the goal of belonging that "belonging exists when all social groups in society are included in critical institutions in society and in their communities; are recognized and accorded visibility within those institutions or communities;

have agency, including the ability to actively participate in shaping those critical institutions and communities; and report a sense of connection or feeling of belonging. Belonging is both perceptual and tangible; a feeling and a practice; subjective and objective" (144).

9. Quoted in Fetner, *How the Religious Right*, 80. Also see Gamson, *Freaks Talk Back*; Gross, *Contested Closets*; Hart-Brinson, *The Gay Marriage Generation*; Hubbs, *Rednecks, Queers, and Country Music*; Signorile, *Queer in America*; Stein, *The Stranger Next Door.*
10. And what exactly is a "social movement"? One helpful definition comes from sociologists of culture Francesca Polletta and Edwin Amenta, who "define social movements as sustained and organized collective actions to effect change in institutions by citizens or members of institutions who are excluded from routine decision-making" ("The Cultural Impact of Social Movements," 281).
11. Although sociologist Amin Ghaziani also wrote that a limitation to the "culture wars" framing of LGBTQ+ social change is that it seems to capture "often the most explosive and violent parts" and not "the experiences we have on our own and with others as we explore our attractions, actions, and identities together—all those tiny moments that mold our minds and hearts" (*Sex Cultures*, 185).
12. Thanks to Nina Mauceri for this reminder and a conversation at a critical point when I was worried about the title.
13. On sexuality, gender identity, and national identity/citizenship, see also Bérubé, *Coming Out Under Fire*; Frank, *Awakening*; Gamson, *Freaks Talk Back*; Seidman, *Beyond the Closet*; Walters, *The Tolerance Trap.*
14. This number remained at 64 percent in 2024 and 2025, as well, though it represents a dip from a high point of 71 percent in 2022 (Gallup, "LGBTQ+ Rights").
15. Gallup, "LGBTQ+ Rights"; Hart-Brinson, *The Gay Marriage Generation*; Pew Research Center, "Attitudes on Same-Sex Marriage"; Pew Research Center, "Growing Support for Gay Marriage"; Public Religion Research Institute, *Americans' Support.*
16. Kiley and Vaisey, "Measuring Stability and Change," 478.
17. Ibid., 494. Also see Ekstam, "The Liberalization of American Attitudes."
18. Liptak, "Civil Rights Law."
19. Burga, "The Implications of Supreme Court's 303 Creative."
20. Duberman, *Has the Gay Movement Failed?*; GLAAD, *Accelerating Acceptance, 2021*; GLAAD, "Incidents of Anti-LGBTQ+ Hate Violence in 2019"; Hauck, "Anti-LGBT Hate Crimes"; Kralik, "'Bathroom Bill' Legislative Tracking"; Movement Advancement Project, *LGBTQ Policy Spotlight*; Signorile, *It's Not Over.*
21. Republican Party, *2024 GOP Platform*, 15.
22. Berman and Hurewitz, "LGBTQ+ Americans"; Cappelletti, "Michigan Adds"; Cawley, "Massachusetts AG"; Harmon and Macur, "Judge Temporarily Stops"; Karnowski, "Minnesota Governor"; Radde, "What Does the Respect for Marriage Act Do?"

23. Bokat-Lindell, "How Trans Children Became a Political Football"; Weigel, "Why Republicans Keep Running Against Trans Rights." For a very useful political overview, also see *The New York Times' The Daily* podcast episode "How the G.O.P. Picked Trans Kids as a Rallying Cry."
24. Choi, "Record Number." Also see Blow, "Yes, We're in an L.G.B.T.Q. State of Emergency."
25. For interactive maps of these 2024 and 2025 bills, see https://www.aclu.org/legislative-attacks-on-lgbtq-rights-2024 and https://www.aclu.org/legislative-attacks-on-lgbtq-rights-2025.
26. Narea and Cineas, "The GOP's Coordinated National Campaign."
27. Astor, "Trump Administration Will End."
28. Diaz, "Florida's Governor Signs."
29. Choi, "Record Number." For an excellent resource for updated policy information, see the state-by-state policy maps produced by the Movement Advancement Project, e.g., *LGBTQ Curricular Laws.*
30. Narea and Cineas, "The GOP's Coordinated National Campaign"; Thompson, "Why American Teens Are So Sad." Also see Blow, "Yes, We're in an L.G.B.T.Q. State of Emergency."
31. Baum, "Devastating Blows"; Cowan, "Hospitals Are Limiting." Also see Baum, "Trump's DOJ."
32. Liptak, "Justices Let Parents"; Liptak, "Supreme Court Upholds."
33. See, e.g., Blee et al., *Out of Hiding*; Caiani and Tranfíc, "Weaving the Transnational Anti-Gender Networks."
34. Beauchamp, "Could Clarence Thomas's Dobbs Concurrence."
35. Pfeiffer, *Battling the Big Lie*, 68.
36. In 2021 surveys, 65 percent of Republicans supported anti-discrimination laws to protect LGBTQ+ people, including 79 percent among moderate Republicans and 60 percent of conservative Republicans. In these surveys, approximately half of Republicans supported marriage equality, including 67 percent of moderate and 41 percent of conservative Republicans (Public Religion Research Institute, *Americans' Support*).
37. Gallup, "LGBTQ+ Rights." Also see Data for Progress, "Americans Are Divided"; and Rector, "Americans Approve."
38. GLAAD, *Accelerating Acceptance, 2021.*
39. Parker et al., "Americans' Complex Views."
40. Human Rights Campaign, "Fatal Violence"; Preston, "The Anatomy of Transmisogynoir." Also see the results of the 2022 US Transgender Survey in James et al., *Early Insights.*
41. Todaro, "LGBTQ+ Adults."
42. Sullivan, "How the Gay Rights Movement." For an incredible rejoinder, see the discussion by Matt Bernstein in his *A Bit Fruity* podcast, entitled "*The New York Times* Thinks Gays Have Gone Too Far."

43. And *social change* can mean many things. As two scholars of the connection between comedy and activism wrote, it can include "building public awareness, shaping individual attitudes and behaviors, shifting social norms and practices, encouraging public engagement, setting a media agenda, and influencing policy" (Chattoo and Feldman, *A Comedian and an Activist*, 5).
44. For this argument that art, culture, pop culture, and sports matter in this way, often in a way that scholars ignore or deny, see, e.g., Gamson, *Claims to Fame*; Halberstam, *The Queer Art of Failure*; Reed, *The Art of Protest*; Rupp and Taylor, *Drag Queens at the 801 Cabaret*; Taylor et al., "Culture and Mobilization"; Zirin, *A People's History of Sports*.
45. See Herlock, "A Playlist."
46. Cooper, "5 Empowering Ads"; Econsultancy, "17 Marketing Campaigns"; Gay, "Fifty Years Ago"; Prinzivalli, "The 10 Most Groundbreaking Beauty Campaigns."
47. On the trailblazing role of progressive TV writer and producer Norman Lear, who created *All in the Family*, among many other groundbreaking shows, see Nussbaum, *I Like to Watch*.
48. Brownstein, *The Power and the Glitter*; Doherty, *Hollywood and Hitler*; Gabler, *An Empire of Their Own*; Renov and Brook, "Editorial Introduction"; Ross, *Hitler in Los Angeles*.
49. Gamson defines Hollywood as "not a geographical term but one describing, often in misleadingly mythical ways, a loose group of professional cultural workers" ("Stopping the Spin," 92n1).
50. Brownstein, *The Power and the Glitter*; Ross, *Hollywood Left and Right*; Signorile, *Queer in America*.
51. For important scholarly attention to this connection between culture and movements for social change around gender and sexuality, see, e.g., Amenta and Polletta, "The Cultural Impact of Social Movements"; Chauncey, *Gay New York*; Faderman and Timmons, *Gay L.A.*; Polletta and Amenta, *Changing Minds*; Polletta et al., "Social Movements in the Commercial Public Sphere"; Van Dyke and Taylor, "The Cultural Outcomes of Social Movements"; White, *Pre-Gay L.A.* And especially on cultural strategies and the marriage movement, see Ghaziani et al., "Cycles of Sameness and Difference"; Moscowitz, *The Battle over Marriage*; Taylor et al., "Culture and Mobilization." And more broadly on social movements, media, and culture, see the recent example of Amenta and Caren, *Rough Draft of History*.
52. James, "Gay Buffalo Teen Commits Suicide"; Kinser, "Gaga's Emotional Tribute."
53. Bryan Rosenberg conducted all of the interviews with me from October 2011 to January 2018. It is my strong impulse to use first-person plural language when I introduce these interviews throughout the book, so that I do not, in any way, erase or minimize Bryan's involvement in and contribution to this project. However, for clarity's sake, I have chosen to use first-person singular language

throughout. The "we" is implied here, and Bryan's contribution to this work has been invaluable.

54. Ohmann, "Knowing/Creating Wants," 224.
55. See Appendix B for a full list of the people I interviewed.
56. While it would be helpful to draw on what celebrities have said to others, I have chosen not to quote many secondary interviews. A number of people I interviewed reported to me that they had the experience of being misquoted or misrepresented by journalists to whom they had granted interviews. For this reason, I have chosen to include secondary quotes—that I did not gather myself—very sparingly, because I cannot be sure that they accurately reflect the words and intended meanings of their speaker. But if quotes have clearly come directly, or in an apparently unmediated way, from people themselves, like in podcast interviews, I have felt that I can responsibly use these as secondary source material.
57. Television and film are not, of course, the only pop cultural forms that have changed in massive ways in recent decades, with the shift to digital delivery of content and to social media as a way to share work and to bring artists closer to their audiences. While I do not focus extensively on music in the book, I recommend, on the history of the music industry and its shifts in recent years, Bullock, *David Bowie Made Me Gay*, and Taylor, *The Sounds of Capitalism*.
58. See Gitlin, *Inside Prime Time*. Or, as sociologist Laura Grindstaff plainly wrote: "The purpose of virtually all television entertainment (and television news as well) is to commodify audiences and sell them to advertisers for profit" (*The Money Shot*, 33).
59. Painter, "How the New York Media Covered the Stonewall Riots."
60. Powdermaker, *Hollywood, the Dream Factory*, 327.
61. Gitlin, *Inside Prime Time*, 16.
62. Also see Auletta, *Three Blind Mice*; Christian, *Open TV*; Gamson, *Claims to Fame*; Gray, *Out in the Country*; Jenkins, *Convergence Culture*; Marcus, *The Drama of Celebrity*.
63. E.g., see Adatto, *Picture Perfect*; Auletta, *Three Blind Mice*; Becker, *Gay TV and Straight America*; Berman, "Reality TV"; Bessner, "The Life and Death of Hollywood"; Caves, *Creative Industries*; Christian, *Open TV*; Jacobs, "Entertainment Media"; Lotz, *After Mass Media*; Martin, *Difficult Men*; Nussbaum, *I Like to Watch*; Ortner, *Not Hollywood*; Poniewozik, *Audience of One*; Powdermaker, *Hollywood, the Dream Factory*; Prindle, *Risky Business*; Spigel, *Make Room for TV*; Tannenbaum and Marks, *I Want My MTV*.
64. Auletta, *Three Blind Mice*. And as Poniewozik explains: "Before cable, TV could only monetize breadth of interest. You made money by airing things a lot of people liked a little. The pay TV model monetized *depth* of interest. HBO made money by airing things a relative few people liked a lot, enough to pay for them" (*Audience of One*, 92).
65. Martin, *Difficult Men*, 10.

66. Network TV is public and subject, therefore, to FCC regulation and the oversight of Standards and Practices monitor.
67. Ron Cowen and Daniel Lipman, interview with author, April 18, 2012. A note on my interviews: I have obtained permission to use real names of participants throughout, unless otherwise noted, and all participants have reviewed their quotes that I have included here, which are transcribed verbatim from audio recordings. The first time in each chapter that I include a quote from a participant, I will note the source, then all subsequent quotations from that person, unless otherwise noted, are from the same interview. In a few cases, to retain anonymity, I explicitly do not attribute some interview quotes.
68. Poniewozik, "'Orange Is the New Black.'" For an excellent profile of Netflix, see season 2 of Vox Media's *Land of the Giants* podcast, entitled *The Netflix Effect*.
69. Andreeva, "Ted Sarandos Marks Decade"; Spangler, "Step Aside, Netflix."
70. Baine, "How Many Streaming Services"; Barnes, "The Streaming Era"; Koblin, "It's Official"; Koblin and Steel, "At the Head of the Pack"; Schneider and Aurthur, "R.I.P. Cable TV"; Weiner, "The Great Race."
71. Adrienne Erickson, interview with author, November 10, 2021.
72. Koblin and Steel, "At the Head of the Pack"; Weiner, "The Great Race."
73. Caves, *Creative Industries*, 314.
74. As media scholar Henry Jenkins explains this broader phenomenon, in his canonical book, *Convergence Culture*: "Fueling this technological convergence is a shift in patterns of media ownership. Whereas old Hollywood focused on cinema, the new media conglomerates have controlling interests across the entire entertainment industry. Warner Bros. produces film, television, popular music, computer games, Web sites, toys, amusement park rides, books, newspapers, magazines, and comics" (16). For some examples of consolidating business deals in recent years, see Baker, "GE to Sell Rest of NBC Stake"; Bart, "Conglomeration Is Snuffing Out Courage"; James, "ViacomCBS Is Renamed."
75. Barnes, "Disney Moves" and "For Disney's Iger."
76. For example, Focus Features is part of NBCUniversal, which is owned by Comcast. On the streaming side, e.g., the merger of HBO's parent company, WarnerMedia, with Discovery made headlines in 2022 when it was revealed that this business deal signaled a threat to the diversity of the HBO/HBO Max team and the content it retained online (see Manno, "Laid-Off HBO Max Execs"). In her book about independent film, anthropologist Sherry B. Ortner writes that the late 1980s and 1990s saw a rise in independent film at a time when the "conglomerization of the studios" produced both a rise in the "blockbuster" films that got their start in the mid-1970s, with Steven Spielberg's *Jaws*, and a boon to independent filmmaking as these same studios developed "specialty divisions." Ortner writes that these "two seemingly contradictory trends were part of a single story, the story of the diversification of studio production and marketing practices in an effort to capture both mass and niche audiences" (*Not Hollywood*, 97).

77. Bessner, "The Life and Death of Hollywood"; Morgan, "What Will the Movie Industry Look Like After Covid?"; Roussel, *Representing Talent*, chap. 2. *The New York Times' The Daily* podcast reported, at the end of 2024, that nine of the top grossing movies of the year were sequels—and the last was *Wicked*, which is also based on existing intellectual property. The *Times* reported this in the context of risk aversion in Hollywood.
78. Herships and Smith, "Is Movie Night Back?"; Lang and Rubin, "How Movie Theaters Fought to Survive"; Sperling, "Hollywood's 'We're Not in Kansas Anymore' Moment."
79. For early reporting on this deal, see Rocha, "What to Know."
80. David Monahan, interview with author, April 27, 2012.
81. On the centrality of television and its impact on "the general public sphere," see Jacobs, "Entertainment Media," 325.

CHAPTER ONE

1. Chris Mosier, interview with author, October 12, 2021. Also see *The New York Times' The Daily* podcast episode "How the G.O.P. Picked Trans Kids as a Rallying Cry."
2. https://www.instagram.com/p/DCFjZ0vy2rJ/?img_index=1.
3. This is a common refrain in the public discussion of queer visibility. See, e.g., Tensley, "The Double-Edged Sword of Queer Visibility."
4. Rosentiel, "Four-in-Ten Americans"; Schmidt, "Americans' Views Flipped." Also see chapter 6.
5. For this finding with gay and lesbian athletes, see Anderson et al., *Out in Sport*.
6. Kramer, "Why Do Straights Hate Gays?"
7. See, e.g., Zhang, "The Radical Act of Invisibility."
8. Gamson, *Freaks Talk Back*, 212; Gossett et al., *Trap Door*; Netflix, *Disclosure*; Steinbock, "The Riotous State." Another must-read on this point is Walters, *All the Rage*.
9. Russo, *The Celluloid Closet*, 248, 219, 178, 325, 322–23. For more on this genius activist, see the documentary "Vito," https://vitorussomovie.com/.
10. For helpful overview discussions and timelines of LGBTQ+ representation, see Bendix, "How Ellen DeGeneres Changed TV History"; Bianco, "20-Year Flashback"; Buzinski and Zeigler, *The Outsports Revolution*; Cavalcante, *Struggling for Ordinary*; Damshenas, "46 of the Best"; D'Arminio, "Gay Teens on TV"; Green, "A Brief History"; Musto, "From Liberace to Sam Smith"; Out.com Editors, "A Timeline." I also recommend consulting the many scholars of and commentators on popular culture that have since identified and critiqued the ways in which LGBTQ+ people appear on stage and screen. Among many useful references, see Alwood, *Straight News*; Becker, *Gay TV and Straight America*; Bendix, "13 Same-Sex TV Kisses"; Bronski, *The Pleasure Principle*; Bullock, *David Bowie Made Me*

Gay; Cagle, "Special Report: The Gay '90s"; Curtin, *"We Can Always Call Them Bulgarians"*; Fetner, *How the Religious Right*; Gamson, *Freaks Talk Back*; Ghaziani, *The Dividends of Dissent*; Gregory, "The 200 Best"; Hart-Brinson, *The Gay Marriage Generation*; Kopay and Young, *The David Kopay Story*; Seidman, *Beyond the Closet*; Serano, *Whipping Girl*; Signorile, *Queer in America*; Streitmatter, *From 'Perverts' to 'Fab Five'*; Walters, *All the Rage* and *The Tolerance Trap*; Warner, "Let's Go, Lesbians"; White, "What 'The Golden Girls' Got Right."

11. Chauncey, *Why Marriage?* On this point and for another good overview, also see Johnson and Lang, "Gay Rights and Hollywood."
12. Gitlin, *Inside Prime Time*. The Gay and Lesbian Alliance Against Defamation (now simply called GLAAD, for broader inclusivity) formed in 1985, specifically to protest the ways in which the news media was covering the AIDS crisis. It then became a broad activist force for positive and inclusive LGBTQ+ representation in American culture (see "GLAAD History and Highlights").
13. Berlant and Freeman, "Queer Nationality"; Bronski, *The Pleasure Principle*; Chauncey, *Why Marriage?*; Gross, *Contested Closets*; Queer Nation, "Queer Nation NY History"; Vaid, *Virtual Equality*.
14. Gross, *Contested Closets*; Masaki, "Today Is the Anniversary."
15. GLAAD publishes annual studies of televisions shows and studio films. These provide excellent data on LGBTQ+ representation and are resources that I consult regularly, especially to understand change over time and to examine intersectionality in representation.
16. See Cramer, "What Does Queer Gen Z Want on TV?"
17. Bendix, "13 Same-Sex TV Kisses"; Fallon, "On 'Glee,' Two Boys Kiss"; Keith, "Life Before Kurt."
18. Nearly seven years after the 2014 cover, *Time* featured its first transgender man, Elliot Page, on its cover (see Holland, "Elliot Page").
19. Romano, "Is J. K. Rowling Transphobic?"
20. See, e.g., Bissinger, "He Says Goodbye, She Says Hello"; Crooked Minis, *Pride on Screen: Trans Visibility*; Lang, "Eddie Redmayne Criticizes"; Meyerowitz, *How Sex Changed*; Natalie, "Laverne Cox's 'Doubt' Love Story"; Pearlman et al. "Arts and Culture"; Steinmetz, "The Transgender Tipping Point"; Wong, "Emmys Tell Non-Binary Star."
21. Jung, "Jeff Varner's Outing." For a clip from this episode, see https://youtu.be/rtdICC9QyZA?si=G9oS6ONC3jt0aUV2.
22. Thanks to Laura Portwood-Stacer for a formative conversation on this framing.
23. Alan Poul, interview with author, April 26, 2012.
24. Paris Barclay, interview with author, April 27, 2012.
25. Bruni, "ABC's Gay Wednesdays" and "Basketball's Gay Paragon"; Harris, *The Rise and Fall of Gay Culture*; Ross, *Hitler in Los Angeles*.
26. Gates, *Double Negative*; Keegan, "On the Necessity of Bad Trans Objects"; Keegan and Horak, "Introduction."

27. On this point of the development of queer representation out of the 1990s and early years of the new millennium, Sender wrote: "In order not to offend mass audiences or the advertisers who sought their attention, lesbian and gay characters had to be beyond reproach. But saints are boring. Before long the contrast was striking between these flattened characters and the complicated, charismatic, three-dimensional antiheroes who populated cable shows. In order to retain audience interest, streaming services portrayed complex LGBTQ+ characters in story arcs characterized by challenging sexual activity, moral ambiguity, and political engagement" ("The Queer Vanguard," 165).
28. Keegan, "On the Necessity of Bad Trans Objects."
29. Gates, *Double Negative*, 26.
30. Wilson Cruz, interview with author, December 7, 2012.
31. Alan Ball, interview with author, January 18, 2012.
32. Samy Nour Younes Figaredo, interview with author, September 27, 2022.
33. Trish Bendix, interview with author, July 24, 2017. See also Bendix, "'Faking It' Finale."
34. Lea DeLaria, interview with author, September 19, 2014.
35. I have made the imperfect choice to include aspects of identity that individual participants, themselves, referenced as important to their experience as intersectional with gender and/or sexuality or when I felt it was important to mark privilege, especially, even if participants did not name it.
36. LZ Granderson, interview with author, April 22, 2013.
37. Meredith Talusan, interview with author, October 10, 2017. Also see Cavalcante, *Struggling for Ordinary*; Mock, *Redefining Realness*; Serano, *Whipping Girl*; and Talusan, "25 Years of Transphobia," "8 Trans Tropes," and *Fairest*.
38. Jen Richards, interview with author, January 11, 2018.
39. E.g., Snorton, *Nobody Is Supposed to Know*.
40. Sedgwick, *Epistemology of the Closet*, 71.
41. Chauncey, *Why Marriage?* and *Gay New York*; Gross, *Contested Closets*; Prindle, *Risky Business*; Seidman, *Beyond the Closet*.
42. Hadleigh, *Hollywood Gays*, 13; Gross, *Contested Closets*. Also see Signorile, *Queer in America*.
43. Bullock, *David Bowie Made Me Gay*; Chauncey, *Gay New York*; Curtin, *"We Can Always Call Them Bulgarians"*; Faderman and Timmons, *Gay L.A.*; Powdermaker, *Hollywood, the Dream Factory*.
44. Jones, "LGBTQ+ Identification"; Parker et al., "Americans' Complex Views"; Rogers, "More Americans Identify."
45. In May 2007, journalist Michael Musto published an *Out* magazine cover story that helped to popularize the term. He wrote that a glass closet is "that complex but popular contraption that allows public figures to avoid the career repercussions of any personal disclosure while living their lives with a certain degree of integrity" ("The Glass Closet"). Also see Musto, "The Glass Closet, Revisited,"

and Signorile, *Queer in America*. C. Riley Snorton, in *Nobody Is Supposed to Know*, connects the concept of the "glass closet" to Sedgwick's work, but adds that the glass closet as both a *durable* and a *fragile* mechanism (17), "a space I define as marked by hypervisibility and confinement, spectacle, and speculation" (4).

46. Armstrong, *Forging Gay Identities*, 89; Sessums, "Jonathan Groff Talks."
47. James Duke Mason, interview with author, October 21, 2011.
48. Yoshino, *Covering*, 18, ix; Goffman, *Stigma*. Pat Griffin also wrote about covering in her classic *Strong Women, Deep Closets*. Griffin identified covering as one of the "identity-management strategies" for lesbian coaches, in that it involved "concealing lesbian identity" though not denying it (135). For recent references to covering theory with respect to pop culture and LGBTQ+ identity, see Signorile, *It's Not Over*; Walters, *The Tolerance Trap*.
49. Badgett and Herman, *Sexual Orientation and Gender Identity Diversity in Entertainment*. Also see Helligar, "Does Hollywood Fail Gay Actors Who Are Out from the Start?" As sociologist Steven Seidman wrote in *Beyond the Closet*: "Shame, fear, terror, and disgust not only are the emotional stuff of the closet, but sustain it" (124).
50. Zeigler, "Pro Sports Are Finally Ready."
51. Amin El Gamal, interview with author, January 13, 2022.
52. On agents and "relationship work," see Roussel, *Representing Talent*, 99.
53. Elliot Page also writes about this kind of professional closeting in his memoir, *Pageboy*, e.g., 106.
54. Russo wrote in the 1980s of the "closet mentality" of "closeted gay people" in Hollywood, whom he called "among the most uptight and uncooperative stumbling blocks in the path of positive gay projects" (*The Celluloid Closet*, xi–xii). Signorile, too, writing about the early '90s, connected the oppressive role of gay people in Hollywood to the role of assimilationist, upwardly mobile Jews in Hollywood in the early twentieth century: "Closeted homosexuals in the business accommodate themselves to the prevailing homophobia. In the same way, Jews in Hollywood accommodated themselves to anti-Semitism in the twenties and thirties" (*Queer in America*, 254).
55. Shadi Petosky, interview with author, October 14, 2021.
56. Aagenes, "Coaches Need to Be Public Allies"; Anderson, *In the Game*.
57. On the "'distraction' myth," see Zeigler, "We Should Never Hear About a Gay NFL Player Being a Media 'Distraction' Ever Again."
58. Griffin, *Strong Women, Deep Closets*, 213. Of course, policing bodies and gender varies by sport and, relatedly, by race, among other factors. See Gittings and Riddell, "WNBA Superstar Sue Bird."
59. Pat Griffin, interview with author, January 9, 2014; also see Aagenes, "Come Out Like a Girl."
60. Street, "JoJo Siwa Explains."
61. Oliver and Yasharoff, "JoJo Siwa Opens Up."

62. Cyphers and Fagan, "Unhealthy Climate"; Griffin, *Strong Women, Deep Closets.*
63. For one excellent profile, see Bachman, "Sherri Murrell."
64. Also see Griffin, "Closeted Lesbian Coaches."
65. Nevin Caple, interview with author, October 8, 2013.
66. Zeigler, "The Number of Out Coaches."
67. Zeigler and Buzinski, "Out in Sports Study."
68. Mock, *Redefining Realness*, 257.
69. Thanks, again, to Laura Portwood-Stacer for a key conversation on this insight.
70. For an example from Hollywood, again see Elliot Page's autobiography, *Pageboy*, e.g., chap. 23.
71. Kopay and Young, *The David Kopay Story*; Pallone with Steinberg, *Behind the Mask*; Tuaolo with Rosengren, *Alone in the Trenches.*
72. Burke with Sherman, *Out at Home.*
73. Tuaolo with Rosengren, *Alone in the Trenches*, 3, 154–56, 206. Also on the cost of the closet for athletes, see Granderson, "Another Ex-Athlete Comes Out?"
74. Bean with Bill, *Going the Other Way.*
75. Billy Bean, interview with author, December 7, 2012.
76. Quote from Bean, "One Pioneering Gay Athlete Thanks Another."
77. Bean with Bill, *Going the Other Way.*
78. Footer, "MLB Names Bean"; Burke with Sherman, *Out at Home*, 181–92.
79. "The coming out imperative" is identified in a different context by Seal, *The Interruption of Heteronormativity in Higher Education*, chap. 10.
80. D'Emilio, *Sexual Politics, Sexual Communities*; Faderman, *The Gay Revolution.*
81. Quoted in Armstrong, *Forging Gay Identities*, 70. Also see Faderman and Timmons, *Gay L.A.*; Meyer and Gamson, "The Challenge of Cultural Elites"; Gross, *Contested Closets*; Seidman et al., "The Politics of Authenticity."
82. Jamie Babbit, interview with author, July 27, 2012.
83. Andrew Goldstein, interview with author, June 11, 2014. Also see Garber, "'Now I Get to Be Like Everybody Else'"; Zeigler, "Robbie Rogers Was Not the First."
84. Brian Ellner, interview with author, February 27, 2012. Also see Hoffman, "A Gay Rights Power Player."
85. Patrick Burke, interview with author, September 17, 2012.
86. Zeigler and Buzinski, "Out in Sports Study."
87. Harper, "Michael Sam Met"; Hod, "How Howard Bragman."
88. Bragman, *Where's My Fifteen Minutes?*, 208; Howard Bragman, interview with author, January 20, 2012. Also see Hod, "How Howard Bragman"; Litman, "Meet the Man." Bragman also sat for an interview with another academic, Julia Himberg, for *The New Gay for Pay*, 84–92.
89. For this paragraph and below, see John Amaechi, interview with author, April 26, 2014. Also see Amaechi with Bull, *Man in the Middle*; Andrews, "John Amaechi"; Jackson, "Why I've Come Out."
90. Amaechi with Bull, *Man in the Middle*, 272, 201.

91. Crary, "New Playbook Emerges"; Wilbon, "Sexuality Disclosed, Ignorance Exposed"; Zeigler, "Players, Coaches and the Media React."
92. For a discussion of outing, see Bronski, *The Pleasure Principle*, 170–82.
93. Collins with Lidz, "The Gay Athlete," 34. On the way that race matters here, also see Arceneaux, "'Black and Gay.'"
94. In February 2022, Griner was stopped in Russia, where she played basketball in the WNBA off-season, when an airport official alleged that Griner was carrying vape cartridges containing cannabis oil. She was detained in Russia for nearly ten months before she was released by the United States in a prisoner swap. The superstar's coach on the Phoenix Mercury, Vanessa Nygaard, referenced the misogyny, racism, and homophobia in the way that Griner's case was covered, noting to the media how this might be handled if Griner's equivalent in men's basketball were facing similar circumstances: "If it was LeBron, he'd be home, right? . . . It's a statement about the value of women. It's a statement about the value of a Black person. It's a statement about the value of a gay person" (quoted in Moore, "Phoenix Mercury Coach").
95. This remains true now, as the mainstream media covers the anti-trans politics and policymaking of the past few years. One study by Media Matters for America and GLAAD found that *The New York Times*, for the year from mid-February 2023 to mid-February 2024, failed to contextualize or fact-check "anti-trans misinformation in quotes" in 18 percent of articles, and often completely omitted trans experts and perspectives from their stories on anti-trans legislation. In 66 percent of these stories, they simply "failed to quote a trans person" (GLAAD, "*The New York Times* Fails").
96. Kye Allums, initial interview with author, March 12, 2013; updated quote here from December 2, 2025.
97. Chris Mosier, interview with author, June 7, 2013.
98. LeBrun, "'This Is Who I Am'"; Russell, as told to Arnovitz, "No Distractions"; Schwab, "Former Cowboys."
99. See Buzinski, "Raiders Player Carl Nassib." And, generally, on social media use among LGBTQ+ Americans and among young Americans, see Pew Research Center, "Social Media Use in 2021" and "A Survey of LGBT Americans."
100. Jacobs, "Lil Nas X"; Andrew, "Why Jojo Siwa's Coming Out"; Coleman, "Lil Uzi Vert"; Draughorne, "Rapper Lil Uzi Vert."
101. Monahan and Sullivan are also, I should disclose, friends of mine.
102. Bonin, "A Gay Kiss."
103. See Nölke, "Making Diversity Conform?"
104. Editors, "Greatest Gay Dads of the Year"; Hogan, "Get to Know"; Lowder, "Stephen Colbert Has Problems"; Wong, "'Family Group' Is Fuming."
105. David Monahan and Larry Sullivan, interview with author, April 27, 2012.
106. Butcher, "Heartstopper Star"; Harris, "Is Celebrity 'Queer Baiting' Really Such a Crime?" Mack, "The Queerbaiting Discourse"; Oliver, "Kit Connor."

107. Anderson, "Kit Connor"; Sim, "*Heartstopper*'s Kit Connor."
108. Hans, "L.G.B.T.Q. Teens."
109. Zackary Drucker, interview with author, August 4, 2025.
110. Chase Joynt, interview with author, July 24, 2025.
111. Zhang, "The Radical Act of Invisibility." Also see Keegan, "On the Necessary of Bad Trans Objects": "In fact, media visibility may ensure further persecution as the wider public becomes familiar with—and more hostile toward—transgender identities" (26).

CHAPTER TWO

1. John Amaechi, interview with author, April 26, 2014. I should note that Amaechi was quite critical of the way that athletes were revered in this way. He said to me: "I know the lessons I learned from sport, and none of them were good. They were that I was more important than normal people. And that other people were normal people and I was extraordinary because I put a ball in a hole."
2. Chattoo and Feldman, *A Comedian and an Activist*, 158.
3. On rescuing some measure of agency in celebrity and fandom, I have learned a lot from Marcus, *The Drama of Celebrity*. Also see Chattoo and Feldman, *A Comedian and an Activist*, and Himberg, *The New Gay for Pay*. My approach draws on scholarship that takes seriously the role of celebrities and of pop culture in politics. See Cooper, *Celebrity Diplomacy*; Ross, *Hollywood Left and Right*; Rupp and Taylor, *Drag Queens at the 801 Cabaret*.
4. While I interviewed people who, of course, agreed to be interviewed and so felt that they had something to say on the topic of pop culture and LGBTQ+ social change, these participants held a wide range of political identities—some identifying to their core as longtime activists and some rejecting these identities almost completely.
5. Scholars who usefully historicize and grapple with the phenomenon and role of fame and celebrity—broadly and as it intersects with politics—include Berlin, *Toxic Fame*; Braudy, *The Frenzy of Renown*; Brownstein, *The Power and the Glitter*; Canon, *Actors, Athletes, and Astronauts*; Cooper, *Celebrity Diplomacy*; Doherty, *Hollywood and Hitler*; Gamson, *Claims to Fame*; Halpern, *Fame Junkies*; Hull, *Same-Sex Marriage*; Marcus, *The Drama of Celebrity*; Marwick, *Status Update*; Meyer and Gamson, "The Challenge of Cultural Elites"; Ross, *Hitler in Los Angeles* and *Hollywood Left and Right*; Street, "Celebrity Politicians"; West and Orman, *Celebrity Politics*; Zirin, *A People's History of Sports*.
6. Also see Hull, *Same-Sex Marriage*, and Lamont, *Seeing Others*, on a strategy that she calls "self-presentation" (103).
7. Burnton, "50 Stunning Olympic Moments"; Louganis with Marcus, *Breaking the Surface*.
8. Greg Louganis, interview with author, December 6, 2012.

9. Denis O'Hare, interview with author, December 14, 2011.
10. Shadi Petosky, interview with author, June 12, 2014.
11. Alec Mapa, interview with author, July 25, 2017.
12. See Richards, "I'm Not One to Go to Protests."
13. https://www.instagram.com/entertainmentlabor4palestine/?hl=en.
14. Amin El Gamal, interviews with author, January 12, 2018, and July 16, 2025.
15. Rory O'Malley, interview with author, April 30, 2013. For one feature on the organization, see Dominick, "Broadway Impact." Also see Baume, *Defining Marriage*. Broadway Impact also created a play, written by Oscar-winning screenwriter Dustin Lance Black, out of the transcripts of the court trial that challenged Proposition 8. They attracted some of the biggest names in Hollywood to perform in the original versions of the show, which was supported by American Foundation for Equal Rights, the organization that had been founded by famous liberal actor/director Rob Reiner and that had backed the lawsuit against Prop. 8. The show, titled 8, was performed in Los Angeles and New York, on Broadway. It was then posted on YouTube and was viewed widely there (https://www.youtube.com/watch?v=qlUG8F9uVgM). The Broadway Impact founders viewed 8 as a community-organizing and education tool. They made the play available (with free licensing) to local and school/college groups, and they provided artistic, marketing and media, and organizing support. There were, ultimately, more than five hundred productions of 8 in all fifty states and in nine countries, according to Jenny Kanelos.
16. https://www.espn.com/espn/photos/gallery/_/id/16797886/version/mobile/bodies-want-2016.
17. I also profiled Mosier in Stulberg, *LGBTQ Social Movements*. Mosier's Nike commercial can be found here: https://youtu.be/y3P6UBZHll8.
18. Chris Mosier, interview with author, June 7, 2013.
19. Rinkunas, "The Trans Athlete." Also for some examples of the extensive coverage of Mosier's accomplishments, see Ennis, "Chris Mosier"; Gleeson, "Transgender Duathlete"; Steele, "Chris Mosier."
20. Also on the ways in which "working conditions" and specifics of "their medium" impact the way that culture workers can impact change, see Lamont, *Seeing Others*, 103.
21. Historian Steven J. Ross makes a related point, noting the ways in which the profession itself might lend itself to actors' liberal politics: "The overwhelmingly liberal orientation of actors, then and now, can be partially understood as a byproduct of the demands of their craft. Playing a variety of characters, many of whom they did not necessarily like, fostered a sense of empathy and ability to understand issues and people outside their personal experience (*Hollywood Left and Right*, 96).
22. Abramovitch, "Joe Biden Cites."
23. On the connection between AIDS, activism, and arts/pop culture, as well as the ways in which AIDS affected arts industries and communities and substantially

spurred new activism in these industries, see Bronski, *The Pleasure Principle*; Bullock, *David Bowie Made Me Gay*; Carney, "AIDS and the Arts"; Faderman and Timmons, *Gay L.A.*; Hadleigh, *Hollywood Gays*; Harris, *The Rise and Fall of Gay Culture*; Prindle, *Risky Business*; Reed, *The Art of Protest*; Román, *Acts of Intervention*; Watney, *Policing Desire*. Also see Lamont's argument in *Seeing Others* that HIV/AIDS presents an example of the ways in which "the process of destigmatization" can come through popular culture, experts and celebrities who provide public support and education and new forms of "recognition" (148–49).

24. Journalist Gabriel Rotello wrote that Hudson's "illness was a great turning point in the epidemic, the moment when AIDS first became a burning national issue" (*Sexual Ecology*, 113). Also see Griffin, *All That Heaven Allows*; Gross, *Contested Closets*; Shilts, *And the Band Played On*; Streitmatter, *From 'Perverts' to 'Fab Five.'*
25. Political scientist Cathy J. Cohen wrote that when Johnson simultaneously announced his HIV status and his retirement from the Los Angeles Lakers, he "forever changed, at least in terms of quantity, the coverage focused on AIDS among African Americans" (*The Boundaries of Blackness*, 149). Also see Gross, *Contested Closets*; Zirin, *A People's History of Sports*.
26. Pearl, "How Nickelodeon Educated a Generation of Kids."
27. Butler and Kois, *The World Only Spins Forward*; Román, *Acts of Intervention*. And for a critical analysis, particularly about the commodification of AIDS and gay identity through theater and film, see Schulman, *Stagestruck*.
28. Larry Kramer, interview with the author, March 7, 2012.
29. On *Philadelphia*, see Seidman, *Beyond the Closet*.
30. Blotcher, "*An Early Frost*"; Duca, "You Have Two Men to Thank"; Gendel, "'An Early Frost.'"
31. Blotcher, "*An Early Frost*"; Duca, "You Have Two Men to Thank"; Harrington, "The Interviews."
32. Watney, *Policing Desire*.
33. Russo, *The Celluloid Closet*, 277.
34. Faderman, *Odd Girls and Twilight Lovers*, 54.
35. Ron Cowen and Daniel Lipman, interview with author, April 18, 2012.
36. Media scholar Larry Gross has written—and spoken with me—about the importance of reality television, and *The Real World* at the origins of this, for queer visibility more broadly. See Gross, "Hollywood's Closet," and Larry Gross, interview with author, July 26, 2012. Going even further back, *An American Family*, often considered to be the very first in the reality TV genre, followed the Loud family of Santa Barbara in 1973 and featured a pathbreaking storyline when one of the sons in the family, Lance, came out as gay (see Sommer, "From '70s Reality TV Star"). Also on the perhaps counterintuitive contribution of reality TV to "deeper considerations of race, gender, class, and sexuality precisely because it is perceived as frivolous, fun, and trashy," see Gates, *Double Negative*, 147. On

the history and cultural centrality of MTV, also see Tannenbaum and Marks, *I Want My MTV*.

37. See Winick, *Pedro and Me*.
38. See Poniewozik, *Audience of One*. *Entertainment Weekly* ranked every season of the thirty-two *Real World* installments, ranking the San Francisco season first and noting: "Zamora remains one of the biggest game changers in television history, both because of his openness about his experience with AIDS (and his death just hours after the show's season finale aired) and his televised commitment ceremony (the first ever) with Sean Sasser" (Heldman and Mercadante, "Ranking All").
39. Judd Winick, interview with author, May 15, 2012.
40. Dave Karger, interview with author, April 9, 2012.
41. Betancourt, "How TV Stories Have Shaped Our Understanding of AIDS."
42. Nisha Ganatra, interview with author, July 24, 2017.
43. Angela Robinson, interview with author, July 25, 2012.
44. Peter Paige, interview with author, June 11, 2014.
45. Peter Paige, interview with author, February 13, 2012; Paige, "The Spirit of 'The Fosters.'" Also see Bergado, "The History-Making Gay Kiss"; Gilchrist, "10 Ways 'The Fosters' Changed TV"; Masters, "Why *The Fosters* Is a Game-Changer."
46. Betancourt, "12 Latinx LGBTQ TV Characters"; Méndez, "The Best Queer Love Scenes."
47. Mark Indelicato, interview with author, February 19, 2013.
48. Eric McCormack, interview with author, March 16, 2012.
49. Eric Stonestreet, interview with author, June 14, 2012.
50. E.g., see McCombs, "Sponsorship of Gay Pride Parades on the Rise."
51. E.g., Rosenbloom, "In Pursuit of the 'Pink Dollar'"; Wolny, "The LGBTQ+ Community." Michael Bronski wrote in 1998: "The growing visibility of the gay and lesbian community in the past decade has been largely a direct result of the emergence of the gay market and the commodification of gay life" (*The Pleasure Principle*, 145). As one sign of how much of a shift in visibility this is, *Queerty* reports that Guinness beer developed a commercial in 1995 featuring a gay couple, but then they never ran the spot (Avery, "St. Patty's Gay"). On this shift, also see Elliott, "Commercials with a Gay Emphasis," and Petrow, "Advertisers Embrace Gay People." Another report notes that IKEA was a leader in this kind of commercial visibility when it ran a 1994 ad, "Dining Room Table," featuring a gay couple. See Italie, "Gay-Themed Ads," and the ad here: https://youtu.be/QCGv1hN6S9E. According to Italie, the commercial only ran once and was then taken off the air after IKEA stores received bomb threats.
52. For the entire commercial, see https://youtu.be/AR-JkiNQ_Ro.
53. Mathewson, "TV Is Biggest Driver." On gender, sports, and platform, one recent analysis found that women's elite sports are a worthwhile investment because interest in them is on the rise, but that they currently struggle to attract media

attention, television viewership, and revenue. For instance: "In 2021, we predict women's sports revenues will be well under a billion dollars—a fraction of the global value of all sports (men's, women's, and mixed), which in 2018 reached US$481 billion, an increase of 45% over 2011" (Lee et al., "Women's Sports").

54. E.g., Anderson, *In the Game*; Griffin, *Strong Women, Deep Closets*; Messner, *Power at Play*; Zirin, *Game Over*.
55. Fagan, "Owning the Middle"; Griffin, "Respect. Just Do It"; Griffin et al., "Nike Hosts"; Woog, "LGBT Sports Movement"; Zeigler, "LGBT Summit Sports Kicks Off." We also recently saw Nike use its clout for institutional change to hasten the name change of the Washington, DC, football team (Lombardo, "Washington").
56. Ariail, "The Pride, Power and Purpose of WNBA Players"; Associated Press, "WNBA to Market"; Given, "WNBA Cashing In"; Macur, "Coast Cleared by Others"; WNBA, "League Debuts"; Ziller and Prada, "The WNBA." Also see Sender, *Business, Not Politics*, chap. 6, on "the lesbian market" (182).
57. Meyersohn, "Target Is the Latest Company," and "Big Brands Are Pulling Back."
58. Holman and Creswell, "Brands Embracing Pride Month."
59. Mulvaney's Bud Light spot can be found here, on Instagram: https://www.instagram.com/p/CqgTftujqZc/?hl=en.
60. Holman and Creswell, "Brands Embracing Pride Month"; Holpuch, "Behind the Backlash"; Roeloffs, "Dylan Mulvaney."
61. Zirin, "On Colin Kaepernick's Nike Ad." Also see Zirin, *A People's History of Sports*, on the history of the rise of Nike in sports.
62. For a foundational articulation, see Schulman, "Israel and 'Pinkwashing.'" Also see Fatoba, "Are Brands Sincere"; Faye, "Gay Pride and Capitalism."
63. https://www.instagram.com/p/DFWAOgSB0wF/?img_index=1.
64. E.g., see Bindel, "The Proud Whopper?"; Bronski, *The Pleasure Principle*.
65. Sender, *Business, Not Politics*, 18. Similarly, Lamont urges: "Many observers have dismissed this 'branding diversity,' calling it a crass marketing gimmick. But this approach has been an effective means for diffusing at scale more inclusive messages about who is worthy" (*Seeing Others*, 151).
66. Some see the *ally* language, itself, as a bit outdated and passive. More recent terminology, particularly in the context of racial justice organizing, includes *accomplice* and *co-conspirator* (e.g., Jana, "The Differences").
67. Stulberg, "One Ally's Story."
68. Armstrong, *Forging Gay Identities*; Faderman, *The Gay Revolution*; Fetner, *How the Religious Right*; Stulberg, *LGBTQ Social Movements*.
69. This is a shift of masculinity that scholar Eric Anderson and his colleagues have termed "inclusive masculinity" (*Out in Sport*, 8).
70. Pat Griffin, interview with author, June 28, 2012; also see Griffin, "Some Thoughts."
71. McCarriston, "Super Bowl Champion."
72. Foxworth, "It's Time for All Jocks."

73. James, "Activism."
74. Long before marriage fights became widespread, 1990s Chicago Bulls super-celebrity Dennis Rodman pushed conversations about and conventions of gender, even as he has claimed that he had no political agenda in doing so. As a 2021 feature of him as a *GQ*'s "style icon" noted: "All of his halter tops and eyeliner did something I wouldn't have been able to appreciate at the time, but can't help thinking about now, in a world populated by the likes of Kid Cudi, Russell Westbrook, and Lil Nas X. He helped set the stage for a broader understanding and acceptance of varied forms of Black masculinity, however shallow that acceptance might be at times" (Smith, "Dennis Rodman"). And as gay former college football player and former Pennsylvania state legislator Brian Sims said of Rodman in my conversation with him in the fall of 2012: "Dennis Rodman, I think, is more responsible for the paradigm shift in becoming an ally than almost anybody that I can name in the last twenty years. He changed it from guilty by association to a sign of your confidence, a sign of how powerful you are in your own skin. And it started to make it easier for allies to come around" (Brian Sims, interview with author, October 25, 2012).
75. See, broadly, his social media presence and his weekly column, Edge of Sports: https://www.edgeofsports.com/.
76. Griffin, "Some Thoughts." On Ben Cohen see, among others, Colman, "A Star Athlete," and Out.com Editors, "Ben Cohen."
77. Hoffman, "A Gay Rights Power Player."
78. Brian Ellner, interview with author, February 27, 2012.
79. Brian Ellner, interview with author, July 23, 2013.
80. On the NFL's tolerance for homophobia, see Zirin's comments that "homophobia is baked so deeply into the cake of football in a way that it's not in other sport" (O'Connell and Radke, "Sports Writer Dave Zirin"). Also see Williams, "Brian Flores," on racial discrimination in coaching in the NFL.
81. According to Zirin, these athletes not only mobilize their normative masculinity in this way, but their very advocacy for LGBTQ+ equality and their public abhorrence of homophobia is part of "redefining a warped vision of manhood in the process" ("Can the NFL").
82. Mathewson, "TV Is Biggest Driver."
83. Quoted in Maraniss, *When Pride Still Mattered*, 471. Also see Kopay and Young, *The David Kopay Story*; Tharrett, "Legendary Football Coach."
84. Fujita, "Acceptance by Example." For Fujita's 2011 marriage equality video, see https://www.youtube.com/watch?v=9pYCEGxfUI8. Also see Zirin, "'It's a New World.'"
85. Scott Fujita, interview with author, September 26, 2013.
86. https://www.allamericanspeakers.com/speakers/389816/Brendon-Ayanbadejo.
87. Ayanbadejo, "Same Sex Marriages."
88. See, e.g., https://youtu.be/VRh_wMrbLZI; https://youtu.be/eCjI8ArDhtQ;

Ayanbadejo, "End Homophobia in Professional Sports"; Ayanbadejo, "Advocacy Acceptance"; Ayanbadejo, "Coming Out a Liberating Move"; Ayanbadejo, "Sam's Draft Prospects"; Ayanbadejo, "My Thoughts on Michael Sam"; Bruni, "Carrying a Cause"; Zirin, "'It's a New World.'"

89. Szabo, "Chris Kluwe."
90. Yahoo Sports, "Maryland Politician's Letter."
91. Kluwe, *Beautifully Unique Sparkleponies*, 6.
92. Kluwe, "They Won't Magically." Also see Zirin, "Chris Kluwe."
93. Gervino, "The Punter Makes His Point"; Kluwe, "Gay Marriage Legalized!"; Linkins, "Chris Kluwe Quits"; Zeigler, "Kick Ass." A number of Kluwe's published pieces are republished in his book: *Beautifully Unique Sparkleponies.*
94. "Brief of Amici Curiae." Also see Karlan, "Broadening Support." This is not the only recent example of elite athletes weighing in on court proceedings of central civil rights claims. In the fall of 2021, more than five hundred female athletes submitted an *amicus* brief with the Supreme Court in support of abortion rights (Streeter, "Why Scores of Female Athletes").
95. Chris Kluwe, interview with author, November 15, 2012.
96. Kluwe, "I Was an NFL Player."
97. Goessling, "Chris Kluwe." Also see Tevlin, "Kluwe Made an Impact."
98. Griffin, "Some Thoughts." Also see Zeigler, "The Effective Role."
99. Burke, "Time for Straight Allies."
100. Branch, "Two Straight Athletes"; Buzinski, "Wrestler Hudson Taylor"; Woog, "Hudson Taylor."
101. Athlete Ally, "About Athlete Ally."
102. See, e.g., Petchesky, "How One Gay Athlete's Coming Out."
103. Brian Ellner, interview with author, November 3, 2021. Ellner was a founding board member of Athlete Ally.
104. Hudson Taylor, interview with author, February 16, 2022.
105. Ross, *Hollywood Left and Right*, 3–4, 20.
106. See Brownstein, *The Power and the Glitter*; Grossman, "The Socialization"; Meyer and Gamson, "The Challenge of Cultural Elites"; Ross, *Hollywood Left and Right*; Rupp and Taylor, *Drag Queens at the 801 Cabaret*; Schmidt, "Americans' Views Flipped."
107. Marcus, *The Drama of Celebrity*.
108. As Ross concludes of these celebrities: "They leverage their celebrity for the public good, not for ratings or income," and they do their homework, "support[ing] their ideas with serious preparation" (*Hollywood Left and Right*, 417). Also see Himberg, *The New Gay for Pay*, who also "rejects the cynical notion that LGBT television advocacy has been so co-opted by partnerships and alliances between industry players and moderate advocacy organizations that it has been rendered politically useless or meaningless—a mere cog in the capitalist machine of marketable LGBT identities and narratives" (52).

CHAPTER THREE

1. Caldwell, *Production Culture*; Gamson, *Claims to Fame*.
2. This builds on the few classic academic studies of Hollywood, like those by Powdermaker, *Hollywood, the Dream Factory*, and Gitlin, *Inside Prime Time*, and draws on the more current examinations of the world of work in Hollywood (e.g., Ortner, *Not Hollywood*; Roussel, *Representing Talent*; Yuen, *Reel Inequality*).
3. Amenta and Polletta, "The Cultural Impact of Social Movements"; Polletta and Amenta, *Changing Minds*.
4. Political scientist David Prindle understood the complexity of this combination of entertainment and late-stage capitalism: "The Hollywood entertainment industry is a *business* whose product is *art*, and that causes the trouble" (*Risky Business*, 4). Also see Caldwell, *Production Culture*; Martin, *Difficult Men*.
5. E.g., Chattoo and Feldman, *A Comedian and an Activist*; Christian, *Open TV*; Nussbaum, *I Like to Watch*; Press, *Stealing the Show*; Vox Media, *Land of the Giants: The Netflix Effect*, episode 4; Yuen, *Reel Inequality*. Importantly, media scholar Amanda D. Lotz argues that it is not *only* streaming that is responsible for "change and expansion in screen storytelling possibilities." Lotz finds, instead, that "two main developments are at the root of this change: digitization and the internationalization of screen industries, especially the business of television," and that these predated the streaming revolution (*After Mass Media*, 26).
6. Christian, "Beyond Branding," 460, 462, 459.
7. Sender, "The Queer Vanguard," 161. Also see Shacklock, "The Category Is."
8. Adalain and Brown, "The Binge Purge"; Barnes, "The Streaming Era."
9. Nisha Ganatra, interview with author, July 24, 2017.
10. Jen Richards, interview with author, January 11, 2018; Lang, "The Only Emmy-Nominated Show." Find the series here: https://www.youtube.com/c/HerStoryShow.
11. Jen Richards, interview with author, February 20, 2024.
12. A July 2024 article noted: "Ticket sales so far this year in North America total $4.3 billion, down roughly 35 percent from the same period in 2019, according to Comscore, which tracks box office data" (Barnes, "Hollywood's Message to Red States").
13. Nielsen, "Connected Devices." And see Adgate, "The Impact COVID-19 Had"; Barnes, "Hollywood's Obituary"; Gura, "Barry Diller Headed"; Herships and Smith, "Is Movie Night Back?"; Lang and Rubin, "How Movie Theaters Fought to Survive"; Shaw, "Here Are the Ways."
14. Bessner, "The Life and Death of Hollywood."
15. Also see Adalain and Brown, "The Binge Purge"; Ovide, "Streaming Is Sadder Now"; Sperling, "Netflix Says." And on the "Great Netflix Correction" of 2022, and its ripple effects throughout the streaming world, see Bloom, "The Great Netflix Correction."

16. Adrienne Erickson, interview with author, November 10, 2021.
17. Gianna Sobol, interview with author, October 14, 2021; Barnes, "The Streaming Era"; Writers Guild of America West, *Inclusion & Equity Report, 2022*, 2.
18. On the creative and labor shortcomings of mini rooms, also see Gross, "Why Writers Are Losing Out"; Maas et al., "One of the Writers Guild's"; and Bessner, "The Life and Death of Hollywood," who writes more broadly about the current precarity of the business—especially for writers.
19. Quoted in Kilkenny, "Fran Drescher Q&A."
20. Brown, "Hollywood Has Left L.A."; Kit and Kilkenny, "Hollywood at Risk."
21. Christian, *Open TV*; Sender, "The Queer Vanguard."
22. Observers have also commented on the ways in which highly nichified and other social media have created and exacerbated cultural and political divisions and extremism (e.g., Poniewozik, *Audience of One*; Reply All, "Louder").
23. Brittani Nichols, interview with author, April 14, 2022. On this point about the reach of network TV, also see Streitmatter, *From 'Perverts' to 'Fab Five.'* Of course, too, streaming spaces range in their degree of niche-ness. See Weprin, "Streaming Profits Are Tough to Find."
24. Also on this point, see Kal Penn's *You Can't Be Serious*, and his discussion of his 2019 NBC sitcom, *Sunnyside*.
25. Peter Paige, interview with author, July 31, 2025.
26. Adalain and Brown, "The Binge Purge"; Bessner, "The Life and Death of Hollywood"; Sender, "The Queer Vanguard"; Uwagba, "Ray of Light."
27. I choose to name the movement as its founder, Tarana Burke, did as "me too" without the hashtag. Burke was a founder of this movement in 2005–6, more than a decade before 2017, when it became a hashtag that applied to sexual misconduct in Hollywood. See Burke, *Unbound*.
28. E.g., Colin, "How Sexist Is Hollywood?"; Erigha, *The Hollywood Jim Crow*; Farrow, *Catch and Kill*; Gross, "'This Changes Everything'"; Hayek, "Harvey Weinstein"; Hunt and Ramón, *Hollywood Diversity Report, 2021*, parts 1 and 2; Kantor and Twohey, *She Said*; Langone, "#MeToo and Time's Up Founders"; Nyong'o, "Lupita Nyong'o: Speaking Out"; Rock, "Chris Rock Pens Blistering Essay"; Sancton, "#MeToo Five Years Later"; Ugwu, "The Hashtag That Changed the Oscars"; Woelfle, "Actor John Leguizamo"; Yamato, "Hollywood Claims to Be Making Strides"; Yuen, *Reel Inequality*.
29. Badgett and Herman, *Sexual Orientation and Gender Identity Diversity in Entertainment*. This study was based on an online survey, conducted in the fall of 2012, of 5,692 SAG-AFTRA members, including 465 self-identified gay men, 61 lesbians, 301 bisexuals, and 7 transgender participants.
30. The Writers Guild of America East and Writers Guild of America West do collect some useful demographic information on TV and film writers, including on LGBTQ+ identification. See, e.g., their *Inclusion & Equity Report, 2025*.

31. Yuen, *Reel Inequality*, 15. Also see Bessner, "The Life and Death of Hollywood"; Cheney-Rice, "Michael B. Jordan Did the Impossible"; Lamont, *Seeing Others*, 103.
32. On this point about the White freedom to fail, also see John Leguizamo's comments in Woelfle, "Actor John Leguizamo."
33. Also on this point, see actor Rizwan Manji's comments on auditions, casting, and White actors on this 2021 panel, Casting Society of America, "A Collective Voice."
34. Also see Yuen, *Reel Inequality*, which makes a similar argument (62). And a 2021 McKinsey & Company report, "Black Representation in Film and TV," found a similar dynamic with Black talent: that they are not given the opportunity to fail (Dunn et al.).
35. Jamie Babbit, interviews with author, July 27, 2012, and January 10, 2018.
36. Sandberg, "Diversity Improves." Also see Oluo, *Mediocre*.
37. Quoted in Piña, "Mark Ruffalo, Ramy Youssef and More."
38. Powdermaker made a similar observation as early as 1950 (*Hollywood, the Dream Factory*, 36–37).
39. For this framing, also see Gross, "Hollywood's Closet"; Prindle, *Risky Business*, 8. Also see Geena Davis's interview with Terry Gross, in which she makes this point that the fact there have always been others around to take their jobs—this "reserve army," in my framing, drawing on Marx—dissuades women from speaking up about the injustices they face in their Hollywood workplace (Gross, "'This Changes Everything'").
40. Again, see similar comments by actor Rizwan Manji, who said on a 2021 panel, "You don't want to be that difficult actor. You don't want to . . . get that branding." See Casting Society of America, "A Collective Voice." This is also a theme in Elliot Page's reflection on his career in *Pageboy* (see, e.g., 186 for this language).
41. Also see Yuen, *Reel Inequality*, on this point.
42. Amir Talai, interview with author, January 10, 2018.
43. Prindle, *Risky Business*, 4; Polletta et al., "Social Movements in the Commercial Public Sphere," 1269. Also see Bielby and Bielby, "'All Hits Are Flukes.'"
44. Sociologist Gitlin, no fan of the industry, wrote in 1983 about how it is the quest for "aggregate eyeballs" that drives decision-making, yet there is a lot of mushiness to measuring audience response and predicting what will draw audiences (*Inside Prime Time*, 56). "Uncertainty," Gitlin wrote, "is the permanent condition of show business" (14). Also see Gamson, *Claims to Fame*; Goldman, *Adventures in the Screen Trade*; Powdermaker, *Hollywood, the Dream Factory*.
45. Russo memorably framed the impact of presuming audience preference this way: "So long as Hollywood has one eye on the box office and the other on the lowest common denominator in the audience, it will always be a chickenshit" (*The Celluloid Closet*, 326). Also see Signorile, *Queer in America*, who wrote of

this dynamic that Hollywood is "a town of so-called liberals selling a product to a country they perceive to be conservative. In that way, when it comes down to the bottom line, the most ardent Hollywood liberal can behave like the most orthodox right-winger. Money is *always* conservative" (255).

46. This kind of coastal exceptionalism reasoning, or "metronormativity," as Jack Halberstam identifies it (*Queer Time and Place*, 36–37), was echoed by many people I spoke with. It is complicated by the fact that much LGBTQ+ civil rights progress, cultural inclusion, and political organizing have been achieved in red states and small towns throughout the country in the past few years, while there has also been anti-LGBTQ+ violence in coastal cities. Another rejoinder to the coastal exceptionalism thesis are the many examples of real-life popular culture that highlight the possibility for openness in "flyover country," like the life and community that the Indigo Girls' Amy Ray and Emily Saliers have built in Georgia; the way that the "Fab Five" on the *Queer Eye* reboot are welcomed and celebrated wherever they go; and the success of Indiana's "Mayor Pete" Buttigieg—and also the absolutely beautiful fictional television show *Somebody Somewhere* (2022–24), set in Manhattan, Kansas. For national state-by-state demographic data, see Williams Institute, "LGBT Proportion of Population: United States." Also see Allen, "Why LGBT People Are Moving" and *Real Queer America*; Barton, *Pray the Gay Away*; Ghaziani, *There Goes the Gayborhood?*; Gray, *Out in the Country*; Halberstam, *In a Queer Time and Place*; Hubbs, *Rednecks, Queers, and Country Music*; Polletta and Amenta, *Changing Minds*; Stein, "In Conservative America"; Stein, *The Stranger Next Door*; Socarides, "The Murder of a Gay Man"; Vaid, *Virtual Equality*; Witosky and Hansen, *Equal Before the Law*.
47. Sociologist Nancy Wang Yuen found this to be the case in her 2017 study of actors' experience with racism in Hollywood. She argues that the "trope of the middle American audience" drives the "blame the market" logic in which Hollywood decision-makers frame their choices as being constrained by their presumed (conservative) audiences (*Reel Inequality*, 62). Also on racial exclusion and the music industry, see Bullock, *David Bowie Made Me Gay*.
48. This was echoed in Bessner's reporting in "The Life and Death of Hollywood." He quotes one creator/showrunner, Kelvin Yu, as saying: "I think that there will be an industry move to the middle in terms of safer, four-quadrant TV. . . . I think a lot of people . . . who were disenfranchised or marginalized—their drink tickets are up."
49. Barnes, "Hollywood's Message to Red States." Also see a post-Trump 2.0 opinion piece contributing to this conversation, Waxman, "Hollywood Is 'Hot, Horny and White' Again."
50. Gianna Sobol, interview with author, July 7, 2025.
51. See Havens, *Black Television Travels*, for an excellent history of the "global television trade" (e.g., 81), its "industry lore" (3), and presumptions it makes about audiences and how this impacts content and representation.

52. This phenomenon of orienting toward international markets is not new, and expansion into international markets after World War I helped Hollywood grow substantially (see Schwartzel, *Red Carpet*). Scholars of Jewish participation in Hollywood have noted a parallel to the years after the Great Depression, when the movie business in the United States was struggling and international markets provided some relief. Movie studio heads, including a number of Jews (and with the exception of Warner Bros., which held the line and actively resisted Nazism, according to Doherty, *Hollywood and Hitler*), bowed to implicit and explicit demands of the German market. There is a bit of historiographic contention about the extent of Hollywood's orientation or acquiescence to Nazi Germany (Baron and Rosenberg, "The Ben Urwand Controversy"; Denby, "How Could Harvard"), but there is agreement that this international market impacted creative decision-making in Hollywood. Russo drew a parallel between Jewish decision-making in Hollywood yielding to Nazism and anti-LGBTQ+ decision-making to capitulate to Christian conservatives: "In 1940, Hollywood producers, many of whom were Jewish, refused to make films that attacked either fascism in general or Nazism in particular simply because they feared losing box office revenue from countries like Germany" (*The Celluloid Closet*, 250). In this example, there is an important institutional point that decision-makers who are part of a marginalized group (e.g., Jews and LGBTQ+ people) can be part of further marginalizing their group in the name of profit and risk aversion. Also see Doherty, *Hollywood and Hitler*; Renov and Brook, *From Shtetl to Stardom*; Ross, *Hitler in Los Angeles*; Urwand, *The Collaboration*.
53. https://help.netflix.com/en/node/14164; Schwartzel, *Red Carpet*, 324; Shaw, "Here Are the Ways"; Vox Media, *Land of the Giants: The Netflix Effect*, episode 7.
54. Yuen, in *Reel Inequality*, notes that there is also a presumption that "film and television shows starring actors of color do not sell overseas," though she notes a number of counterexamples to this (67).
55. Havens, *Black Television Travels*. Also see especially journalist Erich Schwartzel's *Red Carpet*. Orientation toward international markets shows up in other areas of popular culture. For example, in the fall of 2019, the general manager of the National Basketball Association's Houston Rockets posted a pro-democracy tweet, an image reading "FIGHT FOR FREEDOM STAND WITH HONG KONG," that he deleted quickly and that generally could not be seen in China because Twitter is blocked there. But China represents a large and growing market for the NBA, and there were immediate repercussions from the tweet (e.g., Chinese television and streaming stopped airing Rockets games) and the NBA—generally considered among the most progressive of the major sports leagues in the United States—was compelled to respond. See Perper, "China and the NBA"; Schwartzel, *Red Carpet*, 271; Valinsky, "How One Tweet."
56. Schwartzel reports that at the behest of censors in China, "gay people stay in the closet or off-screen," and that, in Kenya, as well, in his reporting, movies

are scrubbed of "gay themes or characters" (*Red Carpet*, 105, 319). Schwartzel wrote, as well, of the 2018 film about Queen and its lead singer Freddie Mercury, *Bohemian Rhapsody*, that three minutes of the film were removed by censors in China (113). For their part, streaming services do not need to run content through censors, so they have more latitude in international markets. But this has not been without controversy when they include LGBTQ+ storylines or characters, as was the case with Netflix's first original Arab film, the adaptation of the Italian *Perfect Strangers*, in January 2022 (Vivarelli, "Netflix Stands By").

57. Erigha, *The Hollywood Jim Crow*, chap. 2.
58. The 2021 McKinsey authors found: "There is also a widespread misperception in the industry that content starring Black actors will not perform well with international audiences. In 2019, the top films with Black leads were distributed in 30 percent fewer international markets on average—yet they earned nearly the same global box-office sales as films with white leads and earned more than those films on a per-market basis" (Dunn et al., "Black Representation in Film and TV").
59. Cheney-Rice, "Michael B. Jordan Did the Impossible"; Rubin, "Ryan Coogler and Michael B. Jordan's 'Sinners.'"
60. See Barnes, "With $218 Million Haul"; Creative Artists Agency and shift7, "Female-Led Films"; Smith, "The Data Behind Hollywood's Sexism"; Ulaby, "The 'Barbie' Movie's Success."
61. Max Mutchnick, interview with author, January 18, 2012.
62. See Roussel, *Representing Talent*.
63. In Gen X star actor Molly Ringwald's words (see Gross, "Molly Ringwald").
64. Harvey Guillén, interview with author, March 20, 2015.
65. A phrase from Jeff Richman, as we were talking about typecasting. Interview with author, April 16, 2013. In another example: In a really engaging 2019 conversation with actor Henry Winkler, who played the iconic role of "The Fonz" on *Happy Days* from 1974 to 1984, Terry Gross asked the actor if it took a while in his career to "un-Fonz" himself "in the eyes of the industry" after the show—and he said, emphatically, that it did. Winkler said that it took him approximately eight years after *Happy Days* to "really get a good acting role" (Gross, "'I Never Had a Plan B'").
66. Dunn et al., "Black Representation in Film and TV." Also see Yuen, *Reel Inequality*, chap. 3.
67. Casting Society of America, "A Collective Voice." Also specifically on casting and race/ethnicity for Middle Eastern, Arab, and South Asian actors, see Al-Kadhi, *Life as a Unicorn*; Talai, "When a Brown Actor"; Wallace, "Riz Ahmed."
68. Amin El Gamal, interviews with author, January 12, 2018, and January 13, 2022.
69. Badgett and Herman, *Sexual Orientation and Gender Identity Diversity in Entertainment*. Also see Stevenson, "Beyond the Gay Role."
70. Also reported by an actor in Badgett and Herman, *Sexual Orientation and Gender Identity Diversity in Entertainment*, 24.

71. Michael Urie, interview with author, March 5, 2013.
72. Also see Lang, "Why Gay Movie Stars"; Yuen, *Reel Inequality*, chap. 3.
73. Peter Paige, interview with author, June 11, 2014.
74. One slightly dated counterexample, but one that came up a lot in my early interviews, is out gay actor Neil Patrick Harris and the highly problematic womanizer that he played on the popular and award-winning CBS sitcom *How I Met Your Mother* (2005–14). NPH was not publicly out until 2006, but he went on to have a long and successful run on the show (see, e.g., Navarro, "Out in Hollywood"). In my conversations about typecasting and whether publicly out gay actors can play straight leads, NPH came up *regularly*. Some explained his role by noting that playing a straight lead on a comedy or on television was different from making the shift to drama or to leading man status in film. Yet they still noted that NPH was an example that a publicly gay actor *could* play a straight—and aggressively straight—lead.
75. And the data is generally collected and reported in this binary way. See Butterly et al., "100 Women"; Saperstein, "Only 7% of Movies"; Statista, "Distribution of Lead Actors."
76. Or even as gay romantic leads in the few roles like this that even now exist. See Billy Eichner's quotes on the casting of leading roles in his 2022 film, *Bros*, in Street, "Here's Why Cis-Het Actors."
77. See Henderson, "*Bridgerton* Proves"; Jordan, "Jonathan Bailey," and for one recent profile, see Chamberlain, "Truly, Madly, Jonny."
78. One older piece seemed to back this up. *Variety* wrote in 2015 that they had commissioned a survey in which "six in 10 adults say they would be less likely to see an action film with a gay leading man or woman, while four in 10 say they'd be more likely to skip an action film with a lead gay character" (Lang, "Why Gay Movie Stars").
79. Writer Michelangelo Signorile wrote in 1993 that this rationale for not casting queer actors "is steeped in fear and grossly underestimates an audience's ability and desire to fantasize." He continued: "If filmgoers are able to believe that an actor is a gladiator or a disciple of Jesus or a general in World War II . . . , why can't they believe in a queer actor playing a heterosexual?" (*Queer in America*, 280).
80. See, e.g., Bendix, "Can Gay Play Straight?'"; Riese, "Can Gay Actors Play Straight Roles?" and "Let Us Now Praise Effeminate Men"; Setoodeh, "From 'Glee' to Sean Hayes"; Vary, "Out Gay Actor Richard Chamberlain."
81. This award buzz might be especially strong if straight actors play gay characters who "die [a] painful death." See Savage, "Straights Who Play Gay." One 2019 article found that twenty-five actors had been nominated for Academy Awards for playing LGBTQ+ roles, and none of them identified as openly LGBTQ+ (Pollard, "'Hollywood Gets Queer Stories Wrong'").
82. Eric McCormack, interview with author, March 16, 2012, and update communication with author, January 15, 2024; Stevenson, "Beyond the Gay Role."

83. See, e.g., Kelly, "Are Straight Actors in Gay Roles the New Blackface?" This casting conversation also has gotten connected to a public conversation about "queer-baiting," which can mean that a celebrity (like singer/actor Harry Styles or singer Bad Bunny) who has not been publicly identified as queer seems to seek attention and queer fans by either (a) being coy about their sexuality in a way that does not deny rumors that they may not be straight or (b) performing their gender, or appropriating markers of queerness, in a way that often raises questions about whether they may be queer. In this context, too, presumed-cisgender and presumed-straight celebrities are accused by some of "oppression tourism" or queer "cosplay" for the purposes of career advancement. See Harris, "Is Celebrity 'Queer Baiting' Really Such a Crime?" Also see Kelleher, "No, Bad Bunny Isn't Queerbaiting," and Mack, "The Queerbaiting Discourse."
84. E.g., Guy, "Cate Blanchett"; Lewis, "Darren Criss"; Pollard, "'Hollywood Gets Queer Stories Wrong'"; Stolworthy, "Darren Criss"; Street, "Here's Why Cis-Het Actors."
85. Peter Paige, interview with author, November 18, 2021.
86. During 2023–24, GLAAD found a decrease in the number of transgender characters on television: "This is the second year in a row that has seen a dramatic decrease in transgender characters, down to 24 from last year's 32. This is the lowest number since the 2017–18 report." Across broadcast, cable, and streaming platforms in 2023–24 "of the 24 trans characters counted, 11 (46 percent) are trans women, five (21 percent) are trans men, and eight (33 percent) are trans nonbinary characters." In addition, GLAAD counted "16 nonbinary characters who are not transgender. However, many of these characters have so little screen time they only barely met our methodology criteria" (GLAAD, *Where We Are on TV, 2023–2024*, 47, 49). For film, this representation was even much smaller. GLAAD noted that 2022 saw a "record high" of "12 trans-inclusive films." But in 2024, there were only *two* transgender characters and *three* nonbinary characters in all of the year's 250 films released in theaters on streaming platforms (GLAAD, *2025 Studio Responsibility Index*, 8, 11). On casting and representation, GLAAD also raised this important critique of the two films with trans characters: "One of those movies had a cisgender actor playing a transgender character—a practice that has been denounced by transgender people and had been nearly eliminated in films and television. . . . This dangerous casting practice, which GLAAD consistently warns against, perpetuates the false narrative that trans people are not who they say they are. The only other film with transgender representation was Netflix's *Emilia Pérez*, which, though authentically cast, chose to perpetuate transphobic stereotypes and harmful tropes" (14).
87. Steinmetz, "The Transgender Tipping Point." And on the complexity of this "tipping point" moment in transgender visibility, see Keegan, "On the Necessity of Bad Trans Objects."

88. See, e.g., among many pieces, Abramovitch, "'Transparent' Star"; Addams, "In Defense of Jared Leto"; Brodesser-Akner, "Can Jill Soloway Do Justice to the Trans Movement?"; Barnes, "Who Gets to Play the Transgender Part?"; D'Addario, "Jared Leto and Michael Douglas' Homophobic Golden Globes Speeches"; Friess, "Don't Applaud"; Goldberg, " Jeffrey Tambor"; O'Donnell, "How Authentic Is 'Transparent'?" Ruiz, "Trans Actors"; Truitt, "The Golden Globes"; Whitney, "An Unfortunate History."
89. When trans writer Meredith Talusan considered this casting choice in a write-up of her interview with Redmayne, she noted that Redmayne approached the role with sensitivity and humility, consulting with trans women as he developed the role. Redmayne also acknowledged to Talusan that there are so few trans parts, and that, in the zero-sum game of casting, hiring cis actors for these roles has an impact on trans actors' livelihood ("Eddie Redmayne's Complicated Masculinity").
90. Richards also noted that this safety concern is primarily for trans *women*, as they are targeted for violence much more frequently than trans men, so she is not *as* concerned when cis women play trans men. And, she noted, she is not as bothered by cisgender women playing transgender women, although she would "always prefer to see a trans actor play a trans part" (Richards, "Matt Bomer").
91. She echoes this point in Street, "Here's Why Cis-Het Actors."
92. Shadi Petosky, interview with author, October 14, 2021.
93. See, e.g., Trans Hollywood on Twitter at https://twitter.com/transholly wood?lang=en. Also on this point about a sizable shift from 2014 to 2017, see Goldberg, "Jeffrey Tambor." And Syd Diaz, interview with author, November 4, 2022.
94. Hicklin, "Scarlett Johansson Withdraws"; Svachula, "Scarlett Johansson."
95. E.g., Showtime's *Billions* (2016–23); Ryan Murphy's *Pose* on FX (2018–21); and Netflix's *The Umbrella Academy* (2019–24), *Sex Education* (2019–23), and *Heartstopper* (2022–24).
96. Rude, "16 TV Shows." Also see Sender, "The Queer Vanguard."
97. Jen Richards, interview with author, July 24, 2025.
98. Shakina Nayfack, interview with author, September 22, 2025.
99. For two high-profile recent examples of the discussion of whether authentic casting means that queer actors should now only play queer roles, see Bagwell, "Rupert Everett," and Heching, "Aaron Sorkin."
100. Deven Hartley, interview with author, July 12, 2022.
101. When I checked quotes with him, Urie wanted to make it clear that he was referencing the *1980s* here, and not the '90s, so I have changed this to *forty* years, from thirty years in his original quote, since we initially spoke in 2013.
102. There is no perfect term to describe this work. While I would like to include "social justice" in the focus here, DEIB reflects, I think, the actual tenor and focus of much of the work in Hollywood. Some of this work, though, is certainly more

focused directly on social justice efforts and, specifically, on directly responding to or fighting against racism, misogyny, and anti-LGBTQ+ work practices and cultures.

103. For example, it was reported in 2017 that the federal government's Equal Employment Opportunity Commission (EEOC) was investigating gender discrimination against women directors, launched as a response to an American Civil Liberties Union investigation. See Thomas and Goodman, "Women Directors."

104. On the closely watched fall 2021 International Alliance of Theatrical Stage Employees (IATSE) union negotiations, for instance, see Barnes, "Hollywood's Behind-the-Scenes Workers."

105. Adrienne Erickson, interview with author, November 10, 2021.

106. For one academic spotlight on this work, see Himberg, *The New Gay for Pay*.

107. For instance, the American Film Institute began the Directing Workshop for Women in 1974, expanding it in later years to include other "underrepresented filmmakers." Robert Redford's Sundance Institute, for instance, dates back to 1981. Outfest has been around since 1982 as a nonprofit organization that sponsors a successful annual film festival, has many training and mentorship programs, and is dedicated to "LGBTQIA+ arts, media and entertainment" (outfest.org). It has been central to professional development and community building for so many LGBTQ+-identified artists that we interviewed. The NAACP has had long-standing partnerships in the industry, especially to increase racial diversity in storytelling and programming (see https://naacp.org/our-work/diversity-entertainment/entertainment-industry-initiatives). Also on the NAACP's late '90s focus on the lack of racial diversity on TV and the industry response, see Weinraub, "Stung by Criticism." And the Geena Davis Institute was founded in 2004. Gamechanger Films dates to 2013 and is an equity fund that finances films, and now television and digital content, that expand diversity. Ryan Murphy launched his Half Initiative in 2016 to hold himself accountable to hiring directors on his shows who are at least 50 percent women, people of color, and LGBTQ+ people—and develop a pipeline through education and mentorship. And sociologist Yuen documented, in her 2017 book, *Reel Inequality* (chap. 7), a number of efforts aimed at boosting the careers of actors of color, like talent showcases run by major networks and studios.

108. For example, the idea of thc *inclusion rider* drew popular attention after actor Frances McDormand mentioned the concept in her Academy Award acceptance speech in 2018. The innovation is credited to USC's Professor Stacy Smith and relies on the idea that a star or someone else with a lot of clout on a project could ensure diversity in hiring by building into their contract that there must be a certain level of diversity in front of and behind the camera (see Belam and Levin, "Woman Behind 'Inclusion Rider'").

109. For instance, casting director Danielle Pretsfelder Demchick, who had focused on youth talent through her work at Nickelodeon, co-led a talent search program

called the Trans Youth Acting Challenge in 2020–21 with trans Nickelodeon actor Michael D. Cohen. She has also been involved, through her leadership work with the Casting Society (CSA), in organizing an open call for trans and nonbinary actors, which has helped to build a database of actors accessible to CSA members who are casting for future roles (Danielle Pretsfelder Demchick, interview with author, April 26, 2022; Ramos, "CSA Announces").

110. Fawzia Mirza, interview with author, March 2, 2022.
111. Harris, "Same Old Script"; Robb, "WGA West Inclusion & Equity Report"; Writers Guild of America West, *Inclusion & Equity Report, 2022*.
112. Like the Warner Bros. Discovery Access Early Career Bootcamp, to name just one of many programs like this.
113. E.g., https://www.wga.org/the-guild/advocacy/inclusion-and-equity/industry-writing-programs; Bergeson, "Issa Rae"; Harris, "Same Old Script"; Zook, "*Queen Sugar*."
114. Andria Wilson Mirza, interview with author, March 8, 2022.
115. Writers Guild of America West and Writers Guild of America East, *Inclusion & Equity Report, 2025*, 8.
116. Barnes, "After #MeToo Reckoning"; Cho and Weprin, "DEI Is Disappearing"; Maddaus et al., "Hollywood Ditches."
117. Zeigler, "NFL Adds 'Sexual Orientation.'"
118. Cyd Zeigler, interview with author, October 21, 2011.
119. E.g., Bouie, "There Is No Dignity"; Brewer, "The Panic"; Hewett, "How Trans Athletes Became Targets"; Krishnakumar, "This Record-Breaking Year."
120. In just a few of the most recent examples, see failed presidential-hopeful Florida governor Ron DeSantis's fight with Disney over its opposition to his "don't say gay" law; attempts across the country's school districts to ban books that feature LGBTQ+ characters and storylines and attacks on librarians that recommend them; and right-wing violent and policy assaults on "drag queen story hours." See, e.g., Kaleem, "How Drag Queen Story Hour"; New York Times, "When Book Bans Came"; Rozsa, "DeSantis Takes on Disney."
121. For another important narrative here, see swimmer Schuyler Bailar's *He/She/They*.
122. Chris Mosier, interview with author, July 29, 2025.
123. Krattenmaker, *Onward Christian Athletes*; Ladd and Mathisen, *Muscular Christianity*; Messner, *Power at Play*; Zirin, *Game Over*.
124. Movement Advancement Project, *Equality Maps: Bans*.
125. White House, "Keeping Men Out." Also see Redfield, "The Impact of Transgender Sports Participation Bans." In March 2025, the Trump administration announced that it would withhold $175 million in federal funds from the University of Pennsylvania because it allowed Lia Thomas, a transgender woman, to swim on the school team during years when Penn was fully abiding by law and policy by allowing Thomas to swim. A few months later, in a move that seemed to

restore this funding, Penn announced that it had "resolved" the "investigation," that it would follow the new NCAA guidelines banning trans women athletes' participation, and that it would "apologize to those [athletes] who experienced a competitive disadvantage or experienced anxiety because of the policies in effect at the time" (Jameson, "Penn's Title IX Resolution"). Also see Knott, "Trump Admin."

126. Barnes and Lavigne, "Transgender Athlete Debate Rolls On"; Macur, "U.S. Olympic Officials," and "N.C.A.A., Following Trump's Order." For other trans-exclusionary policy moves, even those that predate Trump's second term, see Negley, "FINA Votes"; Olson, "NAIA All but Bans"; Zeigler, "World Athletics."
127. Ermyas and Wakeam, "Wave of Bills."
128. Foran and Talbot, "GOP-Led House Votes."
129. Danne Diamond, interview with author, November 5, 2021.
130. Chris Mosier, interview with author, October 12, 2021.
131. Branch, "The Shame of College Sports"; New York Times, "A New Era in College Sports"; Nocera and Strauss, *Indentured*; Zirin, *Game Over*, chap. 6. As Branch writes of the racial power politics of college sports and the role of the NCAA: "to survey the scene . . . is to catch an unmistakable whiff of the plantation" ("The Shame of College Sports").
132. Ennis, "NCAA Takes a Stand"; NCAA, "NCAA Board of Governors Statement"; NCAA Office of Inclusion, *NCAA Inclusion of Transgender Student-Athletes*. Also see a recent discussion of how the NCAA's trans inclusion policy should be updated, particularly to include nonbinary athletes (Ryan, "The NCAA Trans Athlete Policy").
133. Ennis, "NCAA Takes a Stand."
134. Antonucci, "Advocates Call"; Azzi, "NCAA Constitution"; Beran, "As the NCAA Debates"; Hoffman, "Athlete Ally and Chris Mosier Respond"; Yurcaba, "NCAA's New Trans Athlete Guidelines."
135. E.g., Duncan, "Yes, Marathons Will Recognize."
136. De la Cretaz, "Living Nonbinary"; Kim, "Trans WNBA Player."
137. Bell, "*Brown v. Board of Education*." And for the terms "Creative Hollywood" and "Corporate Hollywood," see Ross, *Hollywood Left and Right*, 10.
138. Anderson, "New CAA Study"; Dunn et al., "Black Representation in Film and TV"; Ge, "Diversity in Hollywood"; Hunt and Ramón, *Hollywood Diversity Report, 2021*, parts 1 and 2.
139. E.g., Out & Equal, "Major Companies Respond"; Schnurman and Wolf, "Texas' Harsh Moves"; Schuppe, "Corporate Boycotts." Also see the critical response by audiences and Netflix employees when Netflix aired a transphobic comedy special, *The Closer*, by comedian Dave Chappelle in the fall of 2021 (e.g., Finke, "Netflix Walkout"). And on this framing of diversity and inclusion, and LGBTQ+ inclusion, as "good for business," see Chattoo and Feldman, *A Comedian and an Activist*; Himberg, *The New Gay for Pay*; Sender, "The Queer Vanguard."

140. See chapter 2 for citations regarding the WNBA. See Becker, *Gay TV and Straight America*, who argues that in the 1990s queer content was used by television executives to bring in new younger, more progressive (straight) audiences. Others have written that new gay markets and the money they represented helped to drive an increase in queer representation at this time, as well. See Cagle, "Special Report: The Gay '90s"; Streitmatter, *From 'Perverts' to 'Fab Five.'*
141. On the resolution of the writers' strike, see Barnes and Koblin, "On Day 146."
142. Hadleigh, *Hollywood Gays*; Rich, "Two Gay Cowboys"; Ross, *Hollywood Left and Right.*
143. Leung and Rizzo, "Paramount Ends DEI Policies"; McFall, "Jon Stewart and Stephen Colbert"; Mullin, "F.C.C. Approves."
144. Another report that this has already begun comes from writer/director/showrunner Will Graham, who wrote in June 2023: "I, along with most other queer writers, can tell you personally that the atmosphere has turned frigid in the past year and a half. . . . While states are passing 'Don't Say Gay' laws, we've seen a corresponding tidal wave of cancellations of shows with strong queer characters—especially female, trans and nonbinary characters" ("'A League of Their Own' Co-creator").

CHAPTER FOUR

1. Oluo, *So You Want to Talk About Race*, 112; Cooper, *Eloquent Rage*, 154.
2. Scholars of popular culture have found a similar aversion among those who make film, television, and music to acknowledge an explicitly political or educational goal purpose of their artistic work. See Caldwell, *Production Culture*; Gitlin, *Inside Prime Time*; Hubbs, *Rednecks, Queers, and Country Music*; Lamont, *Seeing Others*; Ortner, *Not Hollywood*. Perhaps this denial of the connection between Hollywood and politics has its historical roots in the ways that McCarthyism targeted and "blacklisted" many in Hollywood as ostensible Communist sympathizers in the early part of the Cold War, beginning in the late 1940s (see Prindle, *Risky Business*, for this history).
3. Gottschall, *The Storytelling Animal*, 148; emphasis in original. Also see Lamont, *Seeing Others*, on the power of *narratives* for social change, and powell and Menendian, *Belonging Without Othering*, who write that "narrative appears to play a central role in both processes of othering and belonging" (223).
4. Wilson Cruz, interview with author, December 7, 2012.
5. See Gould, *Moving Politics*; Polletta and Chen, "Narrative and Social Movements"; Reed, *The Art of Protest*; Rupp and Taylor, *Drag Queens at the 801 Cabaret.*
6. Dan Bucatinsky, interview with author, July 25, 2017.
7. Laura Zak, interview with author, January 11, 2018. This is echoed in the academic literature, as well. Social movements scholars note: "Narrative research has also

identified an important condition for stories' persuasive power. Stories have no effect if their message is too explicit [cite omitted]. This is not surprising. Readers resist being beaten over the head with the moral of the story" (Polletta and Chen, "Narrative and Social Movements," 493). Also see Polletta and Amenta, *Changing Minds*.

8. Amin El Gamal, interview with author, January 13, 2022.
9. Ellen D. Williams, interview with author, February 15, 2022.
10. Abraham Higginbotham, interview with author, April 26, 2012.
11. Media scholars and others have long believed that popular culture—from television and film to news/social media—can be the site of active and agentic identity-building and community, especially for young people, for queer people, and for others who are marginalized and who seek and find solace in each other. See Chauncey, *Gay New York*; Faderman, *Odd Girls and Twilight Lovers*; Fisherkeller, *Growing Up with Television*; Gray, *Out in the Country*; Gross, "Gideon Who Will Be 25"; Ito et al. *Hanging Out, Messing Around, and Geeking Out*; Jenkins, *Convergence Culture*; Miller, "Television"; Polletta and Jasper, "Collective Identity and Social Movements"; Rupp and Taylor, *Drag Queens at the 801 Cabaret*; Shapiro, *Turn the Beat Around*; Turino, *Music as Social Life*. And now, social media can build interactive audience/fan communities that have a strong sense of connection around their fandom. Social media can create a kind of common culture and language and a shared experience in an online space. At its most explicitly political, the online world provides the space for "networked social movements" (Castells, *Networks of Outrage and Hope*, 3), like the Arab Spring. Of course, on the flip side, the world knows the ways in which social media spaces can be highly commodified surveillance tools that serve as self-reinforcing echo chambers that are highly detrimental to democracy, to critical thinking, and to the triumph of truth (see, e.g., Beauchamp, "Social Media Is Rotting Democracy from Within"; Marwick, *Status Update*).
12. Also see Barracks, "No One Talks to Me in the Locker Room"; Kopay and Young, *The David Kopay Story*.
13. As sociologist Bernadette Barton writes, the organized movement tends to "sponsor the telling of stories as a political strategy" (*Pray the Gay Away*, 235).
14. E.g., Branch, "Confronting an Enduring Taboo."
15. See Buzinski and Zeigler, *The Outsports Revolution*, 23.
16. See https://www.outsports.com/comingout.
17. Cyd Zeigler, interview with author, December 6, 2012.
18. Zeigler, "Former College Football Captain."
19. Zeigler, "Brian Sims Story."
20. Brian Sims, interview with author, October 25, 2012.
21. Andrew Goldstein, interview with author, June 11, 2014.
22. E.g., Ryzik, "The Comedy-Destroying, Soul-Affirming Art"; Wired Staff, "Seriously."
23. Gadsby, "*Nanette* Transcript."

24. Scholars of comedy Caty Borum Chattoo and Lauren Feldman argue that we can think of "contemporary mediated comedy" as having five main genres, which they identify as *sketch, satirical news, scripted episodic TV, stand-up,* and *documentary* (*A Comedian and an Activist*, 5, 12, and chap. 3).
25. Chattoo and Feldman, *A Comedian and an Activist*, 191. Also, specifically on comedy's reliance on homophobia and transphobia, see, e.g., Cagle, "Tracy Morgan"; Talusan, "25 Years of Transphobia."
26. Chattoo and Feldman, *A Comedian and an Activist*, 26. Also on the role comedy in social change, see Himberg, *The New Gay for Pay*, and Reed, *The Art of Protest.*
27. Garber, "How Comedians Became Public Intellectuals."
28. D'Lo, interview with author, July 30, 2025.
29. Fawzia Mirza, interview with author, March 2, 2022. On these same themes, also see Mirza's TedX Talk, "Not Your Ordinary Brown Girl."
30. This theme of comedians' intent, along with the fact that many comedians were "motivated first and foremost by making people laugh and entertaining them" (187), is echoed in Chattoo and Feldman, *A Comedian and an Activist*, who write that artists' intent does not have to matter, primarily: "comedy's influence on social change can happen with or without the intent of the comedian" (57). On this theme, also see the oral history of *The Daily Show*: Smith, *The Daily Show (The Book)*.
31. Alec Mapa, interview with author, July 25, 2017. Lamont, in *Seeing Others*, also said that the Hollywood creatives she interviewed sometimes spoke of a strategy that Lamont came to call "the Trojan horse": "the subtle inclusion of social messages in seemingly neutral entertainment" (101).
32. E.g., Lea DeLaria, interview with author, September 19, 2014; also see Gadsby, "*Nanette* Transcript." See similar metaphors used by comedy professionals in Chattoo and Feldman's *A Comedian and an Activist*, e.g., 147, 155, 176; and see Lamont, *Seeing Others*, 99.
33. Many of the queer comedians in the 2024 Netflix documentary *Outstanding* make these points about how comedy works, as well. In *A Comedian and an Activist*, Chattoo and Feldman also argue that one of the mechanisms of social change for comedians is "creating intimacy" and bonds with their audiences: "Through this bond comes empathy and understanding, which can reduce stigma and foster more positive attitudes" (71).
34. Harvey Guillén, interview with author, March 20, 2015.
35. Eric Stonestreet, interview with author, June 14, 2012.
36. Also on the educative power of comedy/sitcoms, see comedian and writer Guy Branum's memoir, *My Life as a Goddess.*
37. Dunn et al., "Black Representation in Film and TV"; Yamato, "Hollywood Claims to Be Making Strides."
38. See, e.g., Henderson, "The Culture Behind Closed Doors"; Heuman, "What Happens in the Writers' Room Stays in the Writers' Room?"

39. Amin El Gamal, interview with author, January 12, 2018; Talai, "When a Brown Actor."
40. Nancy Wang Yuen writes about this, as well: "Actors of color can also reject roles as a form of advocacy" (*Reel Inequality*, 127). She writes broadly of this phenomenon of actors of color using their place in the room, as well.
41. Also see actor Andrew Rannells's stories in his memoir of refusing auditions for roles that he felt were problematic. "There would be no more gay clowning," he wrote (*Too Much Is Not Enough*, 160).
42. Abraham Higginbotham, interview with author, April 26, 2012; Jeff Richman, interview with author, April 16, 2013.
43. Jen Richards, interview with author, January 11, 2018.
44. Bradley, "The Privilege of Mediocrity."
45. On this finding, also see Gitlin, *Inside Prime Time*.
46. Dan Jinks, interview with author, October 20, 2011.
47. As Todd Gitlin observed of television in much earlier days, given the lack of clarity around why certain shows are successful, networks turn to those with clout to hopefully bring them their next big hit (*Inside Prime Time*, 156). Also see Bielby and Bielby, "'All Hits Are Flukes.'"
48. Adrienne Erickson, interview with author, November 10, 2021.
49. As superstar filmmaker Ava DuVernay said of Rhimes: "Shonda says, 'I'm not taking notes,' and network executives say, 'Yes, ma'am'" (quoted in Zook, "*Queen Sugar*"). And for background and discussion of Murphy, see Nussbaum, *I Like to Watch*.
50. GLAAD, *Where We Are on TV, 2020–2021*, 4.
51. Bourdieu, "The Forms of Capital"; Coleman, "Social Capital." Roussel, too, in *Representing Talent*, frames the work of Hollywood agents as "relationship work" that relies on "professional social capital" (99).
52. Gitlin, *Inside Prime Time*, 142, 156. Political scientist David Prindle also wrote that close relationship building in Hollywood is a way to guard against the uncertainty and risk in the business: "A search for powerful friends," he wrote, "is probably the primary psychological strategy . . . for dealing with the industry's emotional risks" (*Risky Business*, 59). Also see Ortner, "Reflections."
53. For some discussion of and reference to the "Gay Mafia," see, e.g., Prindle, *Risky Business*, 71; Signorile, *It's Not Over*, 18; Streitmatter, *From 'Perverts' to 'Fab Five,'* 184.
54. For the history of GLAAD and the organizations that preceded it with a similar purpose of supporting queer media and art, see Faderman and Timmons, *Gay L.A.*; Russo, *The Celluloid Closet*; Signorile, *Queer in America*.
55. Jamie Babbit, interview with author, January 10, 2018.
56. Ayanbadejo, "Coming Out a Liberating Move"; Fagan, "Derrick Gordon Openly Smiling"; Garber, "Impact Martina Navratilova Had"; Harper, "Michael Sam Met"; Hod, "How Howard Bragman"; Nianias, "Jason Collins"; Petchesky, "How

One Gay Athlete's Coming Out"; Tuaolo with Rosengren, *Alone in the Trenches*; Zeigler, "'The Eagle Has Landed.'"

57. See, e.g., the earlier experience of baseball player Billy Bean. See Buzinski, "Moment #7."
58. For another recent example, see the 2023 public coming-out story of NFL associate football coach Kevin Maxen (Zeigler, "Jacksonville Jaguars Strength Coach").
59. Prindle, *Risky Business*, 61. Also see Yuen, *Reel Inequality*.
60. Sarah Schulman writes powerfully on this point: "Historically, dominant people have always been comfortable with the idea of oppressed people as secretly powerful. The easiest example, of course, is how for almost two thousand years, dominant groups of various stripes have convinced themselves that they were ruled over by a secret cabal of Jews. Not only does this relieve the dominant group of responsibility for the pain they have inflicted on marginalized groups, but it further allows them to exercise their supremacy while falsely conceptualizing of themselves as disadvantaged" (*Stagestruck*, 124–25).
61. Among many others who have made this point, see Warner, "Introduction," xvi–xvii.
62. Scott Turner Schofield, interview with author, October 10, 2025.
63. See Bradley, "The Privilege of Mediocrity"; Oluo, *Mediocre*.
64. Warner, *The Trouble with Normal*, 76. Similarly, Jack Halberstam makes a case that "failure" as a new "queer art" can provide a way to critique traditional understandings of merit and success in Hollywood and beyond (*The Queer Art of Failure*).

CHAPTER FIVE

1. For a summary of these pervasive strands of theory and movement orientation and strategy and their proponents, see Stulberg, *LGBTQ Social Movements*. And, of course, the normal/queer binary is messy and complex, rather than fixed and always mutually exclusive (see, e.g., Cavalcante, *Struggling for Ordinary*). But this binary itself has been a central one in LGBTQ+ politics, organizing, and culture. Cavalcante offers the term "queerly ordinary": "a state of being a little bit queer and a little bit ordinary" or "fucking with gender while simultaneously sitting at the bar at Applebee's, having a cocktail and chatting with others" (177, 178).
2. See, e.g., Bernstein and Taylor, "Marital Discord"; Kimport, *Queering Marriage*.
3. Quoted in D'Emilio, *Sexual Politics, Sexual Communities*, 42. Also see Bérubé, *Coming Out Under Fire*.
4. Chauncey, *Why Marriage?*, 41.
5. For example, Trump's January 2025 executive order that moved to ban trans people from military service called into question their character and fitness to serve their country: "adoption of a gender identity inconsistent with an individual's sex conflicts with a soldier's commitment to an honorable, truthful, and

disciplined lifestyle, even in one's personal life" and "is not consistent with the humility and selflessness required of a service member" (White House, "Prioritizing Military Excellence and Readiness").

6. "We'll never be normal," wrote one commentator in June 2023 (Morgan, "As a Gay Man").
7. Yoshino, *Covering*, 77.
8. Gamson, *Freaks Talk Back*; Seidman, *Beyond the Closet*. See also Bronski, *The Pleasure Principle*; Duberman, *Has the Gay Movement Failed?*; Engel, *The Unfinished Revolution*; Garber, *Bisexuality*; Halberstam, *The Queer Art of Failure*; Harris, *The Rise and Fall of Gay Culture*; Kies, "First Comes Love"; Russo, *The Celluloid Closet*; Streitmatter, *From 'Perverts' to 'Fab Five.'* In addition, HBO's 2013 documentary *The Out List* touches on many of these themes, as referenced by high-profile actors, musicians, athletes, and other culture workers (Greenfield-Sanders, *The Out List*).
9. Syd Diaz, interview with author, November 4, 2022.
10. E.g., Engel, *The Unfinished Revolution*; Seidman, *Beyond the Closet*; Sender, *Business, Not Politics*.
11. Rhimes, "'You Are Not Alone.'"
12. In its January 2025 survey, GLAAD found that media representation works in this way and that non-LGBTQ+ adults report a growth of 23–34 percent in "comfortability interacting with our community in various scenarios in life" and "familiarity with our community" when they "see us in the media" (*Accelerating Acceptance, 2025*).
13. For the finding that "television-mediated contact may be especially effective in changing attitudes," because of the particularities of storytelling and delivery of these stories in TV, see Polletta and Amenta, *Changing Minds*, 100.
14. In the context of a discussion of "transgender belonging," media scholar Andre Cavalcante argues for the use of the word *ordinary* and (the *everyday*) instead of *normal*, writing: "I use the word 'ordinary' strategically to move away from the clinical, diagnostic, and deeply moralistic connotations of the word 'normal'" (*Struggling for Ordinary*, 20–21).
15. Guinevere Turner, interview with author, December 7, 2012.
16. Cagle, "Special Report: The Gay '90s"; Poul, "Preserving Our Queer Legacy." Also see Ghaziani, *The Dividends of Dissent*, especially the chapter entitled "The People Next Door: Lesbian and Gay Life in the Late 1980s and Early 1990s."
17. As Peter Paige said about TV: "Television, in particular, even more than movies, is so powerful because we reach people in their homes. . . . We reach people in their homes week after week at their most vulnerable. . . . It's how friendships happen" (Peter Paige, interview with author, June 11, 2014). Also see Himberg, *The New Gay for Pay*, for the note that television, in particular, "encourage[s] a sense of familiarity and closeness" (58).

18. Feiler, "What 'Modern Family' Says"; Zurawik, "'Modern Family.'"
19. Although there is some sociological evidence from the real world that this kind of integration and cultural resemblance might not always be welcome. In her book on small-town Oregon, Arlene Stein wrote that for some Christian conservatives in the town, it was the *fact* of the integration of gay neighbors who might be indistinguishable from them that was problematic to them: "What really seemed to disturb people was that queer people, lacking a ghettoized bar culture, lived in their world: the strangers in their midst looked very much like them" (*The Stranger Next Door*, 16).
20. Hale, "'The Holiday Sitter' Review."
21. Scholar Suzanna Danuta Walters sums up this change with the following periodization: The pre-social movements period until the 1960s "was marked either by absence, coded and subterranean images, or the pathos of abject stereotypes." The next phase of visibility, the late 1980s and early 1990s, "spurred by social movements, Hollywood niche marketing, commodification, and disease—irrevocably brought gays out of the closet but into the problematic space of public spectacle, a space to finally be *seen* but not necessarily to be *known* in any meaningful way." Then a third, current phase after this, which she questions the desirability of: "a phase of banal inclusion, normalization, assimilation, and everyday unremarkable queerness in which tolerance seems finally achieved" (*The Tolerance Trap*, 8).
22. On these impacts of *Will & Grace* and *Modern Family*, in particular, also see Galanes, "At Lunch"; VanArendonk, "*Will & Grace*'s Best Trump Joke"; Zakarin, "Ty Burrell."
23. Jen Richards, interview with author, January 11, 2018.
24. Jen Richards, interview with author, July 24, 2025.
25. Abraham Higginbotham, interview with author, April 26, 2012.
26. Polletta et al.'s "Social Movements in the Commercial Public Sphere" is a great resource on this point. They note: "Audiences' wants are imagined by commercial entitles for the purpose of profit—but the result may be to influence real audiences' beliefs about movements and movement issues" (1304).
27. Jamie Babbit, interview with author, July 27, 2012.
28. See discussion in chapters 1 and 2.
29. Billson, "Harry's Razors Backlash"; Holpuch, "Behind the Backlash."
30. For one of just many examples over the years, see *US Weekly*'s "Excited to Wed" profile on Neil Patrick Harris and David Burtka, who announced their engagement right after same-sex marriage became legal in New York in 2011.
31. Steve Buckley, interview with author, April 5, 2013. Also see Belanger, "A Conversation with Steve Buckley."
32. Chattoo and Feldman, *A Comedian and an Activist*, 67; GLAAD, *2020 Studio Responsibility Index*; Gottschall, "The Power of Fake Gay (and Black) Friends"; Hart-Brinson, *The Gay Marriage Generation*; Lamont, *Seeing Others*; NPR Staff, "How

TV Brought Gay People into Our Homes"; Ortner, *Not Hollywood*; Polletta and Amenta, *Changing Minds*; Polletta et al., "Social Movements in the Commercial Public Sphere"; Schiappa et al., "The Parasocial Contact Hypothesis"; Seidman; *Beyond the Closet*; Streitmatter, *From 'Perverts' to 'Fab Five.'*

33. E.g., Polletta and Amenta, *Changing Minds*; Rupp and Taylor, *Drag Queens at the 801 Cabaret*; Schmidt, "Americans' Views Flipped." Also recall Vice President Joe Biden's statement in 2012 that *Will & Grace* could be substantially credited with a shift in public opinion on marriage equality (see chap. 2 and Walters, *The Tolerance Trap*, 156).
34. Several scholars and commentators note that this theory of familiarity and social attitudes can be traced back to mid-twentieth-century social scientists, like Gordon Allport and his *contact hypothesis*. See, e.g., Allport, *The Nature of Prejudice*; Amenta and Polletta, "The Cultural Impact of Social Movements"; Barton, *Pray the Gay Away*; Chattoo and Feldman, *A Comedian and an Activist*; Schmidt, "Americans' Views Flipped."
35. Gross, *Contested Closets.*
36. See, e.g., Amenta and Polletta, "The Cultural Impact of Social Movements"; Frank, *Awakening*; Ghaziani, *Sex Cultures*; Pew Research Center, "A Survey of LGBT Americans"; Rector, "Americans Approve."
37. Rory O'Malley, interview with author, April 30, 2013.
38. GLAAD, *Accelerating Acceptance, 2025*. These numbers differ only slightly from a Data for Progress poll that sampled all US adults in March 2025, which found that 62, 55, 42, 29, and 20 percent of adults report knowing someone who is gay, lesbian, bisexual, transgender, and nonbinary, respectively ("Americans Are Divided").
39. Data for Progress, "Americans Are Divided."
40. A well-known example from *politics* is former Ohio Republican senator Rob Portman, who famously changed his public stance on marriage equality when his son came out to him as gay. Journalist Josh Barro called this the "gay-relative effect" (see Barro, "How Rob Portman Will Change the Gay Marriage Debate").
41. Patrick Burke, interview with author, September 17, 2012.
42. See, among many examples in sports, Buzinski, "Houston Texan"; Dye, "Magic Johnson"; Friend, "Kenneth Faried"; McCarriston, "Super Bowl Champion"; Zeigler, "10 Black Pro Athletes," "Michael Irvin," and "NFL Commissioner." Also, relatedly, see Pryor, "African American Gay Men Lead the Way."
43. Quoted in Clark, "Dwyane Wade's Unflinching Support"; and see Piña, "Dwyane Wade."
44. Bastidas, "Gabrielle Union and Dwyane Wade."
45. On pop cultural normalization, Katherine Sender argues, in *Business, Not Politics*, that "the 'just like you' claim sets up a false equivalence between economically privileged gays and socially, legally, and economically privileged heterosexuals,

minimizing the very real differences between these groups in terms of interpersonal and institutionalized discrimination" (239).

46. Bronski, *The Pleasure Principle*, 206; emphasis in original.
47. See chap. 1 for a discussion of the "trap" of visibility in this way.
48. See note 10 in chap. 1 for a wide range of scholarly and popular discussions and critiques of this representation. Also see Tison Pugh, who wrote in *The Queer Fantasies of the American Family Sitcom* of the impulse of this response: "From the early days of television . . . the history of gay television representation inevitably has prompted both celebration and disappointment over each milestone: celebration that queer lives are represented onscreen yet disappointment that many of these depictions seem trapped by tired preconceptions of queer lives" (170).
49. Reid, "The Burden of Sole Representation."
50. Abraham Higginbotham, email to author, December 4, 2025.
51. Also see Reid, "The Burden of Sole Representation," who then provides a nuanced analysis of this critique.
52. For just a *very* small sample of the media coverage, see Bruni, "ABC's Gay Wednesdays"; Feiler, "What 'Modern Family' Says"; Poniewozik, "Modern Family Watch"; Portwood, "The New Normal." For an academic reading of the "queer potential latent in the sitcom genre" in general and in *Modern Family* in particular, see Pugh, *The Queer Fantasies of the American Family Sitcom*, 161–62. And see 177–79 for Pugh's analysis of "The Kiss" episode of *Modern Family*.
53. Stack, "Love, Simon."
54. Tobia, "Does Gay Hollywood?"
55. Scholar Lisa Duggan defines homonormativity as "a politics that does not contest dominant heteronormative assumptions and institutions, but upholds and sustains them, while promising the possibility of a demobilized gay constituency and a privatized, depoliticized gay culture anchored in domesticity and consumption" (*The Twilight of Equality?*, 50).
56. With this critique of assimilation into culture, there is an analogous conversation and fear about the loss of queer spaces. See, e.g., Ghaziani, *There Goes the Gayborhood?*
57. Du Bois, *The Souls of Black Folk*, 5.
58. hooks, *Feminist Theory*. Also see hooks, "Choosing the Margin."
59. Collins, "Learning from the Outsider Within," S29. Also see Collins, *Black Feminist Thought*, and Cooper, *Eloquent Rage*. And for a much older—and foundational—contribution from sociology, see Georg Simmel's 1908 essay "The Stranger."
60. Harris, *The Rise and Fall of Gay Culture*.
61. See, e.g., Avilez, "Uncertain Freedom"; Bronski, *The Pleasure Principle*; Schulman, *Stagestruck*.
62. Sarah Schulman, interview with author, May 3, 2013.
63. When I checked to confirm that I had not gotten this term from anyone else, I found an article on physics education by McNeill et al., "Leveraging Queer

Epistemic Subjectivity to Advance Justice Through Physics Teaching," which also examines the contribution that "queer and trans*" students can make to physics through their standpoint and ways of knowing. Elliot Page also uses the phrase in his memoir, writing: "Hollywood is built on leveraging queerness. Tucking it away when needed, pulling it out when beneficial, while patting themselves on the back" (*Pageboy*, 106).

64. Hudson Taylor, interview with author, September 20, 2012. Also see Woog, "Hudson Taylor."
65. Scott Fujita, interview with author, September 26, 2013. Also see Fujita, "Acceptance by Example."
66. Signorile, "Brendon Ayanbadejo."
67. Kluwe, *Beautifully Unique Sparkleponies*, 94–95, 135. And Chris Kluwe, interview with author, November 15, 2012; Gervino, "The Punter Makes His Point"; Zeigler, "Kick Ass."
68. Also see Galanes, "At Lunch," who illustrates this point, as well, in his conversation with Jesse Tyler Ferguson and Eric McCormack: "As a gay kid, I was very watchful of how straight people behaved. I didn't want to get teased, so I wanted to act how they were acting." Actor Michael Kearns, who has spoken publicly about a sexual encounter he had with Rock Hudson and the author of a theater piece about Hudson, said in an interview to author Mark Griffin, for *All That Heaven Allows*, a biography of Hudson: "Rock was a brilliant actor, though not necessarily on the screen. His most brilliant performance was playing 'Rock Hudson' all his life. . . . I mean, from the very beginning of his life, this is someone who had to act just to *survive*" (359; emphasis in original).
69. Bridget McManus, interview with author, March 14, 2023.
70. John Amaechi, interview with author, April 26, 2014.
71. On this theme in sports, see Louganis, "The Toughest Sissy." Also on the theme of pain, trauma, and marginalization providing an outsider's "perspective" that can be channeled into artistic work, see singer Jake Shears's essay "Art from Rage" and his interview in HBO's *The Out List*.
72. Piepenburg, "The Day New Queer Cinema."
73. As noted above, for example, in just the past couple of years, even just the suggestion that trans people did *everyday* things like shave and drink beer was enough to draw substantial and hateful backlash for Bud Light and Harry's razors. See Billson, "Harry's Razors Backlash"; Holpuch, "Behind the Backlash."
74. For anyone interested in a deeper dive into theory on this point, see Michel Foucault's work, e.g., *Discipline and Punish* and *The History of Sexuality*.
75. Again, there is a parallel to draw here to new American Jews at the beginning of the Hollywood studio system, who historically did shape the center of popular culture through Hollywood. In this case, we can see a similarity in the way that they leveraged their influential yet culturally marginalized space in the industry to work assiduously to assimilate into and shape American culture—*and* the

way they actively avoided "flaunting Hollywood's Jewishness, behind or on the screen" (Renov and Brook, "Editorial Introduction," ix). Neal Gabler writes of the "paradox" of Hollywood's origins, that the industry "was founded and for more than thirty years operated by Eastern European Jews who themselves seemed to be anything *but* the quintessence of America. The much-vaunted 'studio system,' . . . was supervised by a second generation of Jews, many of whom also regarded themselves as marginal men trying to punch into the American mainstream" (Gabler, *An Empire of Their Own*, 1–2). Also see Brownstein, *The Power and the Glitter*.

76. See, e.g., Morgan, "As a Gay Man"; Seidman et al., "The Politics of Authenticity."

CONCLUSION

1. Burns, "Why Trump's Latest"; Harmon, "Transgender Americans Say"; Villagran, "'Page Not Found'"; White House, The Inaugural Address; White House, "Protecting Children."
2. For example, see the federal assault on gender-affirming care (e.g., Holzman, "Will Democrats"). The Supreme Court also seems to be signaling, as well, that it will certify the anti-LGBTQ+ agenda of the Right. See, e.g., the 2023 ruling in *303 Creative LLC v. Elenis* that refusing to serve gay customers was protected speech (Burga, "The Implications of Supreme Court's 303 Creative").
3. Simmons-Duffin, "Trans Health Care."
4. Dodds, "Trump's Blitz"; Rector, "Americans Approve"; Thomas, "What's Really Behind."
5. Writer and activist Michael Bronski provides this compelling analysis of the stakes of the clash between margin and center, assimilationism and the assertion of a distinct culture: "All unmodified subcultures pose a threat to the perceived cohesion of the dominant culture. This threat is usually decreased through the process of assimilation, but when subcultures exert influence rather than undergo assimilation, the threat they pose may remain intact. Thus, subculture and dominant culture coexist in an uneasy truce, haunted by the possibility that underlying tensions will erupt: culture wars" (*The Pleasure Principle*, 62).
6. I understand that this framing does not always feel like winning to everyone. For a discussion of LGBTQ+ politics on this point, see Arlene Stein's *The Stranger Next Door*. For a more general discussion that frames recent US politics in this way, see sociologist Arlie Hochschild's *Strangers in Their Own Land*.
7. For thoughtful critiques that have informed my thinking here, see a few excellent titles that take a highly critical yet complex approach to LGBTQ+ politics and culture, such as Harris's *The Rise and Fall of Gay Culture*; Sender's *Business, Not Politics*; and Walters's *All the Rage* and *The Tolerance Trap*.
8. Polletta et al., "Social Movements in the Commercial Public Sphere."
9. Also see Stulberg, *LGBTQ Social Movements*, 1.

10. Lorde, *Sister Outsider*, 44.
11. Relatedly, social movement scholars Nella Van Dyke and Verta Taylor note: "Yet for many social movements, cultural changes are often their most significant and lasting effects, especially when we take into account that most movements ultimately fail to achieve their stated policy objectives" ("The Cultural Outcomes of Social Movements," 482).
12. See the introduction and Pfeiffer, *Battling the Big Lie*.
13. See note 44 in the introduction and note 1 in appendix A, for citations here.
14. For an inspiring example in the recent fight to retain gender-affirming care, see Masterson, "Illinois Joins Lawsuit," and Schorsch, "Chicago Hospitals."
15. For an active public debate—albeit now a few years old—about the future of the LGBTQ+ movement and its victories and continuing fights, see, on one side, e.g., Kirchick, "The Struggle for Gay Rights Is Over," and, on the other, e.g., Duberman, *Has the Gay Movement Failed?* and Signorile, *It's Not Over*.
16. Kushner, *Angels in America*, 290.

APPENDIX A

1. Craig, "Coming Out of the Television"; Gamson, *Claims to Fame* and *Freaks Talk Back*; Himberg, *The New Gay for Pay*; Rupp and Taylor, *Drag Queens at the 801 Cabaret*; Sender, *Business, Not Politics*. And more broadly on pop culture and social change, see Chattoo and Feldman, *A Comedian and an Activist*; Lamont, *Seeing Others*.
2. The classic exceptions are Dunne, *The Studio*; Gitlin, *Inside Prime Time*; Powdermaker, *Hollywood, the Dream Factory*. Some important, more recent exceptions include Caldwell, *Production Culture*; Christian, *Open TV*; Dessauer, "Sousveillance Work"; Grindstaff, *The Money Shot*; Henderson, "The Culture Behind Closed Doors"; Ortner, *Not Hollywood*; Roussel, *Representing Talent*; Yuen, *Reel Inequality*.
3. E.g., Becker, *Gay TV and Straight America*; Chambers, *The Queer Politics of Television*; DeAngelis, *Reading the Bromance*; Hubbs, *Rednecks, Queers, and Country Music*; Pugh, *The Queer Fantasies of the American Family Sitcom*; San Filippo, *The B Word*; Seidman, *Beyond the Closet*; Streitmatter, *From 'Perverts' to 'Fab Five.'*
4. Joshua Gamson reflected: "Relationships are indeed more central to the way things get done in Hollywood than in other more stable industries with more formalized roles. They are both the barrier and the facilitator to access" ("Stopping the Spin," 86).
5. In addition to Ortner's reflections on access to Hollywood production, see those of Caldwell, *Production Culture*; Gamson, "Stopping the Spin"; Lamont, *Seeing Others*; Mayer, "Studying Up."
6. Ortner, "Reflections," 212, 213.

7. On name-dropping in recruiting of this kind, also see Mayer, “Studying Up,” 144.
8. Stulberg, “One Ally’s Story.”
9. Lamont, *Seeing Others*, 9, 177.
10. Lamont, *Seeing Others*, 2, 62.
11. E.g., Flavell, “10 Most Powerful”; Refinery29, “The LGBTQ+ YouTubers.” Also see Gross, *Up from Invisibility*, on LGBTQ+ visibility in comics.

WORKS CITED

Aagenes, A. "Coaches Need to Be Public Allies of LGBT Athletes." *Huffington Post*, May 23, 2013. https://www.huffpost.com/entry/coaches-need-to-be-public-allies-of-lgbt-athletes_b_3319330.

Aagenes, A. "Come Out Like a Girl: Why Athletes Like Brittney Griner Deserve Our Applause and Our Attention." *Huffington Post*, April 22, 2013. https://www.huffpost.com/entry/brittney-griner-coming-out_b_3130781.

Abramovitch, S. "Joe Biden Cites 'Will & Grace' in Endorsement of Same-Sex Marriage" (video). *The Hollywood Reporter*, May 6, 2012. https://www.hollywoodreporter.com/live-feed/joe-biden-cites-will-grace-320724-0.

Abramovitch, S. "'Transparent' Star Alleges Jeffrey Tambor Sexually Harassed Her, 'Got Physical.'" *The Hollywood Reporter*, November 16, 2017. https://www.hollywoodreporter.com/news/general-news/transparent-star-alleges-jeffrey-tambor-sexually-harassed-her-got-physical-1059306/.

Abramowitz, R. *Is That a Gun in Your Pocket?: Women's Experience of Power in Hollywood.* Random House, 2000.

Adalain, J., and L. Brown. "The Binge Purge." *Vulture*, June 6, 2023. https://www.vulture.com/2023/06/streaming-industry-netflix-max-disney-hulu-apple-tv-prime-video-peacock-paramount.html.

Adatto, K. *Picture Perfect: The Art and Artifice of Public Image Making*. Basic Books, 1993.

Addams, C. "Op-Ed: In Defense of Jared Leto." *Advocate*, March 5, 2014. https://www.advocate.com/commentary/2014/03/05/op-ed-defense-jared-leto.

Adgate, B. "The Impact COVID-19 Had on the Entertainment Industry in 2020." *Forbes*, April 13, 2021. https://www.forbes.com/sites/bradadgate/2021/04/13/the-impact-covid-19-had-on-the-entertainment-industry-in-2020/.

Al-Kadhi, A. *Life as a Unicorn: A Journey from Shame to Pride and Everything in Between.* Fourth Estate, 2020.

Allen, S. *Real Queer America: LGBT Stories from Red States*. Little, Brown, 2019.

Allen, S. "Why LGBT People Are Moving to Red States." *Daily Beast*, March 9, 2016. https://www.thedailybeast.com/why-lgbt-people-are-moving-to-red-states/.

Allport, G. W. *The Nature of Prejudice*. 1954. 25th Anniversary Edition. Basic Books, 1979.

Alwood, E. *Straight News: Gays, Lesbians, and the News Media*. Columbia University Press, 1996.

Amaechi, J., with C. Bull. *Man in the Middle*. ESPN Books, 2007.

Amenta, E., and N. Caren. *Rough Draft of History: A Century of US Social Movements in the News*. Princeton University Press, 2022.

Amenta, E., and F. Polletta. "The Cultural Impact of Social Movements." *Annual Review of Sociology* 45 (2019): 279–99.

Anderson, E. *In the Game: Gay Athletes and the Cult of Masculinity*. State University of New York Press, 2005.

Anderson, E., R. Magrath, and R. Bullingham. *Out in Sport: The Experiences of Openly Gay and Lesbian Athletes in Competitive Sports*. Routledge, 2016.

Anderson, J. "Kit Connor Gets a Therapy Session from Jonathan Anderson." *Interview*, August 17, 2023. https://www.interviewmagazine.com/television/kit-connor-gets-a-therapy-session-from-jonathan-anderson.

Anderson, T. "New CAA Study Says Diverse Casting Increases Box Office Potential Across All Budgets." *Los Angeles Times*, June 21, 2017. https://www.latimes.com/entertainment/movies/la-et-mn-caa-diversity-study-exclusive-20170622-story.html.

Andreeva, N. "Lil Nas X Suffers Wardrobe Malfunction During Performance on 'Saturday Night Live.'" *Deadline*, May 23, 2021. https://deadline.com/2021/05/lil-nas-x-wardrobe-malfunction-saturday-night-live-pats-ripped-montero-1234762568/.

Andreeva, N. "Ted Sarandos Marks Decade of Netflix Original Series on Anniversary of 'Lilyhammer' Premiere." *Deadline*, February 6, 2022. https://deadline.com/2022/02/ted-sarandos-lilyhammer-decade-netflix-original-series-anniversary-premiere-1234927208/.

Andrew, S. "Why JoJo Siwa's Coming Out Is Such a Massively Big Deal." CNN, January 30, 2021. https://amp.cnn.com/cnn/2021/01/30/us/jojo-siwa-coming-out-significance-wellness-trnd/index.html.

Andrews, K. "John Amaechi: How the First NBA Player to Come Out Is Now Teaching Us All About White Privilege." *The Guardian*, September 17, 2020. https://www.theguardian.com/society/2020/sep/17/john-amaechi-first-nba-player-to-come-out-now-teaching-us-all-about-white-privilege.

Antonucci, L. "Advocates Call for NCAA to Add Nondiscrimination Protections to New Constitution." NBC Sports, January 20, 2022. https://onherturf.nbcsports.com/2022/01/20/advocates-call-for-ncaa-to-add-nondiscrimination-protections-to-new-constitution/.

Arceneaux, M. "'Black and Gay': How Race Plays a Role in Jason Collins' Coming Out." The Grio, April 30, 2013. https://thegrio.com/2013/04/30/black-and-gay-how-race-plays-a-role-in-jason-collins-coming-out/.

Ariail, C. "The Pride, Power and Purpose of WNBA Players." Swish Appeal, June 21, 2020. https://www.swishappeal.com/wnba/2020/6/21/21293983/wnba-pride-lgbtq-gender-sexuality-race-black-lives-matter-activism-brittney-griner-layshia-clarendon.

Armstrong, E. A. *Forging Gay Identities: Organizing Sexuality in San Francisco, 1950–1994*. University of Chicago Press, 2002.

Armstrong, E. A., and M. Bernstein. "Culture, Power, and Institutions: A Multi-Institutional Politics Approach to Social Movements." *Sociological Theory* 26, no. 1 (March 2008): 74–99.

Aronstein, A. J. "'All in the Family' and the First Gay Sitcom Character." *Vulture*, May 30, 2012. https://www.vulture.com/2012/05/all-in-the-family-and-the-first-gay-sitcom-character.html.

Associated Press. "WNBA to Market to LGBT Community." *USA Today*, May 21, 2014. https://www.usatoday.com/story/sports/wnba/2014/05/21/ap-newsbreak-wnba-to-market-to-lgbt-community/9364893/.

Astor, M. "Trump Administration Will End L.G.B.T.Q. Suicide Prevention Service." *The New York Times*, June 18, 2025. https://www.nytimes.com/2025/06/18/well/lgbtq-988-suicide-prevention.html.

Athlete Ally. "About Athlete Ally." https://www.athleteally.org/about/.

Auletta, K. *Three Blind Mice: How the TV Networks Lost Their Way*. Vintage, 1992.

Avery, D. "St. Patty's Gay: Vintage Guinness Ad Features Same-Sex Couple." *Queerty*, March 17, 2013. https://www.queerty.com/st-pattys-gay-vintage-guinness-ad-features-same-sex-couple-20130317.

Avilez, G. "Uncertain Freedom: RuPaul, Sylvester, and Black Queer Contingency." *The Black Scholar* 49, no. 2 (2019): 50–64.

Ayanbadejo, B. "Advocacy Acceptance Goes Case-by-Case in NFL." FOX Sports, January 4, 2014. https://www.foxsports.com/stories/nfl/opinion-advocacy-acceptance-goes-case-by-case-in-nfl.

Ayanbadejo, B. "Coming Out a Liberating Move for Michael Sam." FOX Sports, March 4, 2020 (updated). https://www.foxsports.com/stories/nfl/ayanbadejo-coming-out-a-liberating-move-for-michael-sam.

Ayanbadejo, B. "End Homophobia in Professional Sports." *USA Today*, February 6, 2013. https://www.usatoday.com/story/opinion/2013/02/06/openly-gay-professional-sports-player/1894721/.

Ayanbadejo, B. "My Thoughts on Michael Sam and LGBT at Sochi." *Huffington Post*, February 19, 2014. https://www.huffpost.com/entry/my-thoughts-on-michael-sam-and-lgbt-at-sochi_b_4816053.

Ayanbadejo, B. "Same Sex Marriages: What's the Big Deal?" *Huffington Post*, May 24, 2009. https://www.huffpost.com/entry/same-sex-marriages-whats_b_190591.

Ayanbadejo, B. "Sam's Draft Prospects Put the Spotlight Squarely Back on NFL." FOX Sports, February 10, 2014. https://www.foxsports.com/stories/nfl/sams-draft-prospects-put-the-spotlight-squarely-back-on-nfl.

Azzi, A. "NCAA Constitution Called Out for Failing to Include Non-Discrimination Policy." NBC Sports, November 12, 2021. https://onherturf.nbcsports.com/2021/11/12/revised-ncaa-constitution-nondiscrimination-policy-athlete-ally-hrc/.

Bachman, R. "Sherri Murrell, After Four Winning Seasons at Portland State, Still Only Publicly Gay Coach in D-1 Basketball." *The Oregonian*, July 19, 2011. https://www.oregonlive.com/vikings/2011/07/sherri_murrell_after_four_winn.html.

Badgett, M. V. L., and J. L. Herman. *Sexual Orientation and Gender Identity Diversity in Entertainment: Experiences and Perspectives of SAG-AFTRA Members*. SAG-AFTRA and Williams Institute, 2013. https://williamsinstitute.law.ucla.edu/wp-content/uploads/SOGI-Entertainment-Sep-2013.pdf.

Bagwell, M. "Rupert Everett Says 'We Shouldn't Be Making Rules' About Gay Actors Playing Gay Roles." *HuffPost*, May 19, 2022. https://www.huffingtonpost.co.uk/entry/rupert-everett-i-dont-think-gay-actors-should-just-play-the-gay-roles_uk_6285e247e4b0556e4a0987ba.

Bailar, S. *He/She/They: How We Talk About Gender and Why It Matters*. Hachette Go, 2023.

Baine, D. "How Many Streaming Services Can People Consume? OTT Services and MVPDs Continue to Soar." *Forbes*, December 22, 2021. https://www.forbes.com/sites/derekbaine/2021/12/22/how-many-streaming-services-can-people-consume-ott-services-vmvpds-continue-to-soar/.

Baker, L. B. "GE to Sell Rest of NBC Stake to Comcast for $16.7 Billion." Reuters, February 12, 2013. https://www.reuters.com/article/us-ge-nbc/ge-to-sell-rest-of-nbc-stake-to-comcast-for-16-7-billion-idUSBRE91B1IM20130212.

Barnes, B. "After #MeToo Reckoning, a Fear Hollywood Is Regressing." *The New York Times*, October 24, 2022. https://www.nytimes.com/2022/10/24/business/media/hollywood-metoo.html.

Barnes, B. "At the Golden Globes, a New Culture War Erupts Onstage." *The New York Times*, January 9, 2017. https://www.nytimes.com/2017/01/09/movies/golden-globes-donald-trump-meryl-streep.html.

Barnes, B. "Disney Moves from Behemoth to Colossus with Closing of Fox Deal." *The New York Times*, March 20, 2019. https://www.nytimes.com/2019/03/20/business/media/walt-disney-21st-century-fox-deal.html.

Barnes, B. "For Disney's Iger, a Bold Move That Will Define His Legacy." *The New York Times*, December 15, 2017. https://www.nytimes.com/2017/12/15/business/media/bob-iger-disney-fox.html.

Barnes, B. "Hollywood's Behind-the-Scenes Workers Reach Deal, Averting Strike." *The New York Times*, October 16, 2021. https://www.nytimes.com/2021/10/16/business/iatse-deal-strike-averted.html.

Barnes, B. "Hollywood's Message to Red States: Our Movies Are for You." *The New York Times*, July 28, 2024. https://www.nytimes.com/2024/07/28/business/media/hollywood-movies-red-state-audiences.html.

Barnes, B. "Hollywood's Obituary, the Sequel. Now Streaming." *The New York Times*,

November 28, 2020. https://www.nytimes.com/2020/11/28/business/media/hollywood-coronavirus-streaming.html.

Barnes, B. "The Streaming Era Has Finally Arrived. Everything Is About to Change." *The New York Times*, November 18, 2019. https://www.nytimes.com/2019/11/18/business/media/streaming-hollywood-revolution.html.

Barnes, B. "Who Gets to Play the Transgender Part?" *The New York Times*, September 3, 2015. https://www.nytimes.com/2015/09/04/movies/who-gets-to-play-the-transgender-part-in-hollywood.html.

Barnes, B. "With $218 Million Haul, 'Black Panther' Smashes Box Office Records." *The New York Times*, February 18, 2018. https://www.nytimes.com/2018/02/18/movies/black-panther-box-office-records.html.

Barnes, B., and J. Koblin. 2023. "On Day 146, Screenwriters Reach Deal with Studios to End Their Strike." *The New York Times*, September 25. https://www.nytimes.com/2023/09/25/business/media/hollywood-writers-strike-deal.html.

Barnes, B., and P. Lavigne. "Transgender Athlete Debate Rolls on Six Months After Executive Order." ESPN, August 6, 2025. https://www.espn.com/olympics/story/_/id/45878971/six-months-president-trump-executive-order-transgender-athlete-debate-persists.

Baron, L., and J. Rosenberg, with a coda by V. Brook. "The Ben Urwand Controversy: Exploring the Hollywood-Hitler Relationship." In *From Shtetl to Stardom: Jews and Hollywood*, edited by Michael Renov and Vincent Brook, 23–46. Purdue University Press for the USC Casden Institution for the Study of the Jewish Role in American Life, 2016.

Barracks, C. "No One Talks to Me in the Locker Room." In *Queer Voices from the Locker Room*, edited by C. T. McGivern and P.C. Miller, 119–26. Information Age, 2018.

Barro, J. "How Rob Portman Will Change the Gay Marriage Debate." Bloomberg, March 15, 2013. https://www.bloomberg.com/view/articles/2013-03-15/how-rob-portman-will-change-the-gay-marriage-debate.

Bart, P. "Conglomeration Is Snuffing Out Courage in Hollywood." *Deadline*, June 30, 2016. https://deadline.com/2016/06/viacom-hollywood-pitfalls-conglomerates-1201782020/.

Barton, B. *Pray the Gay Away: The Extraordinary Lives of Bible Belt Gays*. New York University Press, 2012.

Bastidas, G. "Gabrielle Union and Dwyane Wade Are Raising the Bar." *Parents*, August 1, 2023. https://www.parents.com/gabrielle-union-and-dwayne-wade-on-parenting-and-partnership-7511693.

Baum, S. "Devastating Blows to Trans Care at Kaiser, Yale and Others." *Erin in the Morning* (blog), July 29, 2025. https://www.erininthemorning.com/p/devastating-blows-to-trans-care-at.

Baum, S. "Trump's DOJ Subpoenas Trans Care Records from 20 Hospitals." *Erin in the Morning* (blog), July 11, 2025. https://www.erininthemorning.com/p/trumps-doj-subpoenas-trans-care-records.

Baume, M. *Defining Marriage: Voices from a Forty-Year Labor of Love*. Self-published, 2015.

Baur, B. "Being an Out Gay Actor." *Huffington Post*, October 9, 2012. https://www.huffpost.com/entry/being-an-out-gay-actor_b_1951568.

Bean, B. "One Pioneering Gay Athlete Thanks Another." ABC News, February 15, 2007. https://abcnews.go.com/Sports/story?id=2859328&page=1.

Bean, B., with C. Bill. *Going the Other Way: Lessons from a Life in and out of Major League Baseball*. Marlowe & Co., 2003.

Beauchamp, Z. "Could Clarence Thomas's Dobbs Concurrence Signal a Future Attack on LGBTQ Rights?" *Vox*, June 24, 2022. https://www.vox.com/2022/6/24/23181723/roe-v-wade-dobbs-clarence-thomas-concurrence.

Beauchamp, Z. "Social Media Is Rotting Democracy from Within." *Vox*, January 22, 2019. https://www.vox.com/policy-and-politics/2019/1/22/18177076/social-media-facebook-far-right-authoritarian-populism.

Becker, R. *Gay TV and Straight America*. Rutgers University Press, 2006.

Belam, M., and S. Levin. "Woman Behind 'Inclusion Rider' Explains Frances McDormand's Oscar Speech." *The Guardian*, March 5, 2018. https://www.theguardian.com/film/2018/mar/05/what-is-an-inclusion-rider-frances-mcdormand-oscars-2018.

Belanger, H. P. "A Conversation with Steve Buckley." The Good Men Project, February 1, 2011. https://goodmenproject.com/featured-content/a-conversation-with-steve-buckley/.

Bell, D. A., Jr. "*Brown v. Board of Education* and the Interest-Convergence Dilemma." *Harvard Law Review* 93, no. 3 (January 1980): 518–33.

Bendix, T. "Can Gay Play Straight?: What Sexuality Has to Do with Winning Roles and Academy Awards." Alternet.org, March 4, 2011. https://www.guernicamag.com/trish_bendix/.

Bendix, T. "'Faking It' Finale Proves MTV Does Not Know Lesbian Sexuality." *The Hollywood Reporter*, June 10, 2014. https://www.hollywoodreporter.com/live-feed/faking-finale-proves-mtv-does-710958.

Bendix, T. "How Ellen DeGeneres Changed TV History." *Elle*, May 1, 2017. https://www.yahoo.com/lifestyle/ellen-degeneres-changed-tv-history-180746123.html.

Bendix, T. "13 Same-Sex TV Kisses That Shocked Viewers." NewNowNext, July 6, 2017. http://www.newnownext.com/gay-kisses-television/07/2017/.

Beran, L. "As the NCAA Debates New Rules, Trans Athletes Are Left Out of the Conversation." *The Nation*, June 20, 2024. https://www.thenation.com/article/society/transgender-student-athletes-ncaa-representation/.

Bergado, G. "The History-Making Gay Kiss: 'The Fosters' Features the Youngest Same-Sex TV Kiss Ever." *Daily Beast*, March 3, 2015. https://www.thedailybeast.com/the-history-making-gay-kiss-the-fosters-features-the-youngest-same-sex-tv-kiss-ever.

Bergeson, S. "Issa Rae: 'There's a Laziness' in Hollywood to Find Diverse Voices After Black Lives Matter." *IndieWire*, September 22, 2022. https://www.indiewire.com/2022/09/issa-rae-hollywood-lazy-diverse-voices-blm-1234765588/.

Berlant, L., and E. Freeman. "Queer Nationality." In *Fear of a Queer Planet: Queer Politics and Social Theory*, edited by M. Warner, 193–229. University of Minnesota Press, 1993.

Berlin, J. *Toxic Fame: Celebrities Speak on Stardom*. Visible Ink, 1996.

Berman, J. "Reality TV Has Reshaped Our World, Whether We Like It or Not." *Time*, August 4, 2022. https://time.com/collection/reality-tv-most-influential-seasons/6199108/reality-tv-influence-on-world/.

Berman, S. B., and D. Hurewitz. "LGBTQ+ Americans: History Is on Our Side." *Advocate*, July 29, 2022. https://www.advocate.com/commentary/2022/7/29/lgbtq-americans-history-our-side.

Bernstein, M. "*The New York Times* Thinks Gays Have Gone Too Far (with Chase Strangio)." *A Bit Fruity with Matt Bernstein* (podcast), July 12, 2025. https://podcasts.apple.com/us/podcast/the-new-york-times-thinks-gays-have-gone-too-far/id1693739175?i=1000716791761.

Bernstein, M., and V. Taylor. "Marital Discord: Understanding the Contested Place of Marriage in the Lesbian and Gay Movement." In *The Marrying Kind?: Debating Same-Sex Marriage Within the Lesbian and Gay Movement*, edited by M. Bernstein and V. Taylor, 1–35. University of Minnesota Press, 2013.

Bérubé, A. *Coming Out Under Fire: The History of Gay Men and Women in World War II*. University of North Carolina Press, 2010.

Bessner, D. "The Life and Death of Hollywood." *Harper's Magazine*, May 2024. https://harpers.org/archive/2024/05/the-life-and-death-of-hollywood-daniel-bessner/.

Betancourt, M. "How TV Stories Have Shaped Our Understanding of AIDS." *Vulture*, February 21, 2021. https://www.vulture.com/article/tv-aids-hiv-television-story-timeline.html.

Betancourt, M. "12 Latinx LGBTQ TV Characters Who Made Us Feel Seen." *ET*, June 12, 2021. https://www.etonline.com/12-latinx-lgbtq-tv-characters-who-made-us-feel-seen-154398.

Bianco, R. "20-Year Flashback: Ellen DeGeneres Came Out, and Paved the Way for More Gay TV Roles." *USA Today*, April 26, 2017. https://www.usatoday.com/story/life/tv/2017/04/26/ellen-degeneres-gay-coming-out-tv-20-year-anniversary/100888584/.

Bielby, W. T., and D. D. Bielby. "'All Hits Are Flukes': Institutionalized Decision Making and the Rhetoric of Network Prime-Time Program Development." *American Journal of Sociology* 99, no. 5 (1994): 1287–313.

Billson, C. "Harry's Razors Backlash Is 'Latest Attempt to Harass Trans People Out of Public Life.' *PinkNews*, August 9, 2023. https://www.thepinknews.com/2023/08/09/harrys-razor-trans-boycott/.

Bindel, J. "The Proud Whopper? This Is Not the Gay Liberation We Fought For." *The Guardian*, July 6, 2014. https://www.theguardian.com/commentisfree/2014/jul/07/proud-whopper-not-gay-liberation-equal-marriage-babies-big-business.

Bissinger, B. "He Says Goodbye, She Says Hello." *Vanity Fair*, July 2015.

Blee, K. M., R. Futrell, and P. Simi. *Out of Hiding: Extremist White Supremacy and How It Can Be Stopped*. Routledge, 2024.

Bloom, D. "The Great Netflix Correction One Year Later: April 19, 2022, the Day That Transformed the Streaming Biz." NextTV, April 16, 2023. https://www.nexttv.com/news/the-great-netflix-correction-one-year-later-april-19-2022-the-day-that-transformed-the-streaming-biz-bloom.

Blotcher, J. "*An Early Frost* 25 Years Later." *Advocate*, November 10, 2010. https://www.advocate.com/arts-entertainment/television/2010/11/10/early-frost-25-years-later.

Blow, C. M. "Yes, We're in an L.G.B.T.Q. State of Emergency." *The New York Times*, June 7, 2023. https://www.nytimes.com/2023/06/07/opinion/pride-lgbtq-laws.html.

Bokat-Lindell, S. "How Trans Children Became a Political Football." *The New York Times*, April 8, 2021. https://www.nytimes.com/2021/04/08/opinion/transgender-children-sports-medical.html.

Bonesteel, M. "The NCAA Led the Opposition to HB2, but Will North Carolina's Repeal Be Enough?" *The Washington Post*, March 30, 2017. https://www.washingtonpost.com/news/early-lead/wp/2017/03/30/the-ncaa-led-the-opposition-to-hb2-but-will-north-carolinas-repeal-be-enough/.

Bonin, L. "A Gay Kiss Heats Up 'Dawson's Creek.'" *Entertainment Weekly*, May 3, 2001. https://ew.com/article/2001/05/03/gay-kiss-heats-dawsons-creek/.

Bouie, J. "There Is No Dignity in This Kind of America." *The New York Times*, February 10, 2023. https://www.nytimes.com/2023/02/10/opinion/trump-desantis-transgender-rights.html.

Bourdieu, P. "The Forms of Capital." In *Handbook of Theory and Research for the Sociology of Education*, edited by J. G. Richardson, 241–58. Greenwood Press, 1986.

Bradley, A. "The Privilege of Mediocrity." *The New York Times Style Magazine*, September 30, 2021. https://www.nytimes.com/2021/09/30/t-magazine/mediocrity-people-of-color.html.

Bragman, H. *Where's My Fifteen Minutes?: Get Your Company, Your Cause, or Yourself the Recognition You Deserve*. Portfolio, 2008.

Branch, J. "Confronting an Enduring Taboo." *The New York Times*, April 7, 2011. https://www.nytimes.com/2011/04/08/sports/08outsports.html.

Branch, J. "Two Straight Athletes Combat Homophobia." *The New York Times*, May 13, 2011. https://www.nytimes.com/2011/05/14/sports/two-straight-athletes-combat-homophobia.html.

Branch, T. "The Shame of College Sports." *The Atlantic*, October 2011. https://www.theatlantic.com/magazine/archive/2011/10/the-shame-of-college-sports/308643/.

Branum, G. *My Life as a Goddess: A Memoir Through (Un)popular Culture*. Atria Books, 2018.

Braudy, L. *The Frenzy of Renown: Fame and Its History*. 1986. Reprint, Vintage, 1997.

Brewer, J. "The Panic over Trans Sports Inclusion." *The Washington Post*, June 6, 2024. https://www.washingtonpost.com/sports/interactive/2024/transgender-sports-debate-politics/.

Brief of Amici Curiae Chris Kluwe and Brendon Ayanbadejo in Support of Respondents. http://www.afer.org/wp-content/uploads/2013/02/12-144-bsac-KluweAyanbadejo.pdf.

Brodesser-Akner, T. "Can Jill Soloway Do Justice to the Trans Movement?" *New York Times Magazine*, August 31, 2014. https://www.nytimes.com/2014/08/31/magazine/can-jill-soloway-do-justice-to-the-trans-movement.html.

Bronski, M. *The Pleasure Principle: Sex, Backlash, and the Struggle for Gay Freedom.* St. Martin's Press, 1998.

Brown, L. "Hollywood Has Left L.A." *Vulture*, June 3, 2025. https://www.vulture.com/article/hollywood-movies-film-industry-los-angeles-california-production.html.

Brownstein, R. *The Power and the Glitter: The Hollywood-Washington Connection.* Vintage, 1992.

Bruni, F. "ABC's Gay Wednesdays." *The New York Times*, March 8, 2012. https://archive.nytimes.com/bruni.blogs.nytimes.com/2012/03/08/abcs-gay-wednesdays/.

Bruni, F. "Basketball's Gay Paragon." *The New York Times*, April 29, 2013. https://www.nytimes.com/2013/04/30/opinion/bruni-basketballs-gay-paragon.html.

Bruni, F. "Carrying a Cause to the Super Bowl." *The New York Times*, January 22, 2013. https://bruni.blogs.nytimes.com/2013/01/22/carrying-a-cause-to-the-super-bowl/.

Bucatinsky, D. *Does This Baby Make Me Look Straight? Confessions of a Gay Dad.* Atria Books, 2012.

Bullock, D. W. *David Bowie Made Me Gay: 100 Years of LGBT Music.* Overlook Duckworth, 2017.

Burga, S. "The Implications of Supreme Court's 303 Creative Decision Are Already Being Felt." *Time*, July 16, 2023. https://time.com/6295024/303-creative-supreme-court-future-implications/.

Burke, G., with E. Sherman. *Out at Home: The True Story of Glenn Burke, Baseball's First Openly Gay Player.* 1995. Reprint, Berkley Books, 2015.

Burke, P. "Time for Straight Allies to Get Out of the Spotlight in the LGBT Sports Movement." Outsports, November 7, 2013. https://www.outsports.com/2013/11/7/5076086/straight-allies-lgbt-sports-movement.

Burke, T. *Unbound: My Story of Liberation and the Birth of the Me Too Movement.* Flatiron Books, 2021.

Burns, K. "Why Trump's Latest Trans Military Ban Is So Much Worse Than in 2016." *San Francisco Chronicle*, February 1, 2025. https://www.sfchronicle.com/opinion/openforum/article/trump-trans-military-ban-20066067.php.

Burnton, S. "50 Stunning Olympic Moments. No 20: Greg Louganis's Perfect Dive 1988." *The Guardian*, March 28, 2012. https://www.theguardian.com/sport/blog/2012/mar/28/greg-louganis-50-stunning-olympic-moments.

Butcher, R. "Heartstopper Star Kit Connor 'Forced' to Come Out as Bisexual." *PinkNews*, October 31, 2022. https://www.thepinknews.com/2022/10/31/kit-connor-bisexual-heartstopper-twitter/.

Butler, I., and D. Kois. *The World Only Spins Forward: The Ascent of "Angels in America."* Bloomsbury, 2018.

Butterly, A., S. Buckley, G. Pearce, and C. McDonald. "100 Women: How Hollywood Fails Women on Screen." *BBC News*, March 2, 2018. https://www.bbc.com/news/world-43197774.

Buzinski, J. "Houston Texan Connor Barwin on Marriage Equality, His Gay Brother and NFL Culture." Outsports, June 11, 2012. https://www.outsports.com/2012/6/11/4053218/houston-texan-connor-barwin-on-marriage-equality-his-gay-brother-and.

Buzinski, J. "Moment #7: Major Leaguer Billy Bean Comes Out, Still Regrets Retiring Early." Outsports, September 27, 2011. https://www.outsports.com/2011/9/27/4051910/moment-7-major-leaguer-billy-bean-comes-out-still-regrets-retiring.

Buzinski, J. "Raiders Player Carl Nassib Comes Out as Gay, First Active Player in NFL History." Outsports, June 21, 2021. https://www.outsports.com/2021/6/21/22544294/raiders-player-carl-nassib-gay-nfl-coming-out.

Buzinski, J. "Wrestler Hudson Taylor a Champion for Gay Rights." Outsports, February 21, 2010. https://www.outsports.com/2010/2/21/3863282/wrestler-hudson-taylor-a-champion-for-gay-rights.

Buzinski, J., and C. Zeigler Jr. *The Outsports Revolution: Truth and Myth in the World of Gay Sports*. Alyson Books, 2007.

Cagle, J. "Special Report: The Gay '90s." *Entertainment Weekly*, September 8, 1995. https://ew.com/article/1995/09/08/special-report-gay-90s/.

Cagle, J. "Tracy Morgan and Hollywood's Nasty Comedy Habit." *Entertainment Weekly*, June 17, 2011. https://ew.com/article/2011/06/17/tracy-morgan-and-hollywoods-nasty-comedy-habit/.

Caiani, M., and I. Tranfíc. "Weaving the Transnational Anti-Gender Networks." *Mobilization* 29, no. 4 (2024): 423–39.

Caldwell, J. T. *Production Culture: Industrial Reflexivity and Critical Practice in Film and Television*. Duke University Press, 2008.

Canon, D. T. *Actors, Athletes, and Astronauts: Political Amateurs in the United States Congress*. University of Chicago Press, 1990.

Cappelletti, J. "Michigan Adds LGBTQ Protections to Anti-Discrimination Law." Associated Press, March 16, 2023. https://apnews.com/article/lgbtq-elliott-larsen-michigan-whitmer-discrimination-6dab85a296020e9612ed417028b6cf09.

Carney B. T. "AIDS and the Arts." *Washington Blade*, July 19, 2012. https://www.washingtonblade.com/2012/07/19/aids-and-the-arts/.

Castells, M. *Networks of Outrage and Hope: Social Movements in the Internet Age*. 2nd ed. Polity, 2015.

Casting Society of America. "A Collective Voice: A South Asian + South East Asian Actor Roundtable." YouTube, May 27, 2021. https://youtu.be/cqKB-p7ZViA.

Cavalcante, A. *Struggling for Ordinary: Media and Transgender Belonging in Everyday Life*. New York University Press, 2018.

Caves, R. E. *Creative Industries: Contracts Between Art and Commerce.* Harvard University Press, 2000.

Cawley, G. "Massachusetts AG Maura Healey Backs Suit Against Florida's 'Don't Say Gay' Law." *Boston Herald*, August 5, 2022. https://www.bostonherald.com/2022/08/05/massachusetts-ag-maura-healey-backs-suit-against-floridas-dont-say-gay-law/.

Chamberlain, V. "Truly, Madly, Johnny: *Wicked*'s Jonathan Bailey Talks Fame, Wanting Kids and Returning to the Stage." *British Vogue*, December 12, 2024. https://www.vogue.co.uk/article/jonathan-bailey-january-2025-interview.

Chambers, S. A. *The Queer Politics of Television.* I. B. Tauris & Co., 2009.

Chattoo, C. B., and L. Feldman. *A Comedian and an Activist Walk into a Bar: The Serious Role of Comedy in Social Justice.* University of California Press, 2020.

Chauncey, G. *Gay New York: Gender, Urban Culture, and the Making of the Gay Male World, 1890–1940.* Basic Books, 1994.

Chauncey, G. *Why Marriage?: The History Shaping Today's Debate over Gay Equality.* Basic Books, 2005.

Cheney-Rice, Z. "Michael B. Jordan Did the Impossible." *Vulture*, June 2, 2025. https://www.vulture.com/article/michael-b-jordan-interview-sinners-thomas-crown-affair-ryan-coogler.html.

Cho, W., and A. Weprin. "DEI Is Disappearing in Hollywood. Was It Ever Really Here?" *The Hollywood Reporter*, March 6, 2025. https://www.hollywoodreporter.com/business/business-news/dei-hollywood-trump-1236155842/.

Choi, A. "Record Number of Anti-LGBTQ Bills Have Been Introduced This Year." CNN, April 6, 2023. https://www.cnn.com/politics/anti-lgbtq-plus-state-bill-rights-dg/index.html.

Christian, A. J. "Beyond Branding: The Value of Intersectionality on Streaming TV Channels." *Television & News Media* 21, no. 5 (2020): 457–74.

Christian, A. J. *Open TV: Innovation Beyond Hollywood and the Rise of Web Television.* New York University Press, 2018.

Clark, V. "Dwyane Wade's Unflinching Support of His Trans Daughter Is a Turning Point." *Vox*, February 14, 2020. https://www.vox.com/first-person/2020/2/14/21137163/dwyane-wade-zaya-transgender-daughter.

Cohen, C. J. *The Boundaries of Blackness: AIDS and the Breakdown of Black Politics.* University of Chicago Press, 1999.

Coleman, C. V., II. "Lil Uzi Vert Finally Explains Changing Their Pronouns and Identifying as Gender Nonconforming." *XXL*, May 31, 2023. https://www.xxlmag.com/lil-uzi-vert-finally-explains-changing-their-pronouns-and-identifying-as-gender-nonconforming/.

Coleman, J. S. "Social Capital in the Creation of Human Capital." *American Journal of Sociology* 94 (1988): S95–S120.

Colin, C. "How Sexist Is Hollywood? Check Out Geena Davis's Spreadsheet." *The New York Times*, May 25, 2023. https://www.nytimes.com/2023/05/25/business/geena-davis-hollywood-sexism-gender.html.

Collins, J., with F. Lidz. "The Gay Athlete." *Sports Illustrated*, May 6, 2013, 34–41.
Collins, P. H. "Learning from the Outsider Within: The Sociological Significance of Black Feminist Thought." *Social Problems* 33, no. 6 (October–December 1986): S14–S32.
Collins, P. H. *Black Feminist Thought: Knowledge, Consciousness, and the Politics of Empowerment*. 30th Anniversary Edition. Routledge, 2022.
Colman, D. "A Star Athlete Makes a Big Move Off the Field." *The New York Times*, June 22, 2012. https://www.nytimes.com/2012/06/24/fashion/ben-cohen-makes-a-move-off-the-rugby-field-to-combat-bullying-and-homophobia.html.
Colón, S. "Pride House LA Is Here to Stay!" *Jejune Magazine*, June 30, 2021. https://www.jejunemagazine.com/home/pridehousela.
Cooper, A. F. *Celebrity Diplomacy*. Paradigm, 2008.
Cooper, B. *Eloquent Rage: A Black Feminist Discovers Her Superpower*. Picador, 2018.
Cooper, G. "5 Empowering Ad Campaigns That Are Breaking the Beauty Mold." *Verily*, July 6, 2016. https://verilymag.com/2016/07/positive-advertising-womens-body-image-beauty-standards-dove-nike.
Cowan, J. "Hospitals Are Limiting Gender Treatment for Trans Minors, Even in Blue States." *The New York Times*, July 22, 2025. https://www.nytimes.com/2025/07/22/us/trump-transgender-healthcare-california-hospitals.html.
Craig, D. R. "Coming Out of the Television: LGBT-Themed Made-for-Television Movies as Critical Media Pedagogy." PhD diss. University of California, Los Angeles, 2014.
Cramer, J. "What Does Queer Gen Z Want on TV? Everything Under the Rainbow." INTO, March 31, 2023. https://www.intomore.com/feature/what-does-queer-gen-z-want-on-tv-everything-under-the-rainbow/.
Crary, D. "New Playbook Emerges as US Gay Athletes Come Out." Associated Press, May 5, 2014. https://apnews.com/article/3f3c23386b4a4ccb9f43eee4aad7f680.
Creative Artists Agency and shift7. "Female-Led Films Outperform at Box Office for 2014–2017." Shift7. https://shift7.com/media-research.
Crooked Minis. *Pride on Screen: Trans Visibility* (podcast), June 2019. https://podcasts.apple.com/us/podcast/crooked-minis/id1292665011?i=1000442815084.
Curtin, K. *"We Can Always Call Them Bulgarians": The Emergence of Lesbians and Gay Men on the American Stage*. Alyson, 1987.
Cyphers, L., and K. Fagan. "Unhealthy Climate." *ESPN The Magazine*, January 26, 2011. https://www.espn.com/ncw/news/story?page=Mag15unhealthyclimate.
D'Addario, D. "Jared Leto and Michael Douglas' Homophobic Golden Globes Speeches Show the Worst of Hollywood." *Salon*, January 13, 2014. https://www.salon.com/2014/01/13/jared_leto_and_michael_douglass_homophobic_golden_globes_speeches_show_the_worst_of_hollywood/.
Damshenas, D. "46 of the Best LGBTQ+ Shows You Can Watch Right Now on Netflix." *Gay Times*, September 22, 2020. https://www.gaytimes.co.uk/culture/the-best-lgbtq-inclusive-shows-you-can-watch-right-now-on-netflix/.

D'Arminio, A. "Gay Teens on TV: A Timeline." *Entertainment Weekly*, June 12, 2015. https://ew.com/gallery/gay-teens-tv-timeline/.

Data for Progress. "Americans Are Divided on Issues Related to Transgender People, but Often Don't Want the Federal Government Involved," March 27, 2025. https://www.dataforprogress.org/blog/2025/3/27/americans-are-divided-on-issues-related-to-transgender-people-but-often-dont-want-the-federal-government-involved.

Davis, B. "GLAAD Response to *Vanity Fair* Cover Featuring Caitlyn Jenner, Releases Updated Tip Sheet for Journalists." GLAAD, June 1, 2015. https://www.glaad.org/blog/glaad-responds-vanity-fair-cover-featuring-caitlyn-jenner-releases-updated-tip-sheet.

DeAngelis, M., ed. *Reading the Bromance: Homosocial Relationships in Film and Television*. Wayne State University Press, 2014.

De la Cretaz, F. "Living Nonbinary in a Binary Sports World." *Sports Illustrated*, April 16, 2021. https://www.si.com/wnba/2021/04/16/nonbinary-athletes-transgender-layshia-clarendon-quinn-rach-mcbride-daily-cover.

D'Emilio, J. *Sexual Politics, Sexual Communities: The Making of a Homosexual Minority in the United States, 1940–1970*. 2nd ed. University of Chicago Press, 1998.

Demirjian, K. "Federal Workers Ordered to Remove Gender Identity from Email Signatures." *The New York Times*, January 31, 2025. https://www.nytimes.com/2025/01/31/us/politics/trump-pronouns.html.

Denby, D. "How Could Harvard Have Published Ben Urwand's 'The Collaboration'?" *The New Yorker*, September 23, 2013. https://www.newyorker.com/culture/culture-desk/how-could-harvard-have-published-ben-urwands-the-collaboration.

Dessauer, J. M. "Sousveillance Work: Monitoring and Managing-Up in Patrimonial Hollywood." *Qualitative Sociology* 48 (2025): 73–95.

Diaz, J. "Florida's Governor Signs Controversial Law Opponents Dubbed 'Don't Say Gay.'" NPR, March 28, 2022. https://www.npr.org/2022/03/28/1089221657/dont-say-gay-florida-desantis.

Dodds, I. "Trump's Blitz of Anti-Trans Ads Probably Worked—but Not for the Reason You Might Think." *Independent*, December 1, 2024. https://www.the-independent.com/news/world/americas/us-politics/trump-anti-trans-campaign-adverts-b2654925.html.

Doherty, T. *Hollywood and Hitler, 1933–1939*. Columbia University Press, 2013.

Dominick, N. "Broadway Impact: A Look Back at an Organization That Made a Difference." *Broadway World*, June 26, 2015. https://www.broadwayworld.com/article/Broadway-Impact-A-Look-Back-at-an-Organization-That-Made-a-Difference-20150626.

Draughorne, K. "Rapper Lil Uzi Vert Seemingly Comes Out as Nonbinary After Changing Instagram Pronouns." *Los Angeles Times*, July 18, 2022. https://www.latimes.com/entertainment-arts/music/story/2022-07-18/lil-uzi-vert-non-binary-they-them-pronouns-instagram-yeat.

Duberman, M. *Has the Gay Movement Failed?* University of California Press, 2018.

Du Bois, W. E. B. *The Souls of Black Folk*. Penguin, 1903.

Duca, L. "You Have Two Men to Thank for the Greatest Strides in LGBT Representation on TV." *Huffington Post*, June 18, 2015. https://www.huffpost.com/entry/ron-cowen-dan-lipman_n_7612400.

Duggan, L. *The Twilight of Equality?: Neoliberalism, Cultural Politics, and the Attack on Democracy*. Beacon Press, 2003.

Duncan, T. A. "Yes, Marathons Will Recognize Nonbinary Runners—but There's a Major Piece Missing." *HuffPost*, October 14, 2022. https://www.huffpost.com/entry/nonbinary-marathon-inclusive-prize-money_n_6349b00ae4b0b7f89f569c36.

Dunn, J., S. Lyn, N. Onyeador, and A. Zegeye. "Black Representation in Film and TV: The Challenges and Impact of Increasing Diversity." McKinsey & Company, March 11, 2021. https://www.mckinsey.com/featured-insights/diversity-and-inclusion/black-representation-in-film-and-tv-the-challenges-and-impact-of-increasing-diversity.

Dunne, J. G. *The Studio*. 1968. Reprint, Vintage, 1998.

Dye, N. "Magic Johnson Says He's 'So Proud' of Son EJ: 'He's Saving a Lot of People's Lives.'" *People*, March 2, 2023. https://people.com/sports/magic-johnson-so-proud-of-son-ej-saving-a-lot-of-peoples-lives/.

Econsultancy. "17 Marketing Campaigns with a Positive Message for Women." November 21, 2018. https://econsultancy.com/17-marketing-campaigns-with-a-positive-message-for-women/.

Ekstam, D. "The Liberalization of American Attitudes to Homosexuality and the Impact of Age, Period, and Cohort Effects." *Social Forces* 100, no. 2 (2021): 905–29.

Elliott, S. "Commercials with a Gay Emphasis Are Moving to Mainstream Media." *The New York Times*, June 25, 2013. https://www.nytimes.com/2013/06/26/business/media/commercials-with-a-gay-emphasis-are-moving-to-mainstream-media.html.

Engel, S. M. *The Unfinished Revolution: Social Movement Theory and the Gay and Lesbian Movement*. Cambridge University Press, 2001.

Ennis, D. "Chris Mosier Is First Out Trans Man to Compete with Team USA." *Advocate*, June 6, 2016. https://www.advocate.com/transgender/2016/6/06/chris-mosier-first-out-trans-man-compete-team-usa-video.

Ennis, D. "NCAA Takes a Stand for Inclusion as States Target Trans Student-Athletes: Is It Enough?" Outsports, February 1, 2021. https://www.outsports.com/2021/2/1/22259830/ncaa-statement-trans-student-athletes-transgender-montana.

Erigha, M. *The Hollywood Jim Crow: The Racial Politics of the Movie Industry*. New York University Press, 2019.

Ermyas, T., and K. Wakeam. "Wave of Bills to Block Trans Athletes Has No Basis in Science, Researcher Says." NPR, March 18, 2021. https://www.npr.org/2021/03/18/978716732/wave-of-new-bills-say-trans-athletes-have-an-unfair-edge-what-does-the-science-s.

Faderman, L. *The Gay Revolution: The Story of the Struggle*. Simon & Schuster, 2015.

Faderman, L. *Odd Girls and Twilight Lovers: A History of Lesbian Life in 20th-Century America*. Columbia University Press, 1991.

Faderman, L., and S. Timmons. *Gay L.A.: A History of Sexual Outlaws, Power Politics, and Lipstick Lesbians*. University of California Press, 2009.

Fagan, K. "Derrick Gordon Openly Smiling." ESPN, April 9, 2014. https://www.espn.com/espnw/news-commentary/story/_/id/10754317/espnw-university-massachusetts-minutemen-starter-derrick-gordon-openly-smiling-decision-come-gay.

Fagan, K. "Owning the Middle." ESPN, May 29, 2013. https://www.espn.com/espn/feature/story/_/id/9316697/owning-middle.

Fallon, K. "On 'Glee,' Two Boys Kiss, Without Controversy." *The Atlantic*, March 16, 2011. https://www.theatlantic.com/entertainment/archive/2011/03/on-glee-two-boys-kiss-without-controversy/72571/.

Farrow, R. *Catch and Kill: Lies, Spies, and a Conspiracy to Protect Predators*. Little, Brown, 2019.

Fatoba, K. "Are Brands Sincere in Their Support for Pride." Highsnobiety, June 8, 2017. https://www.highsnobiety.com/p/companies-supporting-lgbt/.

Faye, S. "Gay Pride and Capitalism: What Is Pinkwashing?" Novara Media, June 19, 2016. https://novaramedia.com/2016/06/19/gay-pride-capitalism-what-is-pinkwashing/.

Feiler, B. "What 'Modern Family' Says About Modern Families." *The New York Times*, January 21, 2011. https://www.nytimes.com/2011/01/23/fashion/23THISLIFE.html.

Fetner, T. *How the Religious Right Shaped Lesbian and Gay Activism*. University of Minnesota Press, 2008.

Finke, L. "Netflix Walkout over Dave Chappelle Is Not Just a Matter of Transgender Rights and Dignity." *USA Today*, October 20, 2021. https://www.usatoday.com/story/opinion/2021/10/20/netflix-walkout-chappelle-transphobic-comments-harmful-the-closer/8525972002/.

Fisherkeller, J. *Growing Up with Television: Everyday Learning Among Young Adolescents*. Temple University Press, 2002.

Flavell, L. "10 Most Powerful LGBT Characters in Comics." CBR, October 4, 2019. https://www.cbr.com/powerful-lgbt-characters-comics/.

Footer, A. "MLB Names Bean Its First Ambassador for Inclusion." MLB.com, July 15, 2014. https://www.mlb.com/news/billy-bean-is-mlbs-first-ambassador-for-inclusion/c-84795004.

Foran, C., and H. Talbot. "GOP-Led House Votes to Ban Transgender Athletes from Women's Sports." CNN Politics, January 14, 2025. https://www.cnn.com/2025/01/14/politics/house-vote-ban-transgender-athletes-womens-sports/index.html.

Foucault, M. *Discipline and Punish: The Birth of the Prison*. Translated by Alan Sheridan. Vintage, 1977.

Foucault, M. *The History of Sexuality*. Vol. 1: *An Introduction*. Translated by Robert Hurley. Vintage, 1978.

Foxworth, D. "It's Time for All Jocks to Embrace Diversity." *Huffington Post*, February 26, 2013. https://www.huffpost.com/entry/gay-athletes_b_2762233.

Frank, N. *Awakening: How Gays and Lesbians Brought Marriage Equality to America*. Belknap Press of Harvard University Press, 2017.

Friend, T. "Kenneth Faried Makes Moms Proud." ESPN, May 6, 2013. https://www.espn.com/espn/e60/story/_/id/9248194/denver-nuggets-kenneth-faried-makes-mothers-proud.

Friess, S. "Don't Applaud Jared Leto's Transgender 'Mammy.'" *Time Magazine*, February 28, 2014. https://time.com/10650/dont-applaud-jared-letos-transgender-mammy/.

Fujita, S. "Acceptance by Example, on the Field and at Home." *The New York Times*, March 23, 2013. https://www.nytimes.com/2013/03/24/sports/football/scott-fujita-acceptance-by-example-in-locker-room-and-at-home.html.

Gabler, N. *An Empire of Their Own: How the Jews Invented Hollywood*. Vintage, 1989.

Gadsby, H. "Hannah Gadsby: *Nanette* (2018)—Transcript." *Scraps from the Loft*, July 21, 2018. https://scrapsfromtheloft.com/comedy/hannah-gadsby-nanette-transcript/.

Galanes, P. "At Lunch with Jesse Tyler Ferguson and Eric McCormack." *The New York Times*, July 26, 2013. https://www.nytimes.com/2013/07/28/fashion/at-lunch-with-jesse-tyler-ferguson-and-eric-mccormack.html.

Gallup. "LGBTQ+ Rights." https://news.gallup.com/poll/1651/gay-lesbian-rights.aspx.

Gamson, J. *Claims to Fame: Celebrity in Contemporary America*. University of California Press, 1994.

Gamson, J. *Freaks Talk Back: Tabloid Talk Shows and Sexual Nonconformity*. University of Chicago Press, 1998.

Gamson, J. "Stopping the Spin and Becoming a Prop: Fieldwork on Hollywood Elites." In *Studying Elites Using Qualitative Methods*, edited by R. Hertz and J. Imber, 83–93. SAGE, 1995.

Garber, G. "Impact Martina Navratilova Had on Jason Collins." ESPN, May 8, 2013. https://www.espn.com/sports/tennis/notebook/_/page/secondservings05082013/tennis-significance-martina-navratilova-had-jason-collins-second-servings.

Garber, G. "'Now I Get to Be Like Everybody Else.'" ESPN, May 27, 2005. https://www.espn.com/college-sports/news/story?id=2069239.

Garber, M. *Bisexuality and the Eroticism of Everyday Life*. Routledge, 2000.

Garber, M. "How Comedians Became Public Intellectuals." *The Atlantic*, May 28, 2015. https://www.theatlantic.com/entertainment/archive/2015/05/how-comedians-became-public-intellectuals/394277/.

Gates, R. J. *Double Negative: The Black Image and Popular Culture*. Duke University Press, 2018.

Gay, R. "Fifty Years Ago, Protesters Took on the Miss America Pageant and Electrified the Feminist Movement." *Smithsonian Magazine*, January 2018. https://www

.smithsonianmag.com/history/fifty-years-ago-protestors-took-on-miss-america-pageant-electrified-feminist-movement-180967504/.

Ge, L. "Diversity in Hollywood Pays Off in Rating and Box Office, New Study Finds." TheWrap, February 21, 2017. https://www.thewrap.com/diversity-in-entertainment-pays-off-new-study-finds/.

Gendel, M. "'An Early Frost' Leaps Ahead in Ratings: Viewers Respond." *Los Angeles Times*, November 13, 1985. https://www.latimes.com/archives/la-xpm-1985-11-13-ca-5419-story.html.

Gervino, T. "The Punter Makes His Point." *The New York Times*, October 19, 2012. https://www.nytimes.com/2012/10/20/sports/football/punter-chris-kluwes-voice-is-heard-in-same-sex-marriage-debate.html.

Ghaziani, A. *The Dividends of Dissent: How Conflict and Culture Work in Lesbian and Gay Marches on Washington*. University of Chicago Press, 2008.

Ghaziani, A. *Sex Cultures*. Polity Press, 2017.

Ghaziani, A. *There Goes the Gayborhood?* Princeton University Press, 2014.

Ghaziani, A., V. Taylor, and A. Stone. "Cycles of Sameness and Difference in LGBT Social Movements." *Annual Review of Sociology* 42 (2016): 165–83.

Gilchrist, T. E. "10 Ways 'The Fosters' Changed TV, as Remembered by Cast and Creator." *Advocate*, June 6, 2018. https://www.advocate.com/arts-entertainment/2018/6/06/10-ways-fosters-changed-tv-remembered-cast-and-creator#media-gallery-media-1.

Gitlin, T. *Inside Prime Time*. 1983. Reprint, University of California Press, 2000.

Gittings, P., and D. Riddell. "WNBA Superstar Sue Bird: 'Women's Soccer Players Generally Are Cute Little White Girls.'" CNN, October 18, 2020. https://edition.cnn.com/2020/10/17/sport/sue-bird-megan-rapinoe-wnba-spt-intl/index.html.

Given, K. "WNBA Cashing in with Pro-LGBT Campaign." WBUR, July 5, 2014. https://www.wbur.org/onlyagame/2014/07/05/wnba-pride-game.

GLAAD. *Accelerating Acceptance, 2021*. https://glaad.org/publications/accelerating-acceptance-2021/.

GLAAD. *Accelerating Acceptance, 2025*. https://glaad.org/accelerating-acceptance-2025.

GLAAD. "GLAAD History and Highlights." https://www.glaad.org/about/history.

GLAAD. "Incidents of Anti-LGBTQ Hate Violence in 2019," June 24, 2019. https://www.glaad.org/blog/incidents-anti-lgbtq-hate-violence-2019.

GLAAD. "*The New York Times* Fails to Include Trans Voices in Majority of Articles About Trans Issues," March 26, 2024. https://glaad.org/the-new-york-times-fails-to-include-trans-voices-in-majority-of-articles-about-trans-issues/.

GLAAD. *2020 Studio Responsibility Index*. GLAAD Media Institute, 2020. https://glaad.org/sri/2020/.

GLAAD. *2025 Studio Responsibility Index*. GLAAD Media Institute. https://assets.glaad.org/m/619bf8f01c5e27d7/original/GLAAD-2025-Studio-Responsibility-Index.pdf.

GLAAD. *Where We Are on TV, 2020–2021*. GLAAD Media Institute, 2020. https://assets.glaad.org/m/6508983b2016bca4/original/GLAAD-2020-21-Where-We-Are-on-TV.pdf.

GLAAD. *Where We Are on TV, 2023–2024*. GLAAD Media Institute, 2024. https://assets.glaad.org/m/7c489f209e120a11/original/GLAAD-2023-24-Where-We-Are-on-TV.pdf.

Gleeson, S. "Transgender Duathlete Chris Mosier's Challenge to N.C. Bill." *USA Today*, May 9, 2017. https://www.usatoday.com/story/sports/2017/05/09/chris-mosier-transgender-duathlete-north-carolina-house-bill-142-bathroom-discrimination-ncaa/101405780/.

Goessling, B. "Chris Kluwe, Vikings Avoid Lawsuit." ESPN, August 19, 2014. https://www.espn.com/nfl/story/_/id/11375100/chris-kluwe-minnesota-vikings-reach-settlement-avert-lawsuit.

Goffman, E. *Stigma: Notes on the Management of Spoiled Identity*. Simon & Schuster, 1963.

Goldberg, L. "Jeffrey Tambor Officially Dropped from 'Transparent' in Wake in Harassment Claims." *The Hollywood Reporter*, February 15, 2018. https://www.hollywoodreporter.com/tv/tv-news/jeffrey-tambor-officially-fired-transparent-wake-harassment-claims-1085236/.

Goldman, W. *Adventures in the Screen Trade: A Personal View of Hollywood and Screenwriting*. Grand Central, 1983.

Gossett, R., E. A. Stanley, and J. Burton, eds. *Trap Door: Trans Cultural Production and the Politics of Visibility*. MIT Press, 2017.

Gottschall, J. "The Power of Fake Gay (and Black) Friends: How Fiction Changes the World." *Psychology Today*, June 20, 2012. https://www.psychologytoday.com/us/blog/the-storytelling-animal/201206/the-power-fake-gay-and-black-friends.

Gottschall, J., ed. *The Storytelling Animal: How Stories Make Us Human*. Mariner Books, 2013.

Gould, D. B. *Moving Politics: Emotion and ACT UP's Fight Against AIDS*. University of Chicago Press, 2009.

Graham, W. "'A League of Their Own' Co-Creator: We Can't Lose Queer Film and TV Projects Amid Studio Caution." *The Hollywood Reporter*, June 17, 2023. https://www.hollywoodreporter.com/tv/tv-news/queer-film-tv-representation-1235517325/.

Granderson, LZ. "Another Ex-Athlete Comes Out? Not Impressed." ESPN, February 8, 2007. https://www.espn.com/espn/page2/story?page=granderson/070207.

Gray, M. L. *Out in the Country: Youth, Media, and Queer Visibility in Rural America*. New York University Press, 2009.

Green, J. "A Brief History of Gay Theater, in Three Acts." *The New York Times Magazine*, February 26, 2018. https://www.nytimes.com/2018/02/26/t-magazine/gay-theater-history-boys-in-the-band.html.

Greenfield-Sanders, T. *The Out List*. HBO, 2013. https://www.hbo.com/movies/the-out-list.

Gregory, D. "The 200 Best Lesbian, Bisexual and Queer Movies of All Time." Autostraddle, January 18, 2022. https://www.autostraddle.com/100-best-lesbian-queer-bisexual-movies-285412/?all=1.

Griffin, M. *All That Heaven Allows: A Biography of Rock Hudson.* Harper, 2018.

Griffin, P. "Closeted Lesbian Coaches: Chicken Shit or Caught in a Web of Homophobia and Sexism?" *Pat Griffin's LGBT Sport Blog*, January 18, 2010. http://ittakesateam.blogspot.com/2010/01/closeted-lesbian-coaches-chicken-shit.html.

Griffin, P. "Respect. Just Do It. Swooshing Toward an LGBT Inclusive Sports World." *Pat Griffin's LGBT Sport Blog*, October 17, 2011. http://ittakesateam.blogspot.com/2011/10/respect-just-do-it-swooshing-toward.html.

Griffin, P. "Some Thoughts on Straight Allies in Sport." *Pat Griffin's LGBT Sport Blog*, June 9, 2011. http://ittakesateam.blogspot.com/2011/06/some-thoughts-on-straight-allies-in.html.

Griffin, P. *Strong Women, Deep Closets: Lesbians and Homophobia in Sport.* Human Kinetics, 1998.

Griffin, P., H. Carroll, and C. Zeigler. "Nike Hosts First Ever LGBT Sports Summit, June 14–16." Outsports, May 30, 2012. https://www.outsports.com/2012/5/30/4053168/nike-hosts-first-ever-lgbt-sports-summit-june-14-16.

Grindstaff, L. *The Money Shot: Trash, Class, and the Making of TV Talk Shows.* University of Chicago Press, 2002.

Gross, L. *Contested Closets: The Politics and Ethics of Outing.* University of Minnesota Press, 1993.

Gross, L. "Gideon Who Will Be 25 in the Year 2012: Growing Up Gay Today." *International Journal of Communication* 1 (November 26, 2007): 121–38.

Gross, L. "Hollywood's Closet Still Closed for Business." *Truthdig*, November 26, 2008. https://www.truthdig.com/articles/hollywoods-closet-still-closed-for-business/.

Gross, L. *Up from Invisibility: Lesbians, Gay Men, and the Media in America.* Columbia University Press, 2001.

Gross, T. "'I Never Had a Plan B': Henry Winkler on His Career, from the Fonz to 'Barry.'" *Fresh Air*, April 11, 2019. https://www.npr.org/2019/04/11/712178030/i-never-had-a-plan-b-henry-winkler-on-his-career-from-the-fonz-to-barry.

Gross, T. "Molly Ringwald." *Fresh Air*, February 12, 2024. https://www.npr.org/2024/02/12/1197962964/molly-ringwald.

Gross, T. "'This Changes Everything': Geena Davis on Empowering Women in Hollywood." *Fresh Air*, August 7, 2019. https://freshairarchive.org/guests/geena-davis.

Gross, T. "Why Writers Are Losing Out in Hollywood." *Fresh Air*, April 25, 2024. https://www.npr.org/2024/04/25/1197965134/end-of-hollywood.

Grossman, A. H. "The Socialization of Lesbian, Gay and Bisexual Youth: Celebrity and Personally Known Role Models." *Journal of Leisure, Media and Visual Culture* 83 (2004): 206–26.

Gura, D. "Barry Diller Headed 2 Hollywood Studios. He Now Says the Movie Business Is Dead." NPR, July 8, 2021. https://www.npr.org/2021/07/08/1014095135

/barry-diller-headed-2-hollywood-studios-he-now-says-the-movie-business-is-dead.

Guy, Z. "Cate Blanchett Doesn't Understand the 'Obsession with Labels.'" *Vulture*, February 13, 2023. https://www.vulture.com/2023/02/cate-blanchett-lesbian-tar-carol.html.

Hadleigh, B. *Hollywood Gays*. Barricade Books, 1996.

Halberstam, J. *The Queer Art of Failure*. Duke University Press, 2011.

Halberstam, J. *In a Queer Time and Place: Transgender Bodies, Subcultural Lives*. New York University Press, 2005.

Hale, L. "'The Holiday Sitter' Review: The Cheesy Holiday Movie the LGBTQ+ Community Needs." Fangirlish, December 12, 2022. https://fangirlish.com/2022/12/12/the-holiday-sitter-review-the-cheesy-holiday-movie-the-lgbtq-community-needs/.

Halpern, J. *Fame Junkies: The Hidden Truths Behind America's Favorite Addiction*. Houghton Mifflin, 2007.

Hans, S. "L.G.B.T.Q. Teens on 'Heartstopper': 'I'm Fine with It Not Being Perfect.'" *The New York Times*, August 4, 2023. https://www.nytimes.com/2023/08/04/arts/television/heartstopper-teens.html.

Harmon, A. "Transgender Americans Say Trump's Orders Are Even Worse Than Feared." *The New York Times*, January 28, 2025. https://www.nytimes.com/live/2025/01/28/us/trump-news-executive-orders/transgender-americans-say-trump-orders-are-even-worse-than-feared.

Harmon, A., and J. Macur. "Judge Temporarily Stops Trump's Plan to End Funds for Trans Youths' Health Providers." *The New York Times*, February 13, 2025. https://www.nytimes.com/2025/02/13/us/trump-trans-youth-health-providers.html.

Harper, Z. "Michael Sam Met with Jason Collins Before Coming Out as Gay." CBS Sports, February 10, 2014. https://www.cbssports.com/nba/news/michael-sam-met-with-jason-collins-before-coming-out-as-gay/.

Harrington, N. "The Interviews: Ron Cowen and Daniel Lipman." Emmys, April 16, 2020. https://www.emmys.com/news/interviews-archive/interviews-ron-cowen-and-daniel-lipman.

Harris, A. "Same Old Script." *Slate*, October 18, 2015. https://www.slate.com/articles/arts/culturebox/2015/10/diversity_in_the_tv_writers_room_writers_and_showrunners_of_color_lag_far.html.

Harris, D. *The Rise and Fall of Gay Culture*. Ballantine, 1997.

Harris, M. "Anderson Cooper and the New Art of Coming Out." *Entertainment Weekly*, July 2, 2012. https://ew.com/article/2012/07/02/anderson-cooper-new-art-of-coming-out/.

Harris, M. "Is Celebrity 'Queer Baiting' Really Such a Crime?" *The New York Times Style Magazine*, February 6, 2023. https://www.nytimes.com/2023/02/06/t-magazine/queer-baiting-harry-styles-bad-bunny.html.

Harrison, S. "On Football Saturdays and Sundays, It's Anti-Trans Ads All the

Time." WFAE, October 14, 2024. https://www.wfae.org/politics/2024-10-14/on-football-saturdays-and-sundays-its-anti-trans-ads-all-the-time.

Hart-Brinson, P. *The Gay Marriage Generation: How the LGBTQ Movement Transformed American Culture*. New York University Press, 2018.

Hauck, G. "Anti-LGBT Hate Crimes Are Rising, the FBI Says. But It Gets Worse." *USA Today*, June 28, 2019. https://www.usatoday.com/story/news/2019/06/28/anti-gay-hate-crimes-rise-fbi-says-and-they-likely-undercount/1582614001/.

Haven, T. *Black Television Travels: African American Media Around the Globe*. New York University Press, 2013.

Hayek, S. "Harvey Weinstein Is My Monster Too." *The New York Times*, December 12, 2017. https://www.nytimes.com/interactive/2017/12/13/opinion/contributors/salma-hayek-harvey-weinstein.html.

Heching, D. "Aaron Sorkin Says Only Casting Gay Actors in Gay Roles Is 'Empty Gesture.'" *People*, December 21, 2021. https://people.com/movies/aaron-sorkin-says-only-casting-gay-actors-in-gay-roles-is-empty-gesture/.

Heldman, B. L., and J. Mercadante. "Ranking All 33 Seasons of *The Real World* (and the Moments We'll Never Forget)." *Entertainment Weekly*, October 21, 2025. https://ew.com/tv/the-real-world-seasons-ranked/?slide=5655258#5655258.

Helligar, J. "Does Hollywood Fail Gay Actors Who Are Out from the Start?" *Queerty*, June 1, 2019. https://www.queerty.com/hollywood-fail-gay-actors-start-20190601.

Henderson, F. D. "The Culture Behind Closed Doors: Issues of Gender and Race in the Writers' Room." *Cinema Journal* 50, no. 2 (2011): 145–52.

Henderson, T. "*Bridgerton* Proves Gay Actors Can Convincingly Play Straight Roles." Pride, March 30, 2022. https://www.pride.com/tv/2022/3/30/bridgerton-proves-gay-actors-can-convincingly-play-straight-roles.

Herlock, Ethan. "A Playlist of Tracks Soundtracking the Black Lives Matter Movement." *The Face*, June 19, 2020. https://theface.com/music/black-lives-matter-playlist.

Herships, S., and S. V. Smith. "Is Movie Night Back?" NPR, June 14, 2021. https://www.npr.org/2021/06/14/1006362151/is-movie-night-back.

Heuman, J. "What Happens in the Writers' Room Stays in the Writers' Room?: Professional Authority in *Lyle v. Warner Bros.*" *Television & News Media* 17, no. 3 (2016): 195–211.

Hewett, H. "How Trans Athletes Became Targets in the Culture Wars." *The Washington Post*, September 18, 2023. https://www.washingtonpost.com/books/2023/09/18/fair-play-gender-sports-book-barnes/.

Hicklin, A. "Scarlett Johansson Withdraws from *Rub & Tug*." *Out*, July 13, 2018. https://www.out.com/out-exclusives/2018/7/13/exclusive-scarlett-johansson-withdraws-rub-tug.

Himberg, J. *The New Gay for Pay: The Sexual Politics of American Television Production*. University of Texas Press, 2017.

Hochschild, A. R. *Strangers in Their Own Land: Anger and Mourning on the American Right*. The New Press, 2016.

Hod, I. "How Howard Bragman Orchestrated Michael Sam's Coming Out." *Daily Beast*, March 12, 2014. https://www.thedailybeast.com/how-howard-bragman-orchestrated-michael-sams-coming-out.

Hoffman, J. "Athlete Ally and Chris Mosier Respond to NCAA New Trans Inclusion Policy." Athlete Ally, January 20, 2022. https://www.athleteally.org/athlete-ally-mosier-respond-ncaa-new-trans-policy/.

Hoffman, J. "A Gay Rights Power Player Who Wields a Mighty Phone." *The New York Times*, June 29, 2011. https://www.nytimes.com/2011/06/30/fashion/brian-ellner-a-gay-rights-power-player-with-many-contacts.html.

Hogan, K. "Get to Know the Cute Campbell's Soup Dads, a.k.a. PEOPLE's Sexiest Pitchmen Alive." *People*, November 18, 2015. https://people.com/celebrity/sexiest-man-alive-2015-campbells-soup-dads/.

Holland, O. "Elliot Page Becomes First Trans Man to appear on *Time Magazine* Cover." CNN, March 17, 2021. https://www.cnn.com/style/article/elliot-page-time-magazine-cover-transgender-man/index.html.

Holman, J., and J. Creswell. "Brands Embracing Pride Month Confront a Volatile Political Climate." *The New York Times*, May 25, 2023. https://www.nytimes.com/2023/05/25/business/target-pride-lgbtq-companies-backlash.html.

Holpuch, A. "Behind the Backlash Against Bud Light." *The New York Times*, June 30, 2023. https://www.nytimes.com/article/bud-light-boycott.html.

Holzman, J. "Will Democrats Let the GOP Gut Trans Health Care?" *Rolling Stone*, December 10, 2024. https://www.rollingstone.com/politics/politics-features/trump-trans-health-care-republicans-democrats-1235198473/.

hooks, b. "Choosing the Margin as a Space of Radical Openness." *Framework: The Journal of Cinema and Media* 36 (1989): 15–23.

hooks, b. *Feminist Theory: From Margin to Center*. South End Press, 1984.

Hubbs, N. *Rednecks, Queers, and Country Music*. University of California Press, 2014.

Hughes, J. "The Subversive Joy of Lil Nas X's Gay Pop Stardom." *The New York Times Magazine*, July 7, 2021. https://www.nytimes.com/2021/07/07/magazine/lil-nas-x.html.

Hull, K. E. *Same-Sex Marriage: The Cultural Politics of Love and Law*. Cambridge University Press, 2006.

Human Rights Campaign. "Fatal Violence Against the Transgender and Gender-Expansive Community in 2024." https://www.hrc.org/resources/fatal-violence-against-the-transgender-and-gender-expansive-community-in-2024.

Hunt, D., and A. Ramón. *Hollywood Diversity Report, 2021. Pandemic in Progress. Part 1: Film*. UCLA Institute for Research on Labor and Employment, 2021. https://socialsciences.ucla.edu/wp-content/uploads/2024/06/UCLA-Hollywood-Diversity-Report-2021-Film-4-22-2021.pdf.

Hunt, D., and A. Ramón. *Hollywood Diversity Report, 2021. Pandemic in Progress. Part 2: Television*. UCLA Institute for Research on Labor and Employment, 2021. https://socialsciences.ucla.edu/wp-content/uploads/2024/06/UCLA-Hollywood-Diversity-Report-2021-Television-10-26-2021.pdf.

Hunter, J. D. *Culture Wars: The Struggle to Define America*. Basic Books, 1991.

Italie, L. "Gay-Themed Ads Are Becoming More Mainstream." *Huffington Post*, March 6, 2013.

It Gets Better Project. "About Our Global Movement." https://itgetsbetter.org/about/.

Ito, M., et al. *Hanging Out, Messing Around, and Geeking Out: Kids Living and Learning with New Media*. MIT Press, 2010.

Jackson, J. "Why I've Come Out." *The Guardian*, March 3, 2007. https://www.theguardian.com/sport/2007/mar/04/features.sport4.

Jacobs, J. "Lil Nas X Comes Out on Last Day of Pride Month." *The New York Times*, July 1, 2019. https://www.nytimes.com/2019/07/01/arts/music/lil-nas-x-c7osure.html.

Jacobs, R. N. "Entertainment Media and the Aesthetic Public Sphere." In *The Oxford Handbook of Cultural Sociology*, edited by J. C. Alexander, R. N. Jacobs, and P. Smith, 318–40. Oxford University Press, 2012.

James, M. "ViacomCBS Is Renamed Paramount in a Nod to Its Past and Streaming Future." *Los Angeles Times*, February 15, 2022. https://www.latimes.com/entertainment-arts/business/story/2022-02-15/viacomcbs-renamed-paramount-in-a-nod-to-its-past-and-streaming-future.

James, S. "Activism, the Black Athlete and Supporting LGBT Equality." *Washington Blade*, October 26, 2016. https://www.washingtonblade.com/2016/10/26/activism-black-athlete-supporting-lgbt-equality/.

James, S. D. "Gay Buffalo Teen Commits Suicide on Eve of National Bullying Summit." ABC News, September 21, 2010. https://abcnews.go.com/Health/gay-buffalo-teen-commits-suicide-eve-national-bullying/story?id=14571861.

James, S. E., J. L. Herman, L. E. Durso, and R. Heng-Lehtinen. *Early Insights: A Report of the 2022 U.S. Transgender Survey*. National Center for Transgender Equality, Washington, DC, 2024. https://transequality.org/sites/default/files/2024-02/2022%20USTS%20Early%20Insights%20Report_FINAL.pdf.

Jameson, J. L. "Penn's Title IX Resolution with the U.S. Department of Education Office for Civil Rights." *Penn Today*, July 1, 2025. https://penntoday.upenn.edu/announcements/penns-title-ix-resolution-us-department-education-office-civil-rights.

Jana, T. "The Differences Between Allies, Accomplices and Co-Conspirators May Surprise You." *An Injustice!*, February 8, 2021. https://aninjusticemag.com/the-differences-between-allies-accomplices-co-conspirators-may-surprise-you-d3fc7fe29c.

Jenkins, H. *Convergence Culture: Where Old and New Media Collide*. New York University Press, 2008.

Johnson, T., and B. Lang. "Gay Rights and Hollywood Still Have a Long Way to Go." *Variety*, June 29, 2015. https://variety.com/2015/film/news/gay-rights-and-hollywood-still-have-a-long-way-to-go-1201529591/.

Jones, J. M. "LGBTQ+ Identification in U.S. rises to 9.3%." Gallup, February 20, 2025. https://news.gallup.com/poll/656708/lgbtq-identification-rises.aspx.

Jordan, J. "Jonathan Bailey Is the Sexiest Man Alive 2025! (We Know. We Nailed It.)" *People*, November 3, 2025. https://people.com/jonathan-bailey-is-sexiest-man-alive-2025-11842000.

Jung, E. A. "Jeff Varner's Outing of Trans Contestant Zeke Smith on *Survivor* Was Despicable." *Vulture*, April 13, 2017. https://www.vulture.com/2017/04/survivor-outing-trans-contestant-zeke-smith-was-vile.html.

Kahrl, C. "The Meaning of Caitlyn Jenner." *Grantland*, June 2, 2015. https://grantland.com/hollywood-prospectus/caitlyn-jenner-vanity-fair-cover-announcement/.

Kaleem, J. "How Drag Queen Story Hour Became a Battle over Gender, Sexuality and Kids." *Los Angeles Times*, February 22, 2023. https://www.latimes.com/world-nation/story/2023-02-22/drag-queen-story-hour.

Kantor, J., and M. Twohey. *She Said: Breaking the Sexual Harassment Story That Helped Ignite a Movement*. Penguin, 2019.

Karlan, S. "Broadening Support for 'Athletes' Brief' on Marriage Equality." *BuzzFeed*, March 22, 2013. https://www.buzzfeed.com/skarlan/broadening-support-for-athletes-brief-on-marriage-equality.

Karnowski, S. "Minnesota Governor Protects Rights to Gender Affirming Care." Associated Press, March 8, 2023. https://apnews.com/article/minnesota-transgender-health-tim-walz-2a702340ec5facdb2bb6496e711facf1.

Keegan, C. M. "On the Necessity of Bad Trans Objects." *Film Quarterly* 75, no. 3 (2022): 26–37.

Keegan, C. M., and L. Horak. "Introduction." *Journal of Cinema and Media Studies* 61, no. 2 (2022): 164–68.

Keith, C. "Life Before Kurt: Rickie from 'My So-Called Life' and Justin from 'Queer as Folk.'" NewNowNext, December 20, 2010. http://www.newnownext.com/life-before-kurt-rickie-from-my-so-called-life-and-justin-from-queer-as-folk/12/2010/.

Kelleher, P. "No, Bad Bunny Isn't Queerbaiting—and Here's Why We Need to Stop Policing Sexuality." *PinkNews*, August 31, 2022. https://www.thepinknews.com/2022/08/31/bad-bunny-harry-styles-queerbaiting/.

Kelly, C. "Are Straight Actors in Gay Roles the New Blackface?" *Salon*, June 12, 2013. https://www.salon.com/2013/06/12/stop_praising_straight_actors_for_playing_gay_roles/.

Kies, B. "First Comes Love, Then Comes Marriage: (Homo)Normalizing Romance on American Television." *Journal of Popular Romance Studies* 5 (July 15, 2016): 2. https://www.jprstudies.org/2016/07/first-comes-love-then-comes-marriage-homonormalizing-romance-on-american-televisionby-bridget-kies/.

Kiley, K., and S. Vaisey. "Measuring Stability and Change in Personal Culture Using Panel Data." *American Sociological Review* 85, no. 3 (2020): 477–506.

Kilkenny, K. "Fran Drescher Q&A on SAG-AFTRA Strike: 'The Digital Age Is Cannibalizing Us.'" *The Hollywood Reporter*, July 13, 2023. https://www.hollywoodreporter.com/business/business-news/actors-strike-sag-aftra-leaders-stakes-hollywood-1235536001/.

Kim, M. H. "Trans WNBA Player Layshia Clarendon Shares Top Surgery Photos in Heartfelt Post, Gets Full Support from Team." *Them*, February 1, 2021. https://www.them.us/story/wnba-layshia-clarendon-top-surgery-photos-team-support.

Kimport, K. *Queering Marriage: Challenging Family Formation in the United States*. Rutgers University Press, 2014.

King, B. J. "My Abortion Story Shows Why the Supreme Court Must Save Roe v. Wade." *The Washington Post*, December 1, 2021. https://www.washingtonpost.com/opinions/2021/12/01/billie-jean-king-mississippi-abortion-supreme-court/.

King, B. J., with F. Deford. *Billie Jean*. Viking Press, 1982.

Kinser, J. "Gaga's Emotional Tribute to Jamey Rodemeyer." *Advocate*, September 25, 2011. https://www.advocate.com/news/daily-news/2011/09/25/gaga-pays-tribute-jamey-rodemeyer.

Kirchick, J. "The Struggle for Gay Rights Is Over." *The Atlantic*, June 28, 2019. https://www.theatlantic.com/ideas/archive/2019/06/battle-gay-rights-over/592645/.

Kit, B., and K. Kilkenny. "Hollywood at Risk of Becoming the 'Next Detroit Auto': L.A. Production Insiders Voice Alarm." *The Hollywood Reporter*, April 15, 2025. https://www.hollywoodreporter.com/business/business-news/post-production-los-angeles-music-tax-incentives-1236190752/.

Kluwe, C. *Beautifully Unique Sparkleponies: On Myths, Morons, Free Speech, Football, and Assorted Absurdities*. Little, Brown, 2013.

Kluwe, C. "Gay Marriage Legalized! What an Amazing Day to Be an American." *Slate*, November 7, 2012. https://slate.com/human-interest/2012/11/gay-marriage-legalized-what-an-amazing-day-to-be-an-american.html.

Kluwe, C. "I Was an NFL Player Until I Was Fired by Two Cowards and a Bigot." Deadspin, January 2, 2014. https://deadspin.com/i-was-an-nfl-player-until-i-was-fired-by-two-cowards-an-1493208214.

Kluwe, C. "'They Won't Magically Turn You into a Lustful Cockmonster': Chris Kluwe Explains Gay Marriage to the Politician Who Is Offended by an NFL Player Supporting It." Deadspin, September 7, 2012. https://deadspin.com/they-wont-magically-turn-you-into-a-lustful-cockmonste-5941348?post=52487943.

Knott, K. "Trump Admin. Reportedly Restores Federal Funding to Penn." *Inside Higher Ed*, July 3, 2025. https://www.insidehighered.com/news/quick-takes/2025/07/03/penn-gets-funding-back-after-agreeing-trumps-demands.

Koblin, J. "It's Official: Streaming Is Now the King of TV." *The New York Times*, June 17, 2025. https://www.nytimes.com/2025/06/17/business/media/streaming-beats-cable-broadcast.html.

Koblin, J., and E. Steel. "At the Head of the Pack, HBO Shows the Way Forward." *The New York Times*, April 12, 2015. https://www.nytimes.com/2015/04/13/business/media/at-the-head-of-the-pack-hbo-shows-the-way-forward.html.

Kopay, D., and P. D. Young. *The David Kopay Story: An Extraordinary Self-Revelation*. Arbor House, 1977.

Kozuch, E. "HRC Responses to New FBI Report Showing Spike in Reported Hate Crimes Targeting LGBTQ People." Human Rights Campaign, November 12, 2019. https://www.hrc.org/press-releases/hrc-responds-to-new-fbi-report-showing-spike-in-reported-hate-crimes-target.

Kralik, J. "'Bathroom Bill' Legislative Tracking." National Conference of State Legislatures, October 24, 2019. https://www.ncsl.org/research/education/-bathroom-bill-legislative-tracking635951130.aspx.

Kramer, L. "Why Do Straights Hate Gays?" *Los Angeles Times*, March 20, 2007. https://www.latimes.com/la-oe-kramer20mar20-story.html.

Krattenmaker, T. *Onward Christian Athletes: Turning Ballparks into Pulpits and Players into Preachers*. Rowman & Littlefield, 2010.

Krishnakumar, P. "This Record-Breaking Year for Anti-Transgender Legislation Would Affect Minors the Most." CNN, April 15, 2021. https://www.cnn.com/2021/04/15/politics/anti-transgender-legislation-2021/index.html.

Kushner, T. *Angels in America: A Gay Fantasia on National Themes*. Rev. ed. Theatre Communications Group, 2013.

Ladd, T., and J. A. Mathisen. *Muscular Christianity: Evangelical Protestants and the Development of American Sport*. Bridgepoint Books, 1999.

Lamont, M. *Seeing Others: How Recognition Works—and How It Can Heal a Divided World*. One Signal, 2023.

Lang, B. "Eddie Redmayme Criticizes J. K. Rowling's Anti-Trans Tweets." *Variety*, June 10, 2020. https://variety.com/2020/film/news/eddie-redmayne-jk-rowling-anti-trans-tweets-harry-potter-fantastic-beasts-1234630226/.

Lang, B. "Why Gay Movie Stars Are Staying Locked in the Closet." *Variety*, June 29, 2015. https://variety.com/2015/film/news/gay-lgbt-movie-stars-staying-locked-in-the-closet-1201529581/.

Lang, B., and R. Rubin. "How Movie Theaters Fought to Survive (Another) Year of Turbulence and Change." *Variety*, December 29, 2021. https://variety.com/2021/film/news/movie-theaters-box-office-2021-pandemic-omicron-1235142992/.

Lang, N. "The Only Emmy-Nominated Show Starring Trans Actors Is the One You're Not Watching." *Esquire*, November 15, 2016. https://www.esquire.com/entertainment/tv/a48589/her-story-emmys-jen-richards-trans-stories/.

Langone, A. "#MeToo and Time's Up Founders Explain the Difference Between the 2 Movements—and How They're Alike." *Time*, March 8, 2018. https://time.com/5189945/whats-the-difference-between-the-metoo-and-times-up-movements/.

LeBrun, P. "'This Is Who I Am': Predators Prospect Luke Prokop Comes Out." *The Athletic*, July 19, 2021. https://theathletic.com/2711747/2021/07/19/luke-prokop/.

Lee, P., K. Westcott, I. Wray, and S. Raviprakash. "Women's Sports Gets Down to Business: On Track for Rising Monetization." Deloitte, December 7, 2020. Excerpts available at "The Week in Women's Football: . . . Deloitte Release 2021 Predictions." OneFootball, February 8, 2021. https://onefootball.com/en/news

/the-week-in-womens-football-goteborg-receive-takeover-news-naomi-osaka-invests-in-nc-deloitte-release-2021-predictions-32345210.

Leung, R., and L. Rizzo. "Paramount Ends DEI Policies, Cites Trump Executive Order." CNBC, February 27, 2025. https://www.cnbc.com/2025/02/27/paramount-ends-dei-policies-cites-trump-executive-order.html.

Lewis, A. "Megan Rapinoe: USWNT Captain, World Cup Winner and Campaigner for Social Justice." CNN, July 4, 2019. https://www.cnn.com/2019/06/28/football/megan-rapinoe-donald-trump-uswnt-spt-intl/index.html.

Lewis, I. "Darren Criss: 'Nobody Wants to Know About the Good Things on Glee—but I Was F***ing There.'" *Independent*, December 20, 2021. https://www.independent.co.uk/arts-entertainment/music/features/darren-criss-glee-versace-straight-b1977894.html.

Linkins, J. "Chris Kluwe Quits St. Paul Pioneer Press over Marriage Equality Amendment Editorial." *Huffington Post*, November 3, 2012. https://www.huffpost.com/entry/chris-kluwe-st-paul-pioneer-press_n_2069240.

Liptak, A. "Civil Rights Law Protects Gay and Transgender Workers, Supreme Court Rules." *The New York Times*, June 15, 2020. https://www.nytimes.com/2020/06/15/us/gay-transgender-workers-supreme-court.html.

Liptak, A. "Justices Let Parents Opt Children Out of Classes with L.G.B.T.Q. Storybooks." *The New York Times*, June 27, 2025. https://www.nytimes.com/2025/06/27/us/politics/supreme-court-lgbtq-books.html.

Liptak, A. "Supreme Court Upholds Tennessee Ban on Transgender Care for Minors." *The New York Times*, June 18, 2025. https://www.nytimes.com/2025/06/18/us/politics/supreme-court-trans-children.html.

Litman, L. "Meet the Man Who Orchestrated Michael Sam's Historic Announcement." *USA Today*, March 4, 2014. https://ftw.usatoday.com/2014/03/michael-sam-howard-bragman.

Lombardo, M. "Washington Redskins Considering Name Change: What Role Did Pressure by Nike, FedEx, Others Play in Overdue Decision?" NJ.com, July 3, 2020. https://www.nj.com/giants/2020/07/washington-redskins-considering-name-change-what-role-did-pressure-by-nike-fedex-others-play-in-overdue-decision.html.

Lorde, A. *Sister Outsider*. The Crossing Press, 1984.

Lotz, A. D. *After Mass Media: Storytelling for Microaudiences in the Twenty-First Century*. New York University Press, 2025.

Louganis, G. "The Toughest Sissy in the World: The Moment I Triumphed over My Bullies." *Huffington Post*, June 5, 2012. https://www.huffpost.com/entry/the-toughest-sissy-in-the-world_b_1569369.

Louganis, G., with E. Marcus. *Breaking the Surface*. Random House, 1995.

Lowder, J. B. "Stephen Colbert Has Problems with That Gay Campbell's Soup Ad." *Slate*, October 15, 2015. https://slate.com/human-interest/2015/10/stephen-colbert-on-gay-campbell-s-soup-ad-one-million-moms-forgot-andy-warhol.html.

Maas, J., J. Otterson, and M. Schneider. "One of the Writers Guild's Biggest Contract Negotiation Issues Is the 'Mini Room' Boom." *Variety*, March 29, 2023. https://variety.com/2023/tv/news/writers-guild-contract-negotiation-mini-room-1235568173/.

Mack, D. "The Queerbaiting Discourse Is Out of Control." *BuzzFeed News*, November 2, 2022. https://www.buzzfeednews.com/article/davidmack/kit-connor-bisexual-queerbaiting-heartstopper.

Macur, J. "Coast Cleared by Others, W.N.B.A. Finally Finds Its Gay Pride." *The New York Times*, June 10, 2014. https://www.nytimes.com/2014/06/11/sports/wnba-finally-advertises-its-gay-pride.html.

Macur, J. "N.C.A.A., Following Trump's Order, Excludes Transgender Athletes from Women's Sports." *The New York Times*, February 6, 2025. https://www.nytimes.com/2025/02/06/us/politics/ncaa-transgender-athletes-ban.html.

Macur, J. "U.S. Olympic Officials Bar Transgender Women from Women's Competitions." *The New York Times*, July 22, 2025. https://www.nytimes.com/2025/07/22/us/politics/us-olympics-trans-women-athletes-ban-trump.html.

Maddaus, G., B. Lang, and A. Jackson. "Hollywood Ditches DEI to Avoid Donald Trump's Wrath." *Variety*, March 4, 2025. https://variety.com/2025/film/news/hollywood-drops-dei-programs-donald-trump-disney-paramount-amazon-1236327202/.

Manno, A. "Laid-Off HBO Max Execs Reveal Warner Bros. Discovery Is Killing Off Diversity and Courting 'Middle America.'" *Daily Beast*, August 25, 2022. https://www.thedailybeast.com/laid-off-hbo-max-execs-reveal-warner-bros-discovery-is-killing-off-diversity-and-courting-middle-america.

Maraniss, D. *When Pride Still Mattered: A Life of Vince Lombardi*. Simon & Schuster, 1999.

Marcus, S. *The Drama of Celebrity*. Princeton University Press, 2019.

Martin, B. *Difficult Men: Behind the Scenes of a Creative Revolution: From "The Sopranos" and "The Wire" to "Mad Men" and "Breaking Bad."* Penguin, 2013.

Marwick, A. E. *Status Update: Celebrity, Publicity, and Branding in the Social Media Age*. Yale University Press, 2013.

Masaki, L. "Today Is the Anniversary of *Thirtysomething*'s 'Strangers' Episode." NewNowNext, November 7, 2007. http://www.newnownext.com/today-is-the-anniversary-of-thirtysomethings-strangers-episode/11/2007/.

Masters, J. "Why *The Fosters* Is a Game-Changer for Trans Representation." *HuffPost*, March 31, 2017. https://www.huffpost.com/entry/why-the-fosters-is-a-game-changer-for-trans-representation_b_58de9d27e4b0d804fbbb727f.

Masterson, M. "Illinois Joins Lawsuit Challenging Trump Administration's Efforts to Restrict Gender-Affirming Care." WTTW, August 1, 2025. https://news.wttw.com/2025/08/01/illinois-joins-lawsuit-challenging-trump-administration-s-efforts-restrict-gender.

Mathewson, T. J. "TV Is Biggest Driver in Global Sport League Revenue." Global Sport Matters, March 7, 2019. https://globalsportmatters.com/business/2019/03/07/tv-is-biggest-driver-in-global-sport-league-revenue/.

Mayer, V. "Studying Up and F**cking Up: Ethnographic Interviewing in Production Studies." *Cinema Journal* 47, no. 2 (2008): 141–48.

Maza, C. "Associated Press Violates Its Own Transgender Guidelines in Caitlyn Jenner Story." Media Matters, June 1, 2015. https://www.mediamatters.org/associated-press/associated-press-violates-its-own-transgender-guidelines-caitlyn-jenner-story.

McCarriston, S. "Super Bowl Champion Launches LGBTQ+ Football Camp, Aims to Create Unifying Safe Space Within Sports." *CBS Sports*, July 5, 2025. ttps://www.cbssports.com/nfl/news/super-bowl-champion-launches-lgbtq-football-camp-aims-to-create-unifying-safe-space-within-sports/.

McCombs, B. "Sponsorship of Gay Pride Parades on the Rise." *USA Today*, June 28, 2014. https://www.usatoday.com/story/money/business/2014/06/28/gay-pride-parades-sponsors/11450345/.

McFall, M. R. "Jon Stewart and Stephen Colbert Face Uncertain Futures." *Newsweek*, July 15, 2025. https://www.newsweek.com/jon-stewart-stephen-colbert-future-paramount-skydance-cbs-comedy-central-trump-2097919.

McNeill, R. T., L. A. Leyva, G. D. White, and N. D. Mitchell. "Leveraging Queer Epistemic Subjectivity to Advance Justice Through Physics Teaching." *2022 PERC Proceedings*, American Association of Physics Teachers, July 16–22, 2022.

Méndez, C. M. "The Best Queer Love Scenes of the Decade Show LGBTQ+ People at Their Most Tender Moments." Popsugar, December 19, 2019. https://www.popsugar.co.uk/entertainment/best-queer-love-scenes-in-tv-movies-decade-47037181?stream_view=1#photo-47037176.

Messner, M. A. *Power at Play: Sports and the Problem of Masculinity*. Beacon Press, 1992.

Meyer, D. S., and J. Gamson. "The Challenge of Cultural Elites: Celebrities and Social Movements." *Sociological Inquiry* 65, no. 2 (1995): 181–206.

Meyerowitz, J. 2002. *How Sex Changed: A History of Transsexuality in the United States*. Harvard University Press.

Meyersohn, N. "Big Brands Are Pulling Back on Pride Merchandise and Events This Year." CNN Business, June 4, 2025. https://www.cnn.com/2025/06/02/business/brands-pride-month-trump-lgbtq.

Meyersohn, N. "Target Is the Latest Company to Roll Back Some DEI Programs." CNN Business, January 24, 2025. https://www.cnn.com/2025/01/24/business/target-dei-companies/index.html.

Miller, Q. "Television." In "Postposttranssexual: Key Concepts for a Twenty-First Century Transgender Studies," edited by P. Currah and S. Stryker. Special issue, *Transgender Studies Quarterly* 1, nos. 1–2 (2014): 216–18.

Mirza, F. "Not Your Ordinary Brown Girl." TEDx Talks, 2016. https://www.youtube.com/watch?v=FLRUKCcZtb8.

Mock, J. *Redefining Realness: My Path to Womanhood, Identity, Love and So Much More*. Atria Books, 2014.

Moore, C. L. "Phoenix Mercury Coach Says Brittney Griner's Detainment Would Be Resolved 'If It Was LeBron.'" *USA Today*, July 5, 2022. https://

www.usatoday.com/story/sports/wnba/2022/07/05/mercury-vanessa-nygaard-brittney-griner-lebron-james/7813812001/.

Morgan, B. "What Will the Movie Industry Look Like After Covid?" *Forbes*, July 12, 2021. https://www.forbes.com/sites/blakemorgan/2021/07/12/what-will-the-movie-industry-look-like-after-covid/.

Morgan, R. "As a Gay Man, I'll Never Be Normal." *The New York Times*, June 25, 2023. https://www.nytimes.com/2023/06/25/opinion/as-a-gay-man-ill-never-be-normal.html.

Moscowitz, L. *The Battle over Marriage: Gay Rights Activism Through the Media*. University of Illinois Press, 2013.

Motion Picture Association. *Theme Report, 2021*. https://www.motionpictures.org/wp-content/uploads/2022/03/MPA-2021-THEME-Report-FINAL.pdf.

Movement Advancement Project. *Equality Maps: Bans on Transgender Youth Participation in Sports*. https://www.lgbtmap.org/equality-maps/youth/sports_participation_bans.

Movement Advancement Project. *LGBTQ Curricular Laws*. https://www.lgbtmap.org/equality-maps/curricular_laws.

Movement Advancement Project. *LGBTQ Policy Spotlight: Mapping LGBTQ Equality: 2010 to 2020*. https://www.lgbtmap.org/file/2020-tally-report.pdf.

Mullin, B. "F.C.C. Approves Skydance's $8 Billion Merger with Paramount." *The New York Times*, July 24, 2025. https://www.nytimes.com/2025/07/24/business/media/fcc-skydance-merger-paramount.html.

Musto, M. "From Liberace to Sam Smith, the Evolution of Gay Music." *Advocate*, May 18, 2015. https://www.advocate.com/arts-entertainment/music/2015/05/18/liberace-sam-smith-evolution-gay-music.

Musto, M. "The Glass Closet." *Out*, May 2007. https://www.out.com/entertainment/2008/09/22/glass-closet.

Musto, M. "The Glass Closet, Revisited." *Out*, April 18, 2012. https://www.out.com/entertainment/2008/09/22/glass-closet.

Narea, N., and F. Cineas. "The GOP's Coordinated National Campaign Against Trans Rights, Explained." *Vox*, April 6, 2023. https://www.vox.com/politics/23631262/trans-bills-republican-state-legislatures.

Natalie. "Laverne Cox's 'Doubt' Love Story Imagines a Better World for Trans Women." Autostraddle, August 9, 2017. https://www.autostraddle.com/laverne-coxs-doubt-love-story-allows-trans-women-to-imagine-a-better-world-389725/.

Navarro, M. "Out in Hollywood: Starring Roles Are Rare." *The New York Times*, September 26, 2008. https://www.nytimes.com/2008/09/28/fashion/28gay.html.

NCAA. "NCAA Board of Governors Statement on Transgender Participation." NCAA.org, April 12, 2021. https://www.ncaa.org/about/resources/media-center/news/ncaa-board-governors-statement-transgender-participation.

NCAA Office of Inclusion. *NCAA Inclusion of Transgender Student-Athletes*. NCAA.org,

August 2011. https://ncaaorg.s3.amazonaws.com/inclusion/lgbtq/INC_TransgenderHandbook.pdf.

Negley, C. "FINA Votes to Restrict Transgender Swimmers, Including Lia Thomas, in Elite Women's Events." Yahoo! Sports, July 19, 2022. https://sports.yahoo.com/fina-votes-to-restrict-transgender-swimmers-in-elite-womens-events-181115435.html.

Netflix. *Disclosure*. 2020. https://www.disclosurethemovie.com/about.

New York Times. "How the G.O.P. Picked Trans Kids as a Rallying Cry." *The Daily* (podcast), June 1, 2023. https://www.nytimes.com/2023/06/01/podcasts/the-daily/anti-trans-bills.html?searchResultPosition=1.

New York Times. "A New Era in College Sports." *The Daily* (podcast), July 1, 2021. https://www.nytimes.com/2021/07/01/podcasts/the-daily/ncaa-college-sports-student-athletes.html.

New York Times. "25 Days to Go." *The Daily* (podcast), October 10, 2024. https://www.nytimes.com/2024/10/10/podcasts/the-daily/election-roundtable.html.

New York Times. "When Book Bans Came to Small-Town New Jersey." *The Daily* (podcast), December 7, 2022. https://www.nytimes.com/2022/12/07/podcasts/the-daily/book-ban-high-school-libraries.html.

New York Times. "The Year in TV and Movies." *The Daily* (podcast), December 26, 2024. https://www.nytimes.com/2024/12/26/podcasts/the-daily/2024-best-tv-movies.html.

Nianias, H. "Jason Collins: Gay NBA Player Mentoring Closeted Athletes, and Says the World Is Ready to 'Accept and Support Them.'" *Independent*, February 17, 2015. https://www.independent.co.uk/news/people/jason-collins-gay-nba-player-mentoring-closeted-athletes-and-says-the-world-is-ready-to-accept-and-support-them-10051145.html.

Nielsen. "Connected Devices Are the Industry's Great Amplifier of Content." Nielsen.com, December 2021. https://www.nielsen.com/insights/2021/connected-devices-are-the-industrys-great-amplifier-of-content/.

Nocera, J., and B. Strauss. *Indentured: The Battle to End the Exploitation of College Athletes*. Portfolio, 2018.

The NOH8 Campaign. "About." NOH8campaign.com, September 30, 2009. http://www.noh8campaign.com/article/about.

Nölke, A. "Making Diversity Conform?: An Intersectional, Longitudinal Analysis of LGBT-Specific Mainstream Media Advertisements." *Journal of Homosexuality* 65, no. 2 (2018): 224–55.

NPR Staff. "How TV Brought Gay People into Our Homes." NPR, May 12, 2012. https://www.npr.org/2012/05/12/152578740/how-tv-brought-gay-people-into-our-homes.

Nussbaum, E. *I Like to Watch: Arguing My Way Through the TV Revolution*. Random House, 2019.

Nyong'o, L. "Lupita Nyong'o: Speaking Out About Harvey Weinstein." *The New York Times*, October 19, 2017. https://www.nytimes.com/2017/10/19/opinion/lupita-nyongo-harvey-weinstein.html.

O'Connell, K., and B. Radke. "Sports Writer Dave Zirin: 'Homophobia Is Baked So Deeply into the Cake of Football.'" KUOW, January 13, 2016. https://www.kuow.org/stories/sports-writer-dave-zirin-homophobia-baked-so-deeply-cake-football.

O'Donnell, N. "How Authentic Is 'Transparent'? A Transgender Activist on Jeffrey Tambor and Other Portrayals." *IndieWire*, October 1, 2014. https://www.indiewire.com/features/general/how-authentic-is-transparent-a-transgender-activist-on-jeffrey-tambor-and-other-portrayals-69529/.

Ohmann, R. "Knowing/Creating Wants." In *Making and Selling Culture*, edited by R. Ohmann, 224–38. Wesleyan University Press/University Press of New England, 1996.

Oliver, D. "Kit Connor and the Dangers of Queerbaiting Accusations." *USA Today*, November 11, 2022. https://www.usatoday.com/story/life/health-wellness/2022/11/11/kit-connor-taylor-swift-queerbaiting-accusations/8291960001/.

Oliver, D., and H. Yasharoff. "JoJo Siwa Opens Up About Being a Part of the LGBTQ Community: 'I Am Just So Happy.'" *USA Today*, January 24, 2021. https://www.usatoday.com/story/entertainment/celebrities/2021/01/24/jojo-siwa-youtube-tiktok-superstar-confirms-she-belongs-lgbtq-community/6677951002/.

Olson, E. "NAIA All but Bans Transgender Athletes from Women's Spots. NCAA Vows to Ensure 'Fair Competition.'" Associated Press, April 8, 2024. https://apnews.com/article/naia-transgender-ban-ad422f3a86ebcc4db618750c6a5d1c5f.

Oluo, I. *Mediocre: The Dangerous Legacy of White Male America*. Seal Press, 2020.

Oluo, I. *So You Want to Talk About Race*. Seal Press, 2018.

Ortner, S. B. *Not Hollywood: Independent Film at the Twilight of the American Dream*. Duke University Press, 2013.

Ortner, S. B. "Reflections on Studying Up in Hollywood." *Ethnography* 11, no. 2 (2010): 211–33.

Out.com Editors. "Ben Cohen: Action Man." *Out*, July 11, 2011. https://www.out.com/entertainment/sports/2011/07/11/ben-cohen-action-man.

Out.com Editors. "Greatest Gay Dads of the Year." *Out*, December 30, 2015. https://www.out.com/out-exclusives/2015/12/30/greatest-gay-dads-year.

Out.com Editors. "A Timeline of (Nearly) Every LGBTQ Couple in TV History." *Out*, September 19, 2018. https://www.out.com/television/2018/9/19/timeline-nearly-every-lgbtq-couple-tv-history.

Out & Equal. "56 Major Companies Respond to Alarming Effort to Erase Transgender People from Legal Protections." Out & Equal, November 1, 2018. https://www.thetaskforce.org/news/56-major-companies-respond-to-alarming-effort-to-erase-transgender-people-from-legal-protections/.

Ovide, S. "Streaming Is Sadder Now." *The New York Times*, July 20, 2022. https://www.nytimes.com/2022/07/20/technology/streaming-netflix.html.

Page, E. *Pageboy: A Memoir*. Flatiron Books, 2023.

Paige, P. "The Spirit of 'The Fosters' Was Always About #TheResistance." *The Hollywood Reporter*, June 6, 2018. https://www.hollywoodreporter.com/tv/tv-news/fosters-series-finale-good-trouble-peter-paige-guest-column-1117339/.

Painter, C. "How the New York Media Covered the Stonewall Riots." *The Conversation*, June 19, 2019. https://theconversation.com/how-the-new-york-media-covered-the-stonewall-riots-117954.

Pallone, D., with A. Steinberg. *Behind the Mask: My Double Life in Baseball.* Signet, 1990.

Parker, K., J. M. Horowitz, and A. Brown. "Americans' Complex Views on Gender Identity and Transgender Issues." Pew Research Center, June 28, 2022. https://www.pewresearch.org/social-trends/2022/06/28/americans-complex-views-on-gender-identity-and-transgender-issues/.

Pearl, M. "How Nickelodeon Educated a Generation of Kids About AIDS During the 1990s." *Vice*, October 14, 2015. https://www.vice.com/en/article/7bde4g/was-nickelodeon-in-the-1990s-the-most-forward-thinking-aids-educator-in-america.

Pearlman, L. I., J. DK Szeszycki-Truesfell, and K. C. Lowrey. "Arts and Culture." In *Trans Bodies, Trans Selves: A Resource for the Transgender Community*, edited by L. Erickson-Schroth, 537–66. Oxford University Press, 2014.

Penn, K. *You Can't Be Serious.* Gallery Books, 2021.

Perper, R. "China and the NBA Are Coming to Blows over a Pro–Hong Kong Tweet. Here's Why." Business Insider, October 22, 2019. https://www.businessinsider.com/nba-china-feud-timeline-daryl-morey-tweet-hong-kong-protests-2019-10.

Petchesky, B. "How One Gay Athlete's Coming Out Led to an Activists' War." Deadspin, May 20, 2014. https://deadspin.com/how-one-gay-athletes-coming-out-led-to-an-activists-war-1579093298.

Petrow, S. "Advertisers Embrace Gay People in an Amazing Year of Firsts for Commercials." *The Washington Post*, December 14, 2015. https://www.washingtonpost.com/lifestyle/style/advertisers-embrace-gay-people-in-an-amazing-year-of-firsts-for-commercials/2015/12/14/a1c52c7c-a013-11e5-8728-1af6af208198_story.html.

Pew Research Center. "Attitudes on Same-Sex Marriage." Pew Research Center, May 14, 2019. https://www.pewforum.org/fact-sheet/changing-attitudes-on-gay-marriage/.

Pew Research Center. "Growing Support for Gay Marriage: Changed Minds and Changing Demographics." Pew Research Center, March 20, 2013. https://www.pewresearch.org/politics/2013/03/20/growing-support-for-gay-marriage-changed-minds-and-changing-demographics/.

Pew Research Center. "Social Media Use in 2021." Pew Research Center, April 7, 2021. https://www.pewresearch.org/internet/2021/04/07/social-media-use-in-2021/.

Pew Research Center. "A Survey of LGBT Americans." Pew Research Center, June 13, 2013. https://www.pewresearch.org/social-trends/2013/06/13/a-survey-of-lgbt-americans/.

Pfeiffer, D. *Battling the Big Lie: How Fox, Facebook, and the MAGA Media Are Destroying America.* Twelve, 2022.

Piepenburg, E. "The Day New Queer Cinema Said: Let's Do This." *The New York Times*, January 20, 2022. https://www.nytimes.com/2022/01/20/movies/new-queer-cinema-anniversary.html.

Piña, C. "Dwyane Wade Explains Why He Moved Out of Florida: 'My Family Would Not Be Accepted.'" *The Hollywood Reporter*, April 27, 2023. https://www.hollywoodreporter.com/lifestyle/lifestyle-news/dwyane-wade-why-he-moved-out-of-florida-ron-desantis-1235405336/.

Piña, C. "Mark Ruffalo, Ramy Youssef and More Call on SAG-AFTRA Leaders to Protect Pro-Palestine Members from Being Blacklisted." *The Hollywood Reporter*, September 11, 2024. https://www.hollywoodreporter.com/news/politics-news/mark-ruffalo-ramy-youssef-call-for-pro-palestine-sag-member-protection-1235993880/.

Pollard, A. "'Hollywood Gets Queer Stories Wrong': Should Straight Actors Play Gay Characters on Screen?" *Independent*, January 13, 2019. https://www.independent.co.uk/arts-entertainment/films/straight-actors-playing-gay-roles-characters-ben-whishaw-darren-criss-cate-blanchett-rachel-weisz-a8723421.html.

Polletta, F., and E. Amenta. *Changing Minds: Social Movements' Cultural Impacts*. Russell Sage Foundation, 2025.

Polletta, F., D. Boka, C. Martinez, and M. Ogaki. "Social Movements in the Commercial Public Sphere: How Women's Magazines Popularized Second-Wave Feminism." *American Journal of Sociology* 130, no. 5 (2025): 1263–314.

Polletta, F., and P. C. B. Chen. "Narrative and Social Movements." In *The Oxford Handbook of Cultural Sociology*, edited by J. C. Alexander, R. N. Jacobs, and P. Smith, 487–506. Oxford University Press, 2012.

Polletta, F., and J. M. Jasper. "Collective Identity and Social Movements." *Annual Review of Sociology* 27 (2001): 283–305.

Poniewozik, J. *Audience of One: Donald Trump, Television, and the Fracturing of America*. Liveright, 2019.

Poniewozik, J. "'Modern Family' Watch: Lips Service." *Time*, September 30, 2010. https://entertainment.time.com/2010/09/30/modern-family-watch-lips-service/.

Poniewozik, J. "'Orange Is the New Black' Taught Us What Netflix Was For." *The New York Times*, July 17, 2019. https://www.nytimes.com/2019/07/17/arts/television/orange-is-the-new-black-final-season.html.

Portwood, J. "The New Normal." *Out*, April 19, 2012. https://www.out.com/entertainment/television/2012/04/19/new-normal-modern-family-gay-fathers.

Poul, A. "Preserving Our Queer Legacy." *Huffington Post*, March 18, 2010. https://www.huffpost.com/entry/preserving-our-queer-lega_b_311511.

Powdermaker, H. *Hollywood, the Dream Factory: An Anthropologist Looks at the Movie-Makers*. 1950. Reprint, Martino, 2013.

powell, j. a., and S. Menendian. *Belonging Without Othering: How We Save Ourselves and the World*. Stanford University Press, 2024.

Press, J. *Stealing the Show: How Women Are Revolutionizing Television*. Atria Books, 2018.

Preston, A. M. "The Anatomy of Transmisogynoir." *Harper's BAZAAR*, September 9, 2020. https://www.harpersbazaar.com/culture/features/a33614214/ashlee-marie-preston-transmisogynoir-essay/.

Prindle, D. F. *Risky Business: The Political Economy of Hollywood*. Westview Press, 1993.

Prinzivalli, L. "The 10 Most Groundbreaking Beauty Campaigns of 2018." *Glamour*, December 22, 2018. https://www.glamour.com/story/inclusive-beauty-campaigns.

Pryor, V. "African American Gay Men Lead the Way in Sports." Outsports, May 13, 2014. https://www.outsports.com/2014/5/13/5716086/michael-sam-gay-nfl-african-american-role-vince-pryor-jason-collins.

Public Religion Research Institute. *Americans' Support for Key LGBTQ Rights Continues to Tick Upward*. PRRI, March 17, 2022. https://www.prri.org/research/americans-support-for-key-lgbtq-rights-continues-to-tick-upward/.

Pugh, T. *The Queer Fantasies of the American Family Sitcom*. Rutgers University Press, 2018.

Queer Nation. "Queer Nation NY History." Queer Nation NY. https://queernationny.org/history.

Radde, K. "What Does the Respect for Marriage Act Do? The Answer Will Vary by State." NPR, December 8, 2022. https://www.npr.org/2022/12/08/1140808263/what-does-the-respect-for-marriage-act-do-the-answer-will-vary-by-state.

Ramos, D-R. "CSA Announces Open Casting Call for Transgender Actors." *Deadline*, October 16, 2017. https://deadline.com/2017/10/casting-society-of-america-csa-open-call-transgender-actors-non-binary-gender-non-conforming-genderqueer-casting-tv-film-1202189398/.

Rannells, A. *Too Much Is Not Enough: A Memoir of Fumbling Toward Adulthood*. Crown Archetype, 2019.

Rector, K. "Americans Approve of LGBTQ+ People Living as They Wish, but Their Support Drops for Trans People, Poll Shows." *Los Angeles Times*, June 6, 2024. https://www.latimes.com/california/story/2024-06-06/lgbtq-trans-people-american-support-poll.

Redfield, E. "The Impact of Transgender Sports Participation Bans on Transgender People in the US." Williams Institute, UCLA School of Law, February 2025. https://williamsinstitute.law.ucla.edu/publications/impact-trans-sports-ban-eo/.

Reed, T. V. *The Art of Protest: Culture and Activism from the Civil Rights Movement to the Present*. 2nd ed. University of Minnesota Press, 2019.

Refinery29. "The LGBTQ+ YouTubers You Need to Know." *Refinery29*, June 10, 2020. https://www.refinery29.com/en-us/lgbt-gay-youtubers.

Reid, J. "The Burden of Sole Representation Led Many Viewers to Be Too Hard on *Will & Grace*." *AV Club*, November 6, 2013. https://www.avclub.com/the-burden-of-sole-representation-led-many-viewers-to-b-1798241729.

Renov, M., and V. Brook. "Editorial Introduction." In *From Shtetl to Stardom: Jews and Hollywood*, edited by M. Renov and V. Brook, ix–xv. Purdue University Press for the USC Casden Institution for the Study of the Jewish Role in American Life, 2017.

Reply All. "Louder," episode 145. *Reply All* (podcast), July 11, 2019. https://gimletmedia.com/shows/reply-all/rnhzlo.

Republican Party. *2024 GOP Platform Make America Great Again!* CNN, July 11, 2024. https://www.cnn.com/2024/07/08/politics/read-2024-republican-party-platform/index.html.

Rhimes, S. "'You Are Not Alone': Shonda Rhimes at the Human Rights Campaign Gala in Los Angeles, 2015." *Medium*, March 16, 2015. https://medium.com/@shondarhimes/you-are-not-alone-69c1a10515ab.

Rich, F. "Two Gay Cowboys Hit a Home Run." *The New York Times*, December 18, 2005. https://www.nytimes.com/2005/12/18/opinion/two-gay-cowboys-hit-a-home-run.html.

Richards, J. "I'm Not One to Go to Protests. Getting Shot by an LAPD Projectile Changed That for Me." *Them*, July 7, 2025. https://www.them.us/story/lapd-ice-protests-resistance-essay-jen-richards.

Richards, J. "Matt Bomer Playing a Trans Woman Is More Than Problematic—It's Dangerous." Logo, June 16, 2017.

Riese. "Can Gay Actors Play Straight Roles, Round 1,246: Luke Evans Edition." Autostraddle, October 24, 2011. https://www.autostraddle.com/can-gay-actors-play-straight-roles-round-1246-luke-evans-edition-117786/.

Riese. "Let Us Now Praise Effeminate Men." Autostraddle, May 14, 2010. https://www.autostraddle.com/let-us-now-praise-effeminate-men-45342/.

Rinkunas, S. "The Trans Athlete Behind the Olympic Committee's New Gender Policy." *The Cut*, January 28, 2016. https://www.thecut.com/2016/01/chris-mosier-transgender-athletes-olympics.html.

Robb, D. "WGA West Inclusion & Equity Report Finds 'Significant' Gains by Women and People of Color." *Deadline*, April 6, 2022. https://deadline.com/2022/04/wga-west-inclusion-report-2022-1234995926/.

Rocha, N. "What to Know About Netflix's $83 Billion Deal for Warner Bros. Discovery." *The New York Times*, December 6, 2025. https://www.nytimes.com/2025/12/06/business/netflix-warner-bros-what-to-know.html.

Rock, C. "Chris Rock Pens Blistering Essay on Hollywood's Race Problem: 'It's a White Industry.'" *The Hollywood Reporter*, December 3, 2014. https://www.hollywoodreporter.com/news/general-news/top-five-filmmaker-chris-rock-753223/.

Roeloffs, M. W. "Dylan Mulvaney Opens Up About Bud Light Controversy: 'Hiring Trans People Should Not Be Political.'" *Forbes*, October 3, 2023. https://www.forbes.com/sites/maryroeloffs/2023/10/03/dylan-mulvaney-opens-up-about-bud-light-controversy-hiring-trans-people-should-not-be-political/.

Rogers, K. "More Americans Identify as LGBTQ+ Than Ever Before, Poll Finds." CNN Health, February 20, 2025. https://www.cnn.com/2025/02/20/health/lgbtq-population-rise-united-states-wellness.

Román, D. *Acts of Intervention: Performance, Gay Culture, and AIDS*. Indiana University Press, 1998.

Romano, A. "The Cruel Truth Behind Trump's New Attacks on Trans People." *Vox*, October 30, 2024. https://www.vox.com/2024-elections/380861/trump-transphobic-anti-trans-ads-scapegoating.

Romano, A. "Is J. K. Rowling Transphobic? Let's Let Her Speak for Herself." *Vox*, March 16, 2023. https://www.vox.com/culture/23622610/jk-rowling-transphobic-statements-timeline-history-controversy.

Rosenbloom, S. "In Pursuit of the 'Pink Dollar.'" *The New York Times*, June 1, 2014.

Rosentiel, T. "Four-in-Ten Americans Have Close Friends or Relatives Who Are Gay." Pew Research Center, May 22, 2007. https://www.pewresearch.org/2007/05/22/fourinten-americans-have-close-friends-or-relatives-who-are-gay/.

Ross, S. J. *Hitler in Los Angeles: How Jews Foiled Nazi Plots Against Hollywood and America*. Bloomsbury, 2017.

Ross, S. J. *Hollywood Left and Right: How Movie Stars Shaped American Politics*. Oxford University Press, 2011.

Rotello, G. *Sexual Ecology: AIDS and the Destiny of Gay Men*. Dutton, 1997.

Roussel, V. *Representing Talent: Hollywood Agents and the Making of Movies*. University of Chicago Press, 2017.

Rozsa, L. "DeSantis Takes on Disney in a Culture War with National Implications." *The Washington Post*, April 13, 2022. https://www.washingtonpost.com/politics/2022/04/13/desantis-disney-dont-say-gay-bill/.

Rubin, R. "Ryan Coogler and Michael B. Jordan's 'Sinners' Takes Box Office Crown with $48 Million." *Variety*, April 20, 2025. https://variety.com/2025/film/box-office/sinners-box-office-opening-weekend-strong-michael-b-jordan-ryan-coogler-1236373417/.

Rude, M. "16 TV Shows with Nonbinary Characters." *Out*, August 30, 2021. https://www.out.com/television/2021/8/30/16-tv-shows-nonbinary-characters#rebelltitem31.

Ruiz, M. "Trans Actors and Hollywood Insiders Discuss the Complicated Reality of Trans Casting." *Cosmopolitan*, October 19, 2015. https://www.cosmopolitan.com/entertainment/celebs/a47797/trans-actors-casting-roundtable-interview/.

Rupp, L. J., and V. Taylor. *Drag Queens at the 801 Cabaret*. University of Chicago Press, 2003.

Russell, R., as told to K. Arnovitz. "No Distractions: An NFL Veteran Opens Up on His Sexuality." ESPN, August 29, 2019. https://www.espn.com/nfl/story/_/id/27484719/no-distractions-nfl-veteran-opens-sexuality.

Russo, V. *The Celluloid Closet: Homosexuality in the Movies*. Rev. ed. Harper & Row, 1987.

Ryan, M. "The NCAA Trans Athlete Policy Was Groundbreaking in 2011—but in 2020, More Must Be Done." PopSugar, July 1, 2020. https://www.popsugar.com/fitness/how-ncaa-policy-for-transgender-athletes-can-evolve-47583204.

Ryzik, M. "The Comedy-Destroying, Soul-Affirming Art of Hannah Gadsby." *The New York Times*, July 24, 2018. https://www.nytimes.com/2018/07/24/arts/hannah-gadsby-comedy-nanette.html.

Sancton, J. "#MeToo Five Years Later: A Timeline of Allegations, Accountability and Activism." *The Hollywood Reporter*, September 29, 2022. https://www.hollywoodreporter.com/news/general-news/metoo-five-years-timeline-allegations-accountability-activism-1235228661/.

Sandberg, B. "Diversity Improves Among TV Actors but Execs Still Largely White and Male, Study Finds." *The Hollywood Reporter*, October 22, 2020.

https://www.hollywoodreporter.com/tv/tv-news/diversity-improves-among-tv-actors-but-execs-still-largely-white-and-male-study-finds-4080967/.

San Filippo, M. *The B Word: Bisexuality in Contemporary Film and Television*. Indiana University Press, 2013.

Saperstein, P. "Only 7% of Movies in 2021 Featured More Women Than Men, Study Finds." *Variety*, March 15, 2022. https://variety.com/2022/film/news/womens-roles-2021-films-men-outnumber-lauzen-study-1235204838/.

Savage, D. Introduction to *It Gets Better: Coming Out, Overcoming Bullying, and Creating a Life Worth Living*, edited by D. Savage and T. Miller, 1–8. Dutton, 2011.

Savage, D., and T. Miller, eds. *It Gets Better: Coming Out, Overcoming Bullying, and Creating a Life Worth Living*. Dutton, 2011.

Savage, S. "Straights Who Play Gay and Die Painful Death Win the Oscar." *IndieWire*, November 15, 2011. https://www.indiewire.com/awards/industry/straights-who-play-gay-and-die-painful-death-win-the-oscar-184094/.

Savin-Williams, R. C. *Mostly Straight: Sexual Fluidity Among Men*. Harvard University Press, 2017.

Schiappa, E., P. B. Gregg, and D. E. Hewes. "The Parasocial Contact Hypothesis." *Communication Monographs* 72, no. 1 (March 2005): 92–115.

Schmidt, S. "Americans' Views Flipped on Gay Rights. How Did Minds Change So Quickly?" *The Washington Post*, June 7, 2019. https://www.washingtonpost.com/local/social-issues/americans-views-flipped-on-gay-rights-how-did-minds-change-so-quickly/2019/06/07/ae256016-8720-11e9-98c1-e945ae5db8fb_story.html.

Schneider, M., and K. Aurthur. "R.I.P. Cable TV: Why Hollywood Is Slowly Killing Its Biggest Moneymaker." *Variety*, July 21, 2020. https://variety.com/2020/tv/news/cable-tv-decline-streaming-cord-cutting-1234710007/.

Schnurman, M., and M. Wolf. "Texas' Harsh Moves Against Transgender Youth Provoke a Backlash from Big Business." *The Dallas Morning News*, March 11, 2022. https://www.dallasnews.com/business/2022/03/11/texas-harsh-moves-against-transgender-youth-provoke-a-backlash-from-big-business/.

Schorsch, K. "Chicago Hospitals Are Scaling Back Trans Care for Youth. A Rapid Response Team Is Stepping In." *Chicago Sun-Times*, July 29, 2025. https://chicago.suntimes.com/health/2025/07/29/chicago-hospitals-are-scaling-back-trans-care-for-youth-a-rapid-response-team-is-stepping-in.

Schulman, S. "Israel and 'Pinkwashing.'" *The New York Times*, November 22, 2011. https://www.nytimes.com/2011/11/23/opinion/pinkwashing-and-israels-use-of-gays-as-a-messaging-tool.html.

Schulman, S. *Stagestruck: Theater, AIDS, and the Marketing of Gay America*. Duke University Press, 1998.

Schuppe, J. "Corporate Boycotts Become Key Weapon in Gay Rights Fight." NBC News, March 26, 2016. https://www.nbcnews.com/news/us-news/corporate-boycotts-become-key-weapon-gay-rights-fight-n545721.

Schwab, F. "Former Cowboys, Bucs DE Ryan Russell Says He Is Bisexual in ESPN Story." Yahoo, August 29, 2019. https://www.yahoo.com/now/former-cowboys-bucs-de-ryan-russell-says-he-is-bisexual-in-espn-story-170336675.html.

Schwartzel, E. *Red Carpet: Hollywood, China, and the Global Battle for Cultural Supremacy*. Penguin, 2022.

Seal, M. *The Interruption of Heteronormativity in Higher Education*. Palgrave Macmillan, 2019.

Sedgwick, E. K. *Epistemology of the Closet*. Updated ed. University of California Press, 2008.

Seidman, S. *Beyond the Closet: The Transformation of Gay and Lesbian Life*. Routledge, 2002.

Seidman, S., C. Meeks, and J. J. Dean. "The Politics of Authenticity: Civil Individualism and the Cultural Roots of Gay Normalization." In *The Oxford Handbook of Cultural Sociology*, edited by J. C. Alexander, R. N. Jacobs, and P. Smith, 507–25. Oxford University Press, 2012.

Sender, K. *Business, Not Politics: The Making of the Gay Market*. Columbia University Press, 2004.

Sender, K. "The Queer Vanguard: How Television Streaming Platforms Promoted Intersectional LGBTQ+ Content to Establish Their Brands." *Journal of Communication* 75, no. 3 (2025): 161–70.

Serano, J. *Whipping Girl: A Transexual Woman on Sexism and the Scapegoating of Femininity*. Seal Press, 2007.

Sessums, K. "Jonathan Groff Talks Looking, Hamilton, and Madonna's iPhone." 429, May 7, 2018. https://fourtwonine.com/jonathan-groff-talks-looking-hamilton-madonnas-iphone/.

Setoodeh, R. "From 'Glee' to Sean Hayes: Gay Actors Play Straight." *Newsweek*, May 9, 2010. https://www.newsweek.com/glee-sean-hayes-gay-actors-play-straight-70225.

Shacklock, Z. "The Category Is: Streaming Queer Television." *New Review of Film and Television Studies* 21, no. 2 (2023): 316–37.

Shapiro, P. *Turn the Beat Around: The Secret History of Disco*. Faber and Faber, 2005.

Shaw, L. "Here Are the Ways the Pandemic Changed Hollywood." *Bloomberg*, May 26, 2021. https://www.bloomberg.com/news/features/2021-05-26/pandemic-and-entertainment-how-hollywood-has-been-changed-by-covid.

Shears, J. "Art from Rage." In *It Gets Better: Coming Out, Overcoming Bullying, and Creating a Life Worth Living*, edited by D. Savage and T. Miller, 125–26. Dutton, 2011.

Shears, J. *Boys Keep Swinging: A Memoir*. Atria Books, 2018.

Shilts, R. *And the Band Played On: Politics, People, and the AIDS Epidemic*. 20th Anniversary Edition. St. Martin's Press, 2007.

Signorile, M. "Brendon Ayanbadejo, Baltimore Ravens Linebacker, Talks Gay Marriage and LGBT Rights." *Huffington Post*, September 12, 2012. https://www.huffpost.com/entry/brendon-ayanbadejo-baltimore-ravens-gay-marriage-homophobia-jamie-kuntz_n_1877048.

Signorile, M. *It's Not Over: Getting Beyond Tolerance, Defeating Homophobia, and Winning True Equality*. Houghton Mifflin Harcourt, 2015.

Signorile, M. *Queer in America: Sex, the Media, and the Closets of Power*. 1993. Reprint, University of Wisconsin Press, 2003.

Sim, B. "*Heartstopper*'s Kit Connor Has Advice to Celebs Pressured to Come Out." *Out*, August 17, 2023. https://www.out.com/celebs/kit-connor-coming-out-advice#rebelltitem1.

Simmel, G. "The Stranger [1908]." In *On Individual and Social Forms*. Edited by G. Simmel and D. N. Levine, 143–49. University of Chicago Press, 1971.

Simmons-Duffin, S. "Trans Health Care Under Trump May Follow the Abortion Playbook and Its Hyde Amendment." NPR, November 22, 2024. https://www.npr.org/sections/shots-health-news/2024/11/22/nx-s1-5188573/transgender-gender-affirming-care-trump-abortion-hyde-amendment.

Sisson, P. "The TikTok Party House Next Door." *Bloomberg*, October 9, 2020. https://www.bloomberg.com/news/articles/2020-10-09/inside-l-a-s-tiktok-party-house-real-estate-boom.

Smith, C. *The Daily Show (the Book): An Oral History as Told by Jon Stewart, the Correspondents, Staff and Guests*. Grand Central, 2016.

Smith, C. C. "The *Survivor* 'Come on in, Guys' Controversy, Explained." Bustle, October 19, 2021. https://www.bustle.com/entertainment/survivor-come-on-in-guys-controversy-explained.

Smith, M. D. "Dennis Rodman, Bad Boy for Life." *GQ*, November 18, 2021. https://www.gq.com/story/dennis-rodman-style-icon-of-the-year-2021.

Smith, S. "The Data Behind Hollywood's Sexism." TED Talk, November 18, 2016. https://www.ted.com/talks/stacy_smith_the_data_behind_hollywood_s_sexism.

Smith, S. L., K. Pieper, and A. Khan. *Inclusion in the Director's Chair: Analysis of Director Gender and Race/Ethnicity Across 1,500 Top Films from 2007 to 2021*. USC Annenberg Inclusion Initiative, February 2022. https://assets.uscannenberg.org/docs/aii-inclusion-directors-chair-2022.pdf.

Snorton, C. R. *Nobody Is Supposed to Know: Black Sexuality on the Down Low*. University of Minnesota Press, 2014.

Socarides, R. "The Murder of a Gay Man in Greenwich Village." *The New Yorker*, May 20, 2013. https://www.newyorker.com/news/news-desk/the-murder-of-a-gay-man-in-greenwich-village.

Sommer, T. "From '70s Reality TV Star to Queer Underground Rock Here: Celebrating Lance Loud." *Billboard*, June 25, 2019. https://www.billboard.com/articles/news/pride/8517598/lance-loud-mumps-queer-rock.

Spangler, T. "Step Aside, Netflix: Amazon's Entering the Original Series Race." *Variety*, October 22, 2013. https://variety.com/2013/biz/news/step-aside-netflix-amazons-entering-the-original-series-race-1200749146/.

Spears, M. J. "'Black Lives Matter, People': How the NBA's Social Justice Efforts Dominated the Season." The Undefeated, October 12, 2020. https://theundefeated.com/features/how-the-nba-social-justice-efforts-dominated-the-season/.

Sperling, N. "Hollywood's 'We're Not in Kansas Anymore' Moment." *The New York Times*, November 22, 2020. https://www.nytimes.com/2020/11/22/business/media/wonder-woman-1984-hollywood-streaming.html.

Sperling, N. "Netflix Says It Lost Nearly 1 Million Subscribers, and Breathes a Sigh of Relief." *The New York Times*, July 19, 2022. https://www.nytimes.com/2022/07/19/business/media/netflix-earnings.html.

Spigel, L. *Make Room for TV: Television and the Family Ideal in Postwar America*. University of Chicago Press, 1992.

Stack, T. "'Love, Simon': Your First Look at 2018's Major Studio Gay Teen Romance." Yahoo News, October 31, 2017. https://www.yahoo.com/news/love-simon-first-look-2018-163138624.html.

Staff Reports. "Remembering Billy Lucas, the Boy Whose Suicide Inspired a Movement." LGBTQ Nation, September 9, 2013. https://www.lgbtqnation.com/2013/09/remembering-billy-lucas-the-boy-whose-suicide-inspired-a-movement/.

Statista Research Department. "Distribution of Lead Actors in Movies in the United States from 2011 to 2021, by Gender." Statista, January 5, 2023. https://www.statista.com/statistics/692465/distribution-lead-actors-gender/.

Steele, L. "Chris Mosier on Making History as First Trans Member of Team USA." *Rolling Stone*, August 2, 2016. https://www.rollingstone.com/culture/culture-sports/chris-mosier-on-making-history-as-first-trans-member-of-team-usa-250971/.

Stein, A. *The Stranger Next Door: The Story of a Small Community's Battle over Sex, Faith, and Civil Rights*. Beacon Press, 2001.

Stein, L. "In Conservative America, Small Cities Stand Up for LGBTQ Rights." NBC News, March 15, 2017. https://www.nbcnews.com/feature/nbc-out/conservative-america-small-cities-stand-lgbtq-rights-n733821.

Steinbock, E. "The Riotous State of Trans Visual Culture." *Journal of Cinema and Media Studies* 61, no. 2 (2022): 169–74.

Steinmetz, K. "The Transgender Tipping Point." *Time Magazine*, June 9, 2014. https://time.com/135480/transgender-tipping-point/.

Stevenson, A. "Beyond the Gay Role." Logo, March 4, 2009. https://www.logotv.com/news/ydf4xb/beyond-the-gay-role.

Stolworthy, J. "Darren Criss Says He'll Never Play a Gay Character Again." *Independent*, December 25, 2018. https://www.independent.co.uk/arts-entertainment/tv/news/darren-criss-gay-roles-lgbtq-actors-gianni-versace-assassination-glee-andrew-cunanan-golden-globes-a8698841.html.

Street, J. "Celebrity Politicians: Popular Culture and Political Representation." *British Journal of Politics and International Relations* 6 (2004): 435–52.

Street, M. "Here's Why Cis-Het Actors Should Not Play LGBTQ+ Roles—for Now." *Out*, December 8, 2020. https://www.out.com/film/2020/12/08/heres-why-cis-het-actors-should-not-play-lgbtq-roles-now#toggle-gdpr.

Street, M. "JoJo Siwa Explains Why She No Longer Identifies as a Lesbian." *Them*, April 23, 2025. https://www.them.us/story/jojo-siwa-lesbian-queer-gender-identity-celebrity-big-brother-uk.

Streeter, K. "Why Scores of Female Athletes Are Speaking Out on Abortion Rights." *The New York Times*, September 27, 2021. https://www.nytimes.com/2021/09/27/sports/women-athletes-abortion-rights-brief.html?referringSource=articleShare.

Streitmatter, R. *From 'Perverts' to 'Fab Five': The Media's Changing Depiction of Gay Men and Lesbians*. Routledge, 2009.

Stroude, Will. "Bridgerton Star Jonathan Bailey Talks Sexuality and Acting with Sir Ian McKellen." *Attitude*, December 29, 2020. https://www.attitude.co.uk/culture/film-tv/bridgerton-star-jonathan-bailey-talks-sexuality-and-acting-with-sir-ian-mckellen-302200/.

Stulberg, L. M. *LGBTQ Social Movements*. Polity, 2018.

Stulberg, L. M. "One Ally's Story in Celebration of Pride Month." *Huffington Post*, May 29, 2015. https://www.huffpost.com/entry/one-allys-story-in-celebration-of-pride-month_b_7465888.

Sullivan, A. "How the Gay Rights Movement Radicalized and Lost Its Way." *The New York Times*, June 26, 2025. https://www.nytimes.com/2025/06/26/opinion/gay-lesbian-trans-rights.html.

Sullivan, A. *Virtually Normal: An Argument About Homosexuality*. Knopf, 1995.

Supreme Court of the United States. *Obergefell et al. v. Hodges: The U.S. Supreme Court Decision on Marriage Equality*. Melville House, 2015.

Svachula, A. "Scarlett Johansson Withdraws from Transgender Role After Backlash." *The New York Times*, July 13, 2018. https://www.nytimes.com/2018/07/13/movies/scarlett-johansson-rub-and-tug-transgender.html.

Swanson, C. "The News Is Out: And the World, Thrillingly, Mostly Yawned." *New York Magazine*, July 16–23, 2012, 8.

Szabo, M. "Chris Kluwe, Fired as Football Coach, Sues Huntington Beach Union High School District." *Los Angeles Times Daily Pilot*, July 28, 2025. https://www.latimes.com/socal/daily-pilot/news/story/2025-07-28/chris-kluwe-fired-as-football-coach-sues-huntington-beach-union-high-school-district.

Talai, A. "Eight Simple Steps to Resisting." *Medium*, January 26, 2017. https://medium.com/@AmirTalai/eight-simple-steps-to-resisting-f1f97df1a3ca.

Talai, A. "Stop Playing Terrorists—and Other Ways for Brown (and Black and White) Actors to Be a Part of the Solution." *Medium*, March 2, 2018. https://medium.com/the-establishment/stop-playing-terrorists-and-other-ways-for-actors-to-be-a-part-of-the-solution-8fc90f812635.

Talai, A. "When a Brown Actor Plays a White Character, Who Really Wins?" *BuzzFeed*, August 21, 2015. https://www.buzzfeednews.com/article/amirtalai/when-a-brown-actor-plays-a-white-character-who-really-wins#.duJxvDx9kR.

Talusan, M. "Eddie Redmayne's Complicated Masculinity." *BuzzFeed*, November 22, 2015. https://www.buzzfeed.com/meredithtalusan/eddie-redmaynes-complicated-masculinity?utm_term=.vyBQ7qjOB4#.rh1y6VmM5X.

Talusan, M. "8 Trans Tropes We Need to Retire in 2016." *BuzzFeed*, January 10, 2016. https://www.buzzfeed.com/meredithtalusan/tired-trans-tropes-we-need-to-retire-in-2016.

Talusan, M. *Fairest: A Memoir*. Viking, 2020.

Talusan, M. "From a Symbol of Athletic Power to a Symbol of Gender Transition." *BuzzFeed*, April 25, 2015. https://www.thenation.com/article/archive/olympic-bravery/.

Talusan, M. "25 Years of Transphobia in Comedy." *BuzzFeed*, February 27, 2016. https://www.buzzfeed.com/meredithtalusan/25-years-of-transphobia-in-comedies.

Tannenbaum, R., and C. Marks. *I Want My MTV: The Uncensored Story of the Music Video Revolution*. Rev. ed. Plume, 2012.

Tarr, K. A. "Bias and the Business of Show: Employment Discrimination in the 'Entertainment' Industry." *University of San Francisco Law Review* 51 (November 22, 2016): 1–13. https://cpb-us-w2.wpmucdn.com/usfblogs.usfca.edu/dist/7/272/files/2017/05/Bias-and-the-Business-of-Show-Tarr-Vol.-51-27qk1oa.pdf.

Taylor, T. D. *The Sounds of Capitalism: Advertising, Music, and the Conquest of Culture*. University of Chicago Press, 2012.

Taylor, V., K. Kimport, N. Van Dyke, and E. A. Andersen. "Culture and Mobilization: Tactical Repertoires, Same-Sex Weddings, and the Impact on Gay Activism." *American Sociological Review* 74 (December 2009): 865–90.

Tensley, B. "The Double-Edged Sword of Queer Visibility." *Pacific Standard*, June 28, 2017. https://psmag.com/social-justice/double-edged-sword-queer-visibi.

Tevlin, J. "Kluwe Made an Impact on, off the Field." *Star Tribune*, May 8, 2013. https://www.startribune.com/tevlin-kluwe-made-an-impact-on-off-the-field/206517841/?refresh=true.

Tharrett, M. "Legendary Football Coach Vince Lombardi Accepted Gay Athletes Nearly 50 Years Ago." *Queerty*, May 7, 2013. https://www.queerty.com/vince-lombardi-was-one-of-the-first-coaches-to-accept-gay-athletes-20130507.

Thomas, G., and M. Goodman. "Women Directors Might Just Get the Hollywood Ending They Have Been Hoping For." *ACLU News & Commentary*, February 18, 2017. https://www.aclu.org/news/womens-rights/women-directors-might-just-get-hollywood-ending-they-have.

Thomas, L. "What's Really Behind the House Bill to Ban Transgender Athletes from School Sports?" *The New Yorker*, January 19, 2025. https://www.newyorker.com/sports/sporting-scene/whats-really-behind-the-house-bill-to-ban-transgender-athletes-from-school-sports.

Thompson, D. "Why American Teens Are So Sad." *The Atlantic*, April 11, 2022. https://www.theatlantic.com/newsletters/archive/2022/04/american-teens-sadness-depression-anxiety/629524/?utm_source=pocket-newtab.

Tobia, J. "Does Gay Hollywood Have Room for Queer Kids?" *The New York Times*, March 28, 2018. https://www.nytimes.com/2018/03/28/opinion/love-simon-gay-femme-hollywood.html.

Todaro, R. "LGBTQ+ Adults Prefer Biden over Trump—but Want Democrats to Do More to Protect Their Rights." Data for Progress, April 18, 2024. https://www.dataforprogress.org/blog/2024/4/19/lgbtq-adults-prefer-biden-over-trump-but-want-democrats-to-do-more-to-protect-their-rights.

Truitt, J. "The Golden Globes Gave Jared Leto an Award for Playing a Trans Woman Because Hollywood Is Terrible." *Feministing* (blog), January 13, 2014. https://feministing.com/2014/01/13/the-golden-globes-give-jared-leto-an-award-for-playing-a-trans-woman-because-hollywood-is-terrible/.

Tuaolo, E., with J. Rosengren. *Alone in the Trenches: My Life as a Gay Man in the NFL*. Sourcebooks, 2006.

Turino, T. *Music as Social Life: The Politics of Participation*. University of Chicago Press, 2008.

Ugwu, R. "The Hashtag That Changed the Oscars: An Oral History." *The New York Times*, February 6, 2020. https://www.nytimes.com/2020/02/06/movies/oscarssowhite-history.html.

Ulaby, N. "The 'Barbie' Movie's Success Puts Her Among History's Top-20 Films." NPR, August 23, 2023. https://www.npr.org/2023/08/23/1195387845/the-barbie-movies-success-puts-her-among-historys-top-20-films.

Urwand, B. *The Collaboration: Hollywood's Pact with Hitler*. Belknap Press of Harvard University Press, 2013.

Us Weekly. "Neil and David Excited to Wed!" *Us Weekly*, July 11, 2011, 44.

Uwagba, O. "Ray of Light: With Issa Rae." *Porter*, January 29, 2024. https://www.net-a-porter.com/en-hk/porter/article-3b30998a5c5ae7c3/cover-stories/cover-stories/issa-rae.

Vaid, U. *Virtual Equality*. Anchor Books, 1995.

Valinsky, J. "How One Tweet Snowballed into the NBA's Worst Nightmare." CNN Business, October 11, 2019. https://www.cnn.com/2019/10/09/business/nba-china-hong-kong-explainer.

VanArendonk, K. "*Will & Grace*'s Best Trump Joke Is Its Setting." *Vulture*, September 28, 2017. https://www.vulture.com/2017/09/will-and-grace-best-trump-joke-is-its-setting.html.

Van Dyke, N., and V. Taylor. "The Cultural Outcomes of Social Movements." In *The Wiley Blackwell Companion to Social Movements*, 2nd ed., edited by D. A. Snow, S. A. Soule, H. Kriesi, and H. McCammon, 482–98. John Wiley & Sons, 2019.

Vary, A. B. "Out Gay Actor Richard Chamberlain Says He 'Wouldn't Advise' Closeted Gay Actors to Come Out. Didn't Seem to Hurt His Career." *Entertainment Weekly*, December 27, 2010. https://ew.com/article/2010/12/27/richard-chamberlain-gay-actors-coming-out/.

Villagran, L. "'Page Not Found': Trump Administration Scrubs Webpages of Gender Reference." *USA Today*, January 31, 2025. https://www.usatoday.com/story/news/politics/2025/01/31/government-webpages-scrub-gender-dei/78093721007/.

Vivarelli, N. "Netflix Stands by Arabic Film 'Perfect Strangers' Amid Sexuality Controversy." *Variety*, January 25, 2022. https://variety.com/2022/film/news/perfect-strangers-controversy-netflix-1235162636/.

Vox Media Podcast Network. *Land of the Giants: The Netflix Effect*. Podcast, 2020.

https://podcasts.apple.com/us/podcast/the-netflix-effect/id1465767420?i=1000478014301.

Wallace, C. "Riz Ahmed Acts His Way Out of Every Cultural Pigeonhole." *The New York Times Magazine*, August 30, 2018. https://www.nytimes.com/interactive/2018/08/29/magazine/riz-ahmed-actor-rapper-venom.html.

Walters, S. D. *All the Rage: The Story of Gay Visibility in America*. University of Chicago Press, 2001.

Walters, S. D. *The Tolerance Trap: How God, Genes, and Good Intentions Are Sabotaging Gay Equality*. New York University Press, 2014.

Warner, M. Introduction to *Fear of a Queer Planet: Queer Politics and Social Theory*, edited by M. Warner, vii–xxxi. University of Minnesota Press, 1993.

Warner, M. *The Trouble with Normal: Sex, Politics, and the Ethics of Queer Life*. Harvard University Press, 1999.

Warner, S. M. "Let's Go, Lesbians: 50 Years of Queer Women on Screen." *Paste*, July 26, 2021. https://www.pastemagazine.com/movies/50-years-queer-womens-cinema/.

Watney, S. *Policing Desire: Pornography, AIDS and the Media*. 3rd ed. University of Minnesota Press, 1996.

Waxman, S. "Hollywood Is 'Hot, Horny and White' Again." *The New York Times*, August 9, 2025. https://www.nytimes.com/2025/08/09/opinion/hollywood-entertainment-woke-progressive.html.

Weigel, D. "Why Republicans Keep Running Against Trans Rights." *The Washington Post*, March 2, 2021. https://www.washingtonpost.com/politics/2021/03/02/trailer-why-republicans-keep-running-against-trans-rights/.

Weiner, J. "The Great Race to Rule Streaming TV." *The New York Times*, July 10, 2019. https://www.nytimes.com/2019/07/10/magazine/streaming-race-netflix-hbo-hulu-amazon.html.

Weinraub, B. "Stung by Criticism of Fall Shows, TV Networks Add Minority Roles." *The New York Times*, September 20, 1999. https://www.nytimes.com/1999/09/20/arts/stung-by-criticism-of-fall-shows-tv-networks-add-minority-roles.html.

Weprin, A. "Streaming Profits Are Tough to Find. Niche Movie and TV Platforms See a Way Forward." *The Hollywood Reporter*, June 26, 2024. https://www.hollywoodreporter.com/business/business-news/streaming-profits-movie-tv-platforms-1235932799/.

West, D. M., and J. Orman. *Celebrity Politics*. Prentice Hall, 2003.

White, B. "What 'The Golden Girls' Got Right About Gay Issues in the '80s." Decider, February 14, 2017. https://decider.com/2017/02/14/golden-girls-gay-rights/.

White, C. T. *Pre-Gay L.A.: A Social History of the Movement for Homosexual Rights*. University of Illinois Press, 2009.

White House. Executive Order: Keeping Men Out of Women's Sports, February 5, 2025. https://www.whitehouse.gov/presidential-actions/2025/02/keeping-men-out-of-womens-sports/.

White House. Executive Order: Prioritizing Military Excellence and Readiness, January 27, 2025. https://www.whitehouse.gov/presidential-actions/2025/01/prioritizing-military-excellence-and-readiness/.

White House. Executive Order: Protecting Children from Chemical and Surgical Mutilation, January 28, 2025. https://www.whitehouse.gov/presidential-actions/2025/01/protecting-children-from-chemical-and-surgical-mutilation/.

White House. The Inaugural Address, January 20, 2025. https://www.whitehouse.gov/remarks/2025/01/the-inaugural-address/.

Whitney, E. O. "An Unfortunate History of Cisgender Actors Playing Transgender Characters." ScreenCrush, June 27, 2017. https://screencrush.com/cis-actors-transgender-movies-characters/.

Wilbon, M. "Sexuality Disclosed, Ignorance Exposed." *The Washington Post*, February 9, 2007. https://www.washingtonpost.com/wp-dyn/content/article/2007/02/08/AR2007020802247.html?nav=rss_email/components.

Williams, J., host. "Brian Flores on Taking a Stand Against the NFL." *The Limits* (podcast), February 3, 2022. https://www.npr.org/transcripts/1077927110.

Williams Institute. "LGBT Proportion of Population: United States." Williams Institute, UCLA School of Law. https://williamsinstitute.law.ucla.edu/visualization/lgbt-stats/?topic=LGBT#density.

Wilson, M. "Trump Says Only American Flag Can Fly at U.S. Outposts." *The Washington Times*, January 22, 2025. https://www.washingtontimes.com/news/2025/jan/22/trump-says-american-flag-fly-u-outposts/.

Winick, J. *Pedro and Me: Friendship, Loss, and What I Learned*. Henry Holt, 2000.

Wired Staff. "Seriously, We Really Need to Talk About *Nanette*." *Wired*, July 31, 2018. https://www.wired.com/story/hannah-gadsby-nanette-discussion/.

Witosky, T., and M. Hansen. *Equal Before the Law: How Iowa Led Americans to Marriage Equality*. University of Iowa Press, 2015.

WNBA Press Release. "League Debuts WNBA Pride Presented by COVERGIRL, a National Platform Celebrating Inclusion and Equality." WNBA, May 21, 2014. https://www.wnba.com/archive/wnba/fever/news/league-debuts-wnba-pride-national-platform-celebrating-inclusion-equality.html.

Woelfle, A. "Actor John Leguizamo's New TV Docuseries Spotlights Latino Culture." NPR, April 13, 2023. https://www.npr.org/2023/04/13/1169130814/actor-john-leguizamos-new-tv-docuseries-spotlights-latino-culture.

Wolny, N. "The LGBTQ+ Community Has $3.7 Trillion in Purchasing Power; Here's How We Want You to Sell to Us." *Entrepreneur*, June 10, 2019. https://www.entrepreneur.com/article/334983.

Wong, C. M. "Emmys Tell Non-Binary Star They Can Choose Their Award Category." *HuffPost*, April 6, 2017. https://www.huffpost.com/entry/asia-kate-dillon-emmy-awards_n_58e66f55e4b07da813248728.

Wong, C. M. "'Family Group' Is Fuming over the Campbell's Soup Ad with Gay Dads." *Huffington Post*, October 11, 2015. https://www.huffpost.com/entry/one-million-moms-campbells_n_56181dc1e4b0dbb8000e9e79.

Woodrow, C. "Going Global: The Evolution of International Film Markets." *Medium*, April 27, 2021. https://medium.com/media-capital-technologies/the-evolution-of-international-film-markets-7fed440319e2.

Woog, D. "Hudson Taylor: The Power of 'Athlete Ally.'" The OutField, June 29, 2012. https://www.camprehoboth.com/letters/2012/june-29-2012-out-field-dan-woog.

Woog, D. "The LGBT Sports Movement Faces Growing Pains." Pride Source, April 27, 2017. https://pridesource.com/article/81064-2/.

Writers Guild of America West. *Inclusion & Equity Report, 2022*. WGA.org, 2022. https://www.wga.org/uploadedfiles/the-guild/inclusion-and-equity/Inclusion-Report-2022.pdf.

Writers Guild of America West and Writers Guild of America East. *Inclusion & Equity Report, 2025*. WGA.org, 2025. https://origin.www.wga.org/uploadedfiles/the-guild/inclusion-and-equity/2025_wga_inclusion_report.pdf.

Yahoo Sports Staff. "Maryland Politician's Letter Denouncing Brendon Ayanbadejo's Support of Gay Marriage." Yahoo! Sports, September 6, 2012. http://sports.yahoo.com/news/nfl—maryland-politician%E2%80%99s-letter-denouncing-brendon-ayanbadejo%E2%80%99s-support-of-gay-marriage.html.

Yamato, J. "Hollywood Claims to Be Making Strides on Inclusion. One Professor's Research Says Otherwise." *Los Angeles Times*, January 4, 2019. https://www.latimes.com/entertainment/movies/la-et-mn-usc-study-representation-stacy-smith-20190104-story.html.

Yoshino, K. *Covering: The Hidden Assault on Our Civil Rights*. Random House, 2007.

Yuen, N. W. *Reel Inequality: Hollywood Actors and Racism*. Rutgers University Press, 2017.

Yurcaba, J. "NCAA's New Trans Athlete Guidelines Sow Confusion Amid Lia Thomas Debate." NBC News, January 21, 2022. https://www.nbcnews.com/nbc-out/out-news/ncaas-new-trans-athlete-guidelines-sow-confusion-lia-thomas-debate-rcna13073.

Zakarin, J. "Ty Burrell: 'Modern Family' Helps Move Gay Rights Forward." *The Hollywood Reporter*, October 3, 2012. https://www.hollywoodreporter.com/news/general-news/ty-burrell-modern-family-gay-marriage-butter-376051/.

Zeigler, C. "Brian Sims Story Still Resonating." Outsports, May 18, 2009. https://www.outsports.com/2009/5/18/4047840/brian-sims-story-still-resonating.

Zeigler, C. "'The Eagle Has Landed.': The Exclusive Behind-the-Scenes Story of How NFL Prospect Michael Sam Came Out." Outsports, February 9, 2014. https://www.outsports.com/2014/2/9/5396036/michael-sam-gay-football-player-missouri-nfl-draft.

Zeigler, C. "The Effective Role of Straight Allies Is as the Supporters, Not Stars, of Our Movement." Outsports, November 26, 2013. https://www.outsports.com/2013/11/26/5147032/straight-allies-proper-role-lgbt-sports-movement.

Zeigler, C. "Former College Football Captain Was Openly Gay." Outsports, April 27, 2009. https://www.outsports.com/out-gay-athletes/2013/2/21/4015526/brian-sims-football-gay.

Zeigler, C. "Jacksonville Jaguars Strength Coach Kevin Maxen Comes Out in the NFL, a First in Major US Men's Pro Sports." Outsports, July 21, 2023. https://

www.outsports.com/2023/7/20/23799193/kevin-maxen-nfl-coach-coming-out-jacksonville-jaguars-boyfriend.

Zeigler, C. "Kick Ass." *Out*, November 2012, 42–47.

Zeigler, C. "LGBT Sports Summit Kicks Off in Portland." Outsports, June 11, 2015. https://www.outsports.com/2015/6/11/8761125/lgbt-sports-summit-portland-2015.

Zeigler, C. "Michael Irvin: The Playmaker Preaches." *Out*, July 11, 2011. https://www.out.com/entertainment/sports/2011/07/10/michael-irvin-playmaker-preaches.

Zeigler, C. "NFL Adds 'Sexual Orientation' Protection to Collective Bargaining Agreement." Outsports, September 24, 2011. https://www.outsports.com/2011/9/24/4051886/nfl-adds-sexual-orientation-protection-to-collective-bargaining.

Zeigler, C. "NFL Commissioner Honored with Gay Son." Outsports, October 13, 2005. https://www.outsports.com/2013/2/20/4010320/paul-tagliabue-gay-son.

Zeigler, C. "The Number of Out Coaches in Women's College Basketball Has Exploded. Why?" Outsports, March 30, 2023. https://www.outsports.com/2023/3/30/23653936/women-college-basketball-coaches-final-four-out.

Zeigler, C. "Players, Coaches and the Media React to John Amaechi Coming Out." Outsports, February 13, 2013. https://www.outsports.com/2013/2/20/4009756/players-coaches-media-react-john-amaechi-coming-out-gay.

Zeigler, C. "Pro Sports Are Finally Ready for a Gay Athlete." Outsports, September 11, 2012. https://www.outsports.com/2012/9/11/4053652/pro-sports-are-finally-ready-for-a-gay-athlete.

Zeigler, C. "Robbie Rogers Was Not the First Out Gay American Pro Team Sports Athlete. Andrew Goldstein Broke the 'Gay Barrier' in 2005." Outsports, May 27, 2013. https://www.outsports.com/2013/5/27/4369410/robbie-rogers-andrew-goldstein-first-gay-athlete.

Zeigler, C. "10 Black Pro Athletes Who Luv Their LGBT Family Members." Outsports, February 18, 2015. https://www.outsports.com/2015/2/18/8057695/this-is-luv-black-athletes-family.

Zeigler, C. "We Should Never Hear About a Gay NFL Player Being a Media 'Distraction' Ever Again." Outsports, September 28, 2017. https://www.outsports.com/2017/9/28/16372232/nfl-protest-gay-distraction.

Zeigler, C. "World Athletics Bans Trans Women from the Female Track and Field Category." Outsports, March 23, 2023. https://www.outsports.com/trans/2023/3/23/23653774/world-athletics-bans-trans-women-female-track-field.

Zeigler, C., and J. Buzinski. "Out in Sports Study: Out LGBTQ Athletes Report Deep, Widespread Acceptance from Teammates." Outsports, October 4, 2021. https://www.outsports.com/out-gay-athletes/2021/10/4/22706376/out-in-sports-study-lgbtq-athletes-high-school-college-acceptance.

Zhang, E. "The Radical Act of Invisibility on Trans Day of Visibility." *The Washington Post*, March 31, 2022. https://www.washingtonpost.com/lifestyle/2022/03/31/trans-day-visibility-erique-zhang/.

Ziller, T., and M. Prada. "The WNBA Has Been at the Forefront of Protesting

Racial Injustice." SB Nation, September 24, 2017. https://www.sbnation.com/2017/9/24/16357206/national-anthem-protest-wnba-history-donald-trump.

Zirin, D. "Can the NFL Tackle Homophobia?" *The Nation*, September 29, 2009. https://www.thenation.com/article/archive/can-nfl-tackle-homophobia/.

Zirin, D. "Chris Kluwe and the Greatest Political Statement by Any Athlete Ever." *The Nation*, September 12, 2012. https://www.thenation.com/article/archive/chris-kluwe-and-greatest-political-statement-any-athlete-ever/.

Zirin, D. *Game Over: How Politics Has Turned the Sports World Upside Down*. The New Press, 2013.

Zirin, D. "'It's a New World': The Super Bowl Becomes a Platform for LGBT Equality." *The Nation*, January 26, 2013. https://www.thenation.com/article/archive/its-new-world-super-bowl-becomes-platform-lgbt-equality/#axzz2fqty9yVF.

Zirin, D. "The Olympic Bravery of Caitlyn Jenner." *The Nation*, June 2, 2015. https://www.thenation.com/article/archive/olympic-bravery/.

Zirin, D. "On Colin Kaepernick's Nike Ad: Will the Revolution Be Branded?" *The Nation*, September 4, 2018. https://www.thenation.com/article/archive/on-colin-kaepernicks-nike-ad-will-the-revolution-be-branded/.

Zirin, D. *A People's History of Sports in the United States: 250 Years of Politics, Protest, People, and Play*. The New Press, 2008.

Zook, K. B. "*Queen Sugar*: How Ava DuVernay Elevated Women Directors (with Oprah's Help)." *Vanity Fair*, October 20, 2022. https://www.vanityfair.com/hollywood/2022/10/queen-sugar-how-ava-duvernay-elevated-women-directors-with-oprahs-help.

Zurawik, D. "'Modern Family'—How a Sitcom Manages to Span Our Partisan Divide." *The Baltimore Sun*, June 8, 2012. https://www.baltimoresun.com/opinion/columnists/zurawik/bal-is-modern-family-abc-obama-romney-20120608-story.html.

INDEX